FASHION IN FILM

Fashion in Film

EDITED BY **ADRIENNE MUNICH**

INDIANA UNIVERSITY PRESS

Bloomington & Indianapolis

This book is a publication of

Indiana University Press
601 North Morton Street
Bloomington, IN 47404-3797 USA

www.iupress.indiana.edu

Telephone orders   800-842-6796
Fax orders   812-855-7931
Orders by e-mail   iuporder@indiana.edu

Library of Congress Cataloging-in-
Publication Data

Fashion in film / edited by Adrienne
Munich.
    p. cm. — (New directions in national
cinemas)
    Includes bibliographical references and
index.
  ISBN 978-0-253-35613-0 (cloth : alk.
paper) — ISBN 978-0-253-22299-2
(pbk. : alk. paper) 1. Fashion in motion
pictures. 2. Costume—Symbolic aspects.
3. National characteristics in motion
pictures. I. Munich, Adrienne.
  PN1995.9.C56F385 2011
  791.43'6564—dc22

                                2010039230

    1 2 3 4 5 16 15 14 13 12 11

This volume is dedicated, with respect and affection, to E. Ann Kaplan, whose feminist work in film and media studies has inspired generations of writers and movie-watchers throughout the world.

NEW DIRECTIONS IN NATIONAL CINEMAS

Jacqueline Reich, editor

CONTENTS

ACKNOWLEDGMENTS

Effusive thanks go, above all, to the authors. I read and reread their contributions for the sheer pleasure of learning from them. The idea of exploring connections between fashion and film surfaced during a conversation with Valerie Steele, Tamsen Schwartzman, and Patricia Mears of the Museum at the Fashion Institute of Technology. Elisabeth Sussman and Matthew Yokobosky offered generous curatorial information. A symposium that supplemented my graduate seminar on fashion and film honored E. Ann Kaplan's contributions to the field of feminist cinema studies and to her shaping of the Humanities Institute at Stony Brook University. *Fashion in Film* evolved from that day with its promise of an unfinished and exciting topic. I thank the Stony Brook President's office under Shirley Kenny, the College of Arts and Sciences dean, James Storos, and chair of the English Department, Stephen Spector, for initial support of the project. Colleen Wallahora, who worked with me when I was chair of Women's and Gender Studies, offered her extraordinary combination of aesthetic and managerial skills. Many authors are either current members of the Columbia University Seminar on Cinema and Interdisciplinary Interpretation or have been former chairs, guest presenters, and responders there. That precious, welcoming, and democratic venue, with its co-chairs Krin Gabbard, William Luhr, and more recently, Jane Gaines, promotes a congenial atmosphere for the exchange of ideas. The editor expresses appreciation to the Warner Fund at the

FASHION IN FILM

Fashion Shows

ADRIENNE MUNICH

Fashion in Film explores the vital synergy between dress and the cinema, a force as old as film itself. To offer but one example of their connection, the annual Academy of Motion Picture Arts and Science Awards (the "Oscars") draws from the very core of the fashion/film dynamic. The fashion parade that opens the Oscars not only adds to the ceremony's buzz but nearly trumps it in hype. This event might seem to be merely a publicity device designed to heat up excitement for the award extravaganza, a trivial byproduct of the truly essential ceremony. Yet in fact, there is a primal connection between the two spectacles, a connection that lies, discreet and often unremarked, in the perceived difference between actors and those film roles that have transported them to the red carpet.[1] Upon reflection, however, we realize that our fascination with the stars and their finery constitutes another layer of their film identity. On the carpet tread carefully crafted performers, whose names may have been inventions and whose ensembles have been donated. Both events, then, are shows, or one big show, part of a ritual; the opening fashion show serves as a processional preceding the bestowal of trophies. As with many relationships, however, the pair aren't always seen together; the Oscars fashion show spins off into other media—reverential or snippy commentary, reviews, and photographs—to assume a life of its own, a life that many follow more avidly than the Oscars themselves.

I use the Oscars to illustrate the connections between fashion and film because it makes a glitzy spectacle of their alliance. Their affiliation spite fashion's definition as inexorably linked to the present moment.[7] Paula Patton, nominated for a Best Supporting Actress Oscar for her role as a teacher in *Precious* (2009), reveals to a *New York Times* reporter what influences her Look: "I always love Grace Kelly. That white dress she wears in 'To Catch a Thief' is to die for. I was thinking I should have it remade for a red-carpet affair. . . . Marilyn Monroe in 'Gentlemen Prefer Blondes' in that purple outfit with the right belt and the right bag—it opened me up."[8] Patton shows that she designs her professional image in relation to earlier great stars; clearly ordinary viewers can do the same.

Patton's language reveals that for her film fashion blends with items in the stars' personal closets. She does not take into account that Kelly's white dress and Monroe's purple outfit were costume designs, not picked up on the swanky Beverley Hills shopping street, Rodeo Drive. That the white dress seems to belong to Grace Kelly and not to the film character who goes unnamed by Patton underlines the point that the costume design appears natural and uncontrived, perfectly worn by the actress who then is remembered through her character's dress. The great and prolific Edith Head designed the costumes for this and other Hitchcock films, including the white dress that now signifies "Grace Kelly." In the case of Monroe's purple dress, William Travilla designed it with the right belt and the right bag. What strikes a newspaper reader seeking fashion news in the *Times* style section in 2009 is that both films were produced in the early 1950s. Yet to Patton, the dresses continue to have an impact on her fashion sensibility, not as quaintly vintage but as right for her own moment and self-image. That is to say, film fashion, bound to star images, endures beyond the confines of the short time periods associated with a typical notion of fashion. According to received wisdom, fashion seems to define itself as a particular Look unique to a brief moment, yet that definition competes with fashion designers' penchant for quotation, for importing the past into their declarations of the *now*. This Janus-like quality in fashion—looking backwards to design forwards—finds its perfect vehicle in film. Moviegoers do not need the fashion industry to act as interpreter in order to understand movie costume of whatever period as a fashion show for their own moment. As Patton envisions herself in sartorial quotation, she exemplifies what Ulrich Lehmann describes as "fashion's dialectical aesthetics," a term describing how fashion's inevitable ephemerality also contains its own opposite, "the eternal."[9]

Viewers quickly grasp the contemporary meanings and values conveyed by costume, even in films about earlier historical moments. Thus, fashion is an essential tool in the craft of conveying meaning through film. Reciprocally, films provide a dictionary, or better, an encyclopedia and an archive for fashionable quotation. Oscar-winning costume designers may not stand at the forefront of the fashion/film alliance. Yet though the Award is not given for the most influential costume design, film influence on fashion is powerful. In 2010, *Avatar,* whose costume designs, produced by collaboration between animators and conventional designers, would have required a reconception of the category, was not nominated; nonetheless it immediately inspired fashion designers.[10] For fashion, movies are a gift that keeps on giving.

Taken as a whole, *Fashion in Film* expands upon conventional understandings of the role of fashion in creating the Look of a film and influencing its meanings. There may be no entirely satisfactory definition of fashion. Joanne Entwistle offers a simple and seemingly unproblematic one: "Fashion is dress that embodies the latest aesthetic."[11] Bringing the notion of historical specificity into a consideration of fashion, Gilles Lipovetsky emphasizes fashion's ephemerality and its importance in defining modernity. Such a focus opens up a consideration of consumer culture and class. No definition is uncontested in fashion studies; the claim that fashion as a concept originates in Western modes of commerce and kinds of political organization is particularly contentious.[12] Lipovetsky, representing a highly politicized view, argues that fashion is a democratic phenomenon, dependent upon modern industry and independent of class because modern capitalistic democracy allows anyone access to fashionable Looks and the freedom to pursue fashion. While we may harbor reservations about his opinions, it is clear at least that film provides a democratic medium of access to Looks. Film opens fashion to huge audiences that exceed the boundaries of a fashion moment and enable viewers and fashion designers to adapt past fashions to their own time. Film offers fashion to the masses and is an avenue to its democratization.

FASHION, NATION, CAMERA

The impact of nation and nationality form a subtext throughout the chapters in *Fashion in Film,* although each chapter takes up the concept of nation from different perspectives. Most chapters recognize how film fashion navigates among national borders. Because of the contradictory yet powerful manner in which fashion operates, it can both assert a fashion identity for a particular country and gesture toward a Look for which national borders seem irrelevant. Indeed, some films include fashion as part of their portrayal of a national character. That such a weighty concept as "nation" could be dependent for its very definition on a cultural practice generally considered superficial, insubstantial, and particularly associated with women's (implicitly or explicitly trivial) preoccupations testifies to fashion's fundamental importance in the modern world.

To add to the complexity of defining nation through fashion, an international context may suggest a national identity by means of a filmic Look. To cite a little-known but pithy example, Doris, the narrator and main character in the 1932 German bestseller, *The Artificial Silk Girl* by Irmgard Keun, visualizes her life as if it were a screenplay:

> I think it will be a good thing if I write everything down because I'm an unusual person. I don't mean a diary—that's ridiculous for a trendy girl like me. But I want to write like a movie, because my life is like that and it's going to become even more so. And I look like Colleen Moore, if she had a perm and her nose were a little more fashionable, like pointing up. And when I read it later on, everything will be like at the movies—I'm looking at myself in pictures.[13]

The pictures that Doris conjures are international, largely from Hollywood, not Germany. Keun endows Doris with a modernity that characterizes her historical moment by showing how she weaves together her identity with fashion awareness and movie fandom. The character doesn't see herself as a film still or a head shot; she sees herself moving and clothed: "And now I'm sitting in my room in my nightgown, which has just slipped off my famous shoulder. . . ."[14] As a self-aggrandizing young woman desiring above all else to appear trendy, her account stitches together the cultural fabrics of film, fashion, identity, and, more complexly, nation. The character seems suspended above a vaguely

Western global map, lifting herself above her tawdry life through a fantasy about being glamorous. She seems to efface her German nationality by visualizing herself as an American film star. And yet, capturing a moment in her nation's history—the transition from the Weimar Republic to Nazi Germany—Doris in her synthetic clothes fits into the milieu of Weimar decadence. Keun's artificial silk girl could be cited as an exemplary figure with a recognizable attitude defining that particular time and place. At the same time, her self-image reflects foreign moving pictures.

Complicating the national mélange even more, Keun consciously adopts and then adapts a memorable device from the American novel *Gentlemen Prefer Blondes* (1925), by Anita Loos. Here, famously, is Loos's character Lorelei Lee: "So I told Mr. Lamson how I write down all of my thoughts and he said he knew I had something to me and when we become better acquainted I am going to let him read my diary."[15] Keun's character claims a fashionable distinction in rejecting Lorelei's obsolete diary in favor of a screenplay.[16] Adding an intertextual layer to these self-styling women-on-the-make, no person after the 1953 film adaptation of Loos's novel can separate Lorelei's self-portrait from the luscious screen presentation of Marilyn Monroe as an updated, 50s-fashioned Lorelei; now Paula Patton wants to bring Marilyn/Lorelei's purple dress into the twenty-first century. When a reader in our moment encounters Doris, she sees her multimedia reflections through Monroe back in time to the liberated flapper, Lorelei, to the silent film star, Colleen Moore. Not only does Doris envision herself as an American movie star, but current readers of the novel are likely to imagine the setting focused through the lens of American film projectors.

The Artificial Silk Girl tracks Keun forming her main character according to a national type, while appropriating fashions from international origins. It's precisely these cosmopolitan tints that color concepts of Weimar decadence. From the very intertextuality of Doris's construction emerges her defining voice. Colleen Moore (1900–1988), who is the model for the artificial silk girl's self-image, built her fame during the silent film era upon her fashionable image as much as her acting ability. Her bobbed haircut (sometimes called a "Dutch-boy," to further expand the internationalism of fashion inspiration) was radical for a moment of

This volume offers many exciting ways of exploring the twists and turns of the two strands.

Fashion in Film is divided into three main sections: Fashioning Film, Filming Fashion, and Fashioning National Identities, with each section preceded by a brief overview. The epilogue, After Fashion, with only one essay, serves as homage to and showcase for its author, E. Ann Kaplan.

NOTES

1. Recognizing the importance of the red carpet, the official website features a link to it. If you click on "Women's Fashion," you can see a fashion show consisting of no fewer than 144 fashion shots of celebrities proceeding alphabetically from Amy Adams to Ziyi Zhang. The show consists of dresses from Academy Awards past (over ten years), and it's interesting that one cannot accurately date the fashion changes. The accompanying caption gives the designer of the gown as well as the source of the accessories. If those 144 dresses are not enough, the site also features a retro fashion link to gowns worn by Academy Award winners, sorted by decade and going back to the 1930s. Not to overlook men's fashion, another link takes you to a gallery of Oscar finery as worn by actors from Ben Affleck to Billy Zane. http://www.oscar.com/redcarpet/.

2. Barbara Klinger, "Contraband Cinema" 114–15.

3. Before film, theater provided a venue for fashion shows, and burlesque anticipated the fashion parade. Earlier books and individual essays have discussed fashions in film. Though not a comprehensive list of titles on the topic, the following are some to consult for more on the topic: Jane Gaines and Charlotte Herzog, *Fabrications*; Sarah Berry, *Screen Style*; Stella Bruzzi, *Undressing Cinema*; David Dresser and Garth Jowell, *Hollywood Goes Shopping*; Pam Cook, *Fashioning the Nation*; Edward Maeder, ed., *Hollywood and History*; and Marketa Uhlirova, ed., *If Looks Could Kill*.

4. Elizabeth Wilson, *Adorned in Dreams*, 157.

5. Amy flamboyantly takes them off to disappear with the other camp followers into the desert sands and "The End."

6. Annie Hall's wardrobe was inspired by Keaton's own wardrobe. Charlotte Herzog, in "'Powder Puff' Promotion," describes a similar interchange between the virtual audience of a fashion show in a film and the actual viewers (144).

7. It is also true that filmic representation of a historical period has changed over time according to fashion. For examples of how historical figures such as Cleopatra and Marie Antoinette have looked in films over a period of time, see Edward Maeder, ed., *Hollywood and History*. On fashion in films as selling glamour to viewers see Jeanine Basinger, *A Woman's View*.

8. Karen Nelson, "Pulse."

9. Ulrich Lehmann, *Tigersprung*, 9–10.

10. After the 2010 Academy Awards, Ruth La Ferla, commenting in the *New York Times* on the intense relationship between fashion and film, asserted "clearly a long and fabled love affair has lost its heat" (E7). Her remarks refer to the costume

awards going to relatively safe costume designs rather than to highly colored and original costumes in such films as *Avatar*, costumes which were immediately translated to runways by such important couturiers as Jean Paul Gaultier and Valentino. La Ferla actually underscores the strong influence of film on fashion, if not the influence of Academy Awards for costume design; her evidence seems to affirm what she denies in illustrating fashion designers' polymorphous attraction to film fashion.

11. Joanne Entwistle, *The Fashioned Body*, 1.

12. For arguments that extend fashion to embrace world cultures and earlier

historical moments, see, among many others, Jean Allman, ed., *Fashioning Africa*; Yuniya Kawamura, *Fashion-ology*; Jennifer Craik, *The Face of Fashion*.

13. Irmgard Keun, *The Artificial Silk Girl*, 3.

14. Ibid.

15. Anita Loos, *Gentlemen Prefer Blondes*, 9.

16. To appreciate more fully Keun's cosmopolitan influences, see Maria Tatar's excellent introduction to the novel: "Inspired by the example of Anita Loos's *Gentlemen Prefer Blondes* (1925), Keun set out to write the German answer to the best-selling novel from the United States" (xvii).

17. "See The Second Floor" (A3).

WORKS CITED

Allman, Jane, ed. *Fashioning Africa: Power and the Politics of Dress*. Bloomington: Indiana University Press, 2004.

Basinger, Jeanine. *A Woman's View: How Hollywood Spoke to Women, 1930–1960*. Middletown, Conn.: Wesleyan University Press, 1995.

Berry, Sarah. *Screen Style: Fashion and Femininity in 1930s Hollywood*. Minneapolis: University of Minnesota Press, 2000.

Bruzzi, Stella. *Undressing Cinema: Clothing and Identity in the Movies*. London: Routledge, 1997.

Cook, Pam. *Fashioning the Nation: Costume and Identity in British Cinema*. London: British Film Institute, 1996.

Craik, Jennifer. *The Face of Fashion: Cultural Studies in Fashion*. London: Routledge, 1994.

Dresser, David, and Garth Jowell, eds. *Hollywood Goes Shopping*. Minneapolis: University of Minnesota Press, 2000.

Entwistle, Joanne. *The Fashioned Body: Fashion, Dress and Modern Social Theory*. Cambridge, U.K.: Polity, 2000.

Gaines, Jane, and Charlotte Herzog, eds. *Fabrications: Costume and the Female Body*. New York: Routledge, 1990.

Herzog, Charlotte. "'Powder Puff' Promotion: The Fashion Show-in-the-Film." In *Fabrications: Costume and the Female Body*, ed. Jane Gaines and Charlotte Herzog, 134–59. New York: Routledge, 1990.

Isherwood, Christopher. *Goodbye to Berlin*. New York: Random House, 1939.

Kawamura, Yuniya. *Fashion-ology: An Introduction to Fashion Studies*. Oxford: Berg, 2005.

Keun, Irmgard. *The Artificial Silk Girl*. Trans. Kathie von Ankum. New York: Other Press, 2002 [1932].

Klinger, Barbara. "Contraband Cinema: Piracy, *Titanic*, and Central Asia." *Cinema Journal* 49 (Winter 2010): 106–124.

La Ferla, Ruth. "Film and Fashion: Just Friends." *The New York Times* (New York) March 4, 2010, (Styles): E1, E7.

Lehmann, Ulrich. *Tigersprung: Fashion in Modernity*. Cambridge, Mass.: MIT Press, 2000.

Lipovetsky, Gilles. *The Empire of Fashion: Dressing Modern Democracy.* Trans. Catherine Porter. Princeton, N.J.: Princeton University Press, 1994.

Loos, Anita. *Gentlemen Prefer Blondes.* 1932. New York: Penguin, 1998.

Maeder Edward, ed. *Hollywood and History: Costume Design in Film.* New York: Thames and Hudson, 1987.

Mulvey, Laura. "Visual Pleasure and Narrative Cinema." *Screen* 16 (Autumn 1975): 6–18.

Nelson, Karen. "Pulse: What I'm Wearing Now." *The New York Times* (New York), November 1 2009, (Styles) 3.

"See the Second Floor." Advertisement. *New York Times* (New York), November 9 2009: A3.

Tatar, Maria. "Introduction." In *The Artificial Silk Girl,* xi–xxi. New York: Other Press, 2002.

Uhlirova, Marketa, ed. *If Looks Could Kill: Cinema's Images of Fashion, Crime and Violence.* London: Koenig Books, 2008.

Wilson, Elizabeth. *Adorned in Dreams: Fashion and Modernity.* New Brunswick: Rutgers University Press, 1985, rev. 2003.

FILMOGRAPHY

Annie Hall. Dir. Woody Allen. Costumes, Ralph Lauren. Rollins-Joffe Productions, 1977.

Avatar. Dir. James Cameron. Costumes, John Harding, Mayes C. Rubeo, Deborah Lynn Scott, and others. 20th Century Fox, Dune Entertainment, Giant Studios, Ingenious Film Partners, Lightstorm Entertainment, 2009.

Cabaret. Dir. Bob Fosse. Costumes, Charlotte Flemming. ABC Pictures, 1972.

The Call of the Wild. Dir. William Wellman. Costumes, Omar Kiam. Twentieth Century Pictures, 1935.

Gentlemen Prefer Blondes. Dir. Howard Hawks. Costumes, William Travilla. 20th Century Fox, 1953.

The Incredibles. Dir. Brad Bird. Walt Disney Pictures, Pixar Animation Studios, 2004.

Morocco. Dir. Josef von Sternberg. Costumes, Ruth Morley. Paramount Pictures, 1930.

Nanook of the North. Dir. Robert J. Flaherty. (Documentary film.) 1922.

Precious. Dir. Lee Daniels. Costumes, Lisa Cortes, Tracey Fields, Anne Kenney. Lee Daniels Entertainment, Smokewood Entertainment Group, 2009.

Titanic. Dir. James Cameron. Costumes, Deborah L. Scott. 20th Century Fox Film Corporation, Paramount Pictures, Lightstorm Entertainment, 1997.

To Catch a Thief. Dir. Alfred Hitchcock. Costumes, Edith Head. Paramount Pictures, 1955.

Unzipped. Dir. Douglas Keeve. (Documentary Film.) Hachette Filipacchi, Miramax Films, 1995.

PART ONE

Fashioning Film

Fashion, in its original sense, indicates the process of making, and thus the title of this section signifies making films by means of fashion. In the introduction, I indicated that Look signifies a fashion statement, and that the overall Look of a whole film contributes to a film genre, and the cinematic method itself of tailoring as a way of making films. In the broadest sense, these four chapters concern fashion's role in making movies and creating their Look.

Drake Stutesman in "Costume Design, or, What Is Fashion in Film?" focuses on the meticulous craft of the costume designer as integral to a given film's meanings. Using examples of some important Hollywood costume designs for both men and women, she demonstrates the centrality of painstaking costume design in constructing the meaning of a film. Stutesman argues, moreover, that, though costumes are not equivalent to "clothes," they include clothing design and as such "helped design what becomes recognizable as an American style." Film costumes have promoted American success in an international economy. Fashioning film, in her sense, also fashions America as a Look. Her point about fashion and its relationship to national identity is taken up in different ways in other sections. To begin *Fashion in Film* with this chapter both emphasizes the crucial role of costume designers and introduces themes that are threaded through the entire collection.

Viewers recognize film genres by means of costumes. "Fashioning Film" touches on the implications of this understanding by focusing on some familiar and enduring genres. Mary Ann Caws in "What to Wear in a Vampire Film" indicates in her very title that there are prescriptions for the vampire Look that we can identify and follow from the early silent vampire films to their recent incarnations in television series and films. Caws demonstrates that all vampire costumes are styled for a formal ritual. The vampire dresses in formal attire to honor the blood rite, which emphasizes the hallowed nature of the performance. Whether male or female, a vampire can be known by a Look. Written in high style, Caws's chapter describes how fashion contributes to the tone of vampire spectacularity that signifies the vampire film as a genre.

Ula Lukszo, in "Noir Fashion and Noir *as* Fashion," takes up the enduring mode of film noir to show that it only retrospectively becomes a genre when later films select fashions that then give the later film its "noir" Look. "The development of film noir as a genre is a post-noir phenomenon" she argues, demonstrating her point with films produced in what is generally considered the post-noir period, that is, after the 1930s and '40s. These later films pick and choose from the fashions of the early noir movement so that eventually the very Look contributes to "the recognition and *creation* of noir as a genre." In that vital sense, fashion shapes the genre.

Giuliana Bruno culminates the section with an elegant description of fashioning film. In "Surface, Fabric, Weave: The Fashioned World of Wong Kar-wai" she provides a paradigm for the visual language of film. Rather than "fashioning," Bruno uses the metaphor of "tailoring" powerfully to indicate the very texture and body-forming nature of both fashion and film. The chapter brings the reader into the exquisitely tailored cinematic world of Wong Kar-wai, refreshing Western eyes with its different aesthetic. At the same time, and while focusing on this one director and his carefully fabricated designs, Bruno's essay opens the eyes to the tailoring of film itself as a supremely aesthetic medium. Her chapter fluidly advances the volume to the next section which focuses on filming fashions.

ONE

Costume Design, or, What Is Fashion in Film?

DRAKE STUTESMAN

Why do we love fabric so much? Why do we love tailoring? A great couturier uses the best material to achieve a garment's ideal flow, stretch, cling, or billow or any other desired aspect of shape, block, and line. Madeleine Vionnet is famous for her bias cut because it caused the material to fall in a mesmerizing way. Paul Poiret is famous for his draping because it revolutionized women's clothing. Charles James is famous for his constructions (such as a hard corset that sustains a floating ball gown) because their anomalous balance uniquely eroticized the wearer.[1]

Great costume designers are equally ingenious. The most influential, on film and in fashion, is Gilbert Adrian (a.k.a. Adrian), MGM's Head of Costume (1928–1941) through its golden decade, who is famous for sculpting the padded shoulder and tapering, sleek silhouette that dominated much of twentieth-century dress.[2] Jean-Louis's corset-based, strapless gown for Rita Hayworth in *Gilda* (1946) is considered to have anticipated Dior's 1947 New Look. Many others have also moved the course of fashion by introducing trends—from Edith Head's flowery bustier for Elizabeth Taylor in *A Place in the Sun* (1951) to Kym Barrett's sinuous, utilitarian, cleric-inspired long black coats for *The Matrix Reloaded* (2003). This level of comparison raises questions. Are fashion and costume design the same? What do they have in common? Where do they depart?

Fashion is now a public sensibility—it is talked about at every level of society; bookstores have huge "fashion" sections; the red carpet is about who is wearing what label; names like Armani, Versace, and Chanel are household words; stars like Puff Daddy have their own clothing houses; and, "experts" on fashion such as, of all people, Joan Rivers, have sprouted up everywhere. No one blinks an eye. Despite Baudelaire's apotheosis of fashion as modern society's litmus test,[3] this attitude toward fashion is relatively recent. In 2000, fashion scholars Stella Bruzzi and Pamela Church Gibson summed up the discomforts of examining the subject: "Finally fashion's fundamental dilemma is that it has inevitably been predicated upon change, obsolescence, adornment and, in the so-called First World, it has been inextricably bound up with the commercial; this has led to the assumption that it is therefore superficial, narcissistic and wasteful."[4]

But a few years later, other fashion scholars could raise the status of their subject. In *Fashion Statements,* Francesca Alfano Miglietti extolled fashion's role, finding it "a reality that belongs essentially to modernity."[5] Christopher Breward shared that sentiment, declaring that "fashion now occupies the centre ground in popular understandings of modern culture. It enjoys unprecedented coverage in the western media and defines the tenor of urban life as no other medium."[6] "Modernity" legitimizes fashion, but Breward underestimates today's preoccupation with it. As early cinema took hold of the public imagination in the early 1910s, costume design and its trendsetting fashions became an implacable and alluring force.

Fashion as a focus has evolved prodigiously in the last ten years (with or without the true homage its creativity deserves) but film fashion, or what is actually *costume design,* has not. It is marginalized, if not ignored, in the way that fashion, as Bruzzi and Church Gibson defined its dismissal, was written off not long ago. Costume design is not only a phenomenal element of the filmic process, it is a phenomenon that has changed international economies. Lenin recognized film as "the most important" of the arts in part because it is the most persuasive.[7] Film spreads a Look or a message faster than any other medium except the internet. This power has allowed costume design, often unsung, to outdo couture's influence.

Film costume design started at the lowest end of the taste scale, Hollywood, and was pitted ultimately against the highest end, Parisian couture, which had dominated the garment trade since the seventeenth century. By the 1930s, this inequality had leveled and the scales began to tip toward the U.S. film industry and its groundbreaking popular costumes. At that time, American film costume design had so great an impact on the world of fashion that the important surrealist couturière Elsa Schiaperelli announced, without irony: "What Hollywood designs today you will be wearing tomorrow."[8]

With this kind of primacy, it could be said that film costume design not only boosted U.S. success in an international economy but, I would argue, went further. It helped to define an American identity, which to this day is still linked with the same adjectives that describe American design generally—inventive, straightforward, streamlined, practical, dynamic, pioneering, and explosive. By the early to mid- twentieth century, costume design had developed a significant connection to the American fashion empires, which began in earnest in the 1930s and 1940s with houses like Hattie Carnegie (who fostered many great costume design and couture talents),[9] John-Frederics, Traina-Norell, Mainbocher, Claire McCardell, and more. As these began to infiltrate the global fashion market and establish a style that was associated with an American Look, the European garment trade realized it was in conflict with a strong rival. Once the U.S. controlled cinema distribution (from the late '10s and early '20s onwards) the extraordinary costume design of American films reached and astonished audiences by the millions. Initial costume designers, such as Clare West and Adrian, recognized costume design as a great force in twentieth-century *haute couture*. Their work, crucial to the establishment of American style as a world competitor, was the first to outstrip the French, who until then had ruled fashion both commercially and artistically. It's arguable that West and Adrian were key figures in laying the groundwork for what is internationally known as the "American Look." They also were extremely vocal in their defense of U.S. fashion over Parisian alternatives and influenced the public to rethink which continent to imitate. Adrian bitterly commented that his designs went to Paris on film and French couturiers stole his ideas and returned them to the States as their own invention.[10] This was so common, he stated, that "every Hollywood designer has had the experience of seeing one of his designs ignored when first flashed on the screen and then a season or two later become the vogue because it had the stamp of approval from Paris."[11]

There have been some partnerships. In the Studio days, such couturiers as Schiaparelli, Chanel, Lucile, Givenchy, Dior, Hartnell, Balmain, Molyneux, Lanvin, Erté, Norell, and Reville designed for films, often in tandem with an in-house costume designer, and today it is not unheard of to see a film credit for Giorgio Armani or Jean-Paul Gaultier. But these were not, and still are not, strong relationships. The cinema costume design world and the couture world are linked but also very separate.

With these intense connections, it is obvious that the costume designer and couturier share a great deal. They each have an intimate knowledge, if not a deep love, of fabric, tailoring, line, and style, and they typically can claim an invaluable imagination and innovative, even wild, aesthetic. But there are many differences. The key one is that costume design is a working craft whose purpose is not to serve or even expand a style but to serve a film. It must express something far beyond the outfit: the costume designer must use clothes to create basic movie elements. They have to meet extreme demands such as coping with the cinematographer's lighting, the dimensions of an actor's body, the story's character, and that unique cinematic feature—the close up—all without being obtrusive. It is a complex task but it succeeds because the audience is well prepared. How so?

What does not seem to have changed in the course of some forty thousand–plus years of human society is the impact of clothing on the psyche. Costume design plays on our deepest responses to clothes and all their aspects (shape, color, texture), aspects which augment, indeed almost stand in for, our perceptions of sex, authority, comfort/discomfort, and stature. Nakedness is eroticized by clothing. Power, class, and wealth are recognized by what is worn. Fashion plays on the same responses and is as old as clothing itself. In 2009, twisted flax fibers, thirty thousand years old and dyed into pinks, blues, and grays, were found in the Republic of Georgia. Elizabeth Barber, an expert on prehistoric textiles, surmised that these threads were not for functional wear but rather for "fashion," as she put it, because, even then, status was beginning to be revealed through cloth.[12] What, then, are , clothes, fashion, and costume design? In a sense, clothes are what one sweats in (a life), fashion is the sweep of a Look (a lifestyle), and costume design is an industrial illusion of both (a desire for a life).

Fashion historian Valerie Steele puts it succinctly, "Fashion is a particular kind of clothing that is 'in style.'"[13] The differentiations of fashion (i.e. high fashion/low fashion) are not elaborate. They are found in the cost, the use, and the tailoring expertise of the clothes. High fashion, or *haute couture* (which loosely means "quality stitching") is only a small part of what is termed the "fashion system." The rest is boutique, ready-to-wear, and—the most lucrative part of any fashion empire—branding.

Costume, on the other hand, is on another planet or, as it were, a parallel universe. Though often breathtaking, it is really a clever cinematic beast of burden, created for a solely cinematic purpose. The former head of the American Costume Designers Guild, costume designer Deborah Nadoolman Landis, sees costume and fashion as "antithetical." She maintains that the starstruck public can't believe that the costume the star wears is a cinematic device that is there only, as Landis sees it, to tell a story.[14] This sounds unilateral and certainly there are many overlaps between fashion and costume design, but she is right that the public doesn't grasp costume design as a piece of film architecture.

Costume is a high art. The costume designer uses the word "build" to describe an outfit's construction. The costume is an object, a literal building that the actor enters, "wears," or inhabits in order to perform. Many actors feel that they understand their character once they have worn the costume. It is a psychic world (it protects the actor's character fantasy) as well as a material one (it must be built to withstand great stresses such as wind, water, fighting, dancing, sweating, tearing, staining, and constant reuse). One even could compare the extremes of costume design, (such as a much toiled-over costume that appears for a few minutes and then is never seen again, like Norma Shearer's ball gown by Adrian in *Marie Antoinette*, 1938), with the extremes of *haute couture*, the original outfits seen on the catwalk. Alexander McQueen, Viktor and Rolf or Hussein Chalayan, to name a few, have often created bizarre clothes for their seasonal collections that are impossible to wear. They are only prototypes and they quickly disappear. In the documentary *The Secret World of Haute Couture* (2007), *haute couture* customers (often requesting anonymity), who have sole access to these original clothes, describe how they refit the single catwalk article, even completely, at great cost. After these clients' retailoring, multiple versions of the clothes emerge until the innovations of the outfit filter into retail mass consumption. Some costumes are unwearable though fans crave their style. For example, Marilyn Monroe's pink gown in the 1953 film *Gentleman Prefer Blondes*, which she wears while singing "Diamonds Are a Girl's Best Friend," was made of upholstery satin and lined with felt by William Travilla.

Costume designers have to tell a story, and they tap into the same stratagems that the first ancient dyed "fashion" threads tapped. They manipulate through tools such as silhouettes, color nuances, design lines, or fabric textures (is silk right for the character or is burlap better?) but they also create an emotional *feel* in the costume through minute details such as moving a shoulder seam further from or closer to the neck or making a jacket a little too tight, too loose, too short, or too long. They must convey considerable information through imperceptible details. Wonderful use of these seemingly innocuous signals is a costume design staple. In the television sitcom, *Two and A Half Men* (2003–present), a silhouette subtly creates part of the comedy. The show is about two brothers—one an immature forty-something, handsome and a swinging bachelor who has a constant stream of beautiful bed partners, and the other an immature forty-something, homely and deeply repressed. The swinger is always dressed in large, square, knee-length shorts, a box cut, vertically lined rayon sport shirt with an open collar, and loafers with white socks. He looks stylish but also somewhat adolescent, as the clothes make him look boyish, reflecting his inner character. The repressed brother wears a polo shirt tucked into a neatly cinched belt, waist-high. His top shirt collar button is always closed but often the button pulls on the buttonhole, making two taut folds. This, a feature obviously sewn into the costume, makes him look pinched, almost childishly dressed in a different way, and underscores his immaturity and psychic discomfort. If the costume designer, Mary T. Quigley, dressed the brothers in fitting, hip, or debonair clothes, they would both look like well-built, handsome men, and the comedy wouldn't work.

Color too dictates what can work and not work in a film and the costume designer has to deal with a host of possible problems—from art direction to the actor's complexion to the lighting, to name a few.

This can range from knowing what not to dress an actor in (if a wall is green, then an actor in a green suit could be lost against it) to knowing the limitations of a color within the context of the film. In *Shaft* (2000), costume designer Ruth Carter was determined to dress the lead character, Shaft, in black, though the cinematographer was against it, concerned black would be lost in the film's many night scenes. Carter had to find a material that flattered actor Samuel L. Jackson's complexion but refracted enough light to offset it *and* would withstand the darkness of the shots. After many tests, she settled on a coal-colored suede whose upright fibers uniquely threw off light as the body moved.[15] Piero Tosi, one of the world's greatest costume designers, who costumed most of Luchino Visconti's films and is known for his perfectionism and historical faithfulness, nevertheless changed the blue of the military uniform in *Ludwig* (1972) because he felt it was not a "believable" color.[16] This nuanced judgment is crucial. The costume designer must know how to convince a modern audience and therefore must not only know the true attire, textiles, patterns, and colors that someone in a given period would have worn—from a cave dweller to a barfly in '60s Hong Kong to a Victorian nun—but be able to deviate from any of it.

Costume designers approach the character not just from the perspective of what suits the storyline (for example, is it a western, a noir, a romance, or a sci-fi?) but from the perspective of what suits the actor. They must, at times, make an actor's character emerge against body type. In the international hit HBO series *The Sopranos*, which ran for eight years (1999–2007), James Gandolfini portrayed domineering, sexual, violent mafia head Tony Soprano. Soprano's clothes had to reflect an unsophisticated New Jersey twenty-first-century mafia look (realism was part of the show's attraction). At the same time, Gandolfini was an overweight, round-faced, balding man and not an obvious seductive lead. Thus costume designer Juliet Polsca had a conflict. She couldn't rely on the ubiquitous Armani suit to glamorize him, as that would be out of character, so she artfully dressed Gandolfini in solid tones of greys, browns, blacks, and tans, and in diamond and striped patterns. The fabric was of good quality and the color tones were elegant, lending him urbanity while the simple, polished lines sexualized his bulk. Though it might be considered a trick Look, Polsca set new styles.[17]

1.1. Moss Mabry cleverly juxtaposed the delicate garments of the middle-aged women who signify vulnerable life against the brainwashed, deadened soldiers' dark, heavy combat uniforms in a recurring nightmare in *The Manchurian Candidate*.
Courtesy of Jerry Ohlinger's Movie Material Store.

The beautiful Grace Kelly, in her Academy Award–winning performance in *The Country Girl* (1954), had to play against type as a dowdy, downtrodden woman married to an older, alcoholic man. In charge of Paramount's Costume Department at the time, Edith Head dressed her in loose, high-collared white blouses, long A-line skirts with little emphasis on her waistline, and flat shoes. Her shapely body was disguised and her character made to seem stifled. In the 1939 romantic comedy, *Ninotchka,* about a Russian commissar, played by Greta Garbo, who comes to Paris and gradually succumbs to the joys of western decadence, the costume fabrics as well as the costume designs revealed her route from disciplinarian to lover. Adrian dressed her for the entrance scene in a stiff wool suit, cut close to her body and tightly buttoned, but, as the film progressed, each time her garment changed, he softened the fabric, until finally she was dancing in an off-the-shoulder chiffon gown.

Costume designer Moss Mabry also used fabric to subliminally underlie the 1962 Cold War thriller, *The Manchurian Candidate,* a film about brainwashed American POWs from the Korean War. A key motif appears in a recurring nightmare where soldiers sit among middle-aged, well-dressed women at a ladies' suburban garden party and the dream women slowly are revealed to be Communist officials watching the POWs commit murder as a test. The dream's atmosphere is both gentle and sardonic. The soldiers are polite, almost bored. When, on command, a soldier, in a detached state, strangles his friend, nothing changes, and the soldiers show no emotion.

Throughout, the camera pans across the women's heads and shoulders and, though they all wear hats, it is their décolletage that stands out. The dresses are made of flowered or patterned silk or cotton, with modest but revealing scoop or V-neck collars (some plain, some flounced). Most of the women wear sparkling, at times gaudy, but tasteful necklaces. Through such details, the audience is unconsciously drawn to their throats. The vulnerable throat (the place where the soldier is killed) stands in for the naturalness that the brainwashed soldiers have suppressed. When the dream portrays the men as apathetic and cold, the talkative, delicately dressed women evoke, in the viewer, what the dream does not reveal—the soldiers' humanity.

A single outfit can also speak volumes. One of cinema's most iconic and most shrewd is Lucinda Ballard's costume for Marlon Brando in the 1951 film based on the 1947 play, *A Streetcar Named Desire,* about two sisters in working-class New Orleans—one married to, and desperately in love with, a crude, stunning, virile man played by Brando, and the other, unmarried, who is trying to hide her sexual past. Sex, and its compulsions, is one of the narrative's driving forces. As such, it played a major role in the costumes.

Ballard dressed Brando in an undershirt and trousers. Figure 1.2 shows a studio shot of Brando, as Stanley, in the costume he wears through some of the film's opening scenes. Casting Brando as Stanley is an obvious choice. His effortless, irresistible, insouciant sexiness is obvious in his pose, but a close look shows that many devices also promote it.

Brando wears an ordinary undershirt and belted trousers, but the clothes are not haphazard. Ballard created this outfit to *seem* as if his clothes are filthy from work, wrinkled from the sweltering New Orleans' heat, and clinging to Brando's flesh. The clothes are so plausible, it's as if he lives in them. But they just have been lifted from a wardrobe rack and, to complicate the job further, since Brando wears these clothes in many scenes, more than one set, exactly alike, would have had to be made.

Though this type of Look had been seen in French and American 1930s films and in the 1940s wartime male, Brando's fame raised it to new heights and it is likely that Ballard took care to perfect the overall eroticism.[18] The undershirt is fairly tight. The sleeves hug the round shoulders and Ballard would have sewn them into caps to snugly fit Brando's muscles, placed the seams to flatter his neck and shoulders, and cut the sleeves to do the same, giving him the most compelling lines possible. The sweat is necessary to the narrative, but where it is placed and how it appears are costume design choices. This sweat enhances Brando's shape. The dark, seemingly wet (though it is oil), stain sits in the middle of his chest, revealing its muscular curves and so making his body accessible and real. The armpit creases are placed so that their V-lines visibly show how active Brando is and how strong. The undershirt's wrinkles cross his tapering body, outlining his contours as if hand drawn, taking our eyes with them, one long fold rolling straight into the front of his pants. His shirt and trousers would have been beaten, washed, or worn to make them appear used, and the edges of the pants' pockets pulled on to give the impression that he would hook his thumbs there often. The fabric is not denim but something softer, hanging off his hips to underscore his build.

As real as this looks, the purpose of the costume is not realism. It is, as Landis argues, to tell a story and, in this case, to make Brando look like a working class stud, his character and key to the plot's progress. Without his sexiness (for his attractiveness is the critical difference between the two sisters) the story fails. Ballard could have dressed Brando in heavier,

1.2. Marlon Brando in *A Streetcar Named Desire* smolders in a carefully constructed costume of an undershirt and belted trousers. *Courtesy of Jerry Ohlinger's Movie Material Store.*

her. He loved what he called "her lavish hand." DeMille hired West in 1918 to oversee costumes at Famous Players-Lasky, the foremost studio at that time, because he knew her genius could "make people gasp."[27] It did.

Christian Esquevin, in his Adrian biography, locates the era of Hollywood's greatest pressure on France in the late '20s when, he argues, a form-fitting gown showing a womanly shape began to glide across the silver screen, simply obliterating Poiret's boyish, cloaked, semi-asexual figure.[28] But this pressure began even earlier with West's talent, with her popularity and the publicity that her work garnered. Her reputation grew more public as her outré, sexy gowns, barely clinging to the bodies of the superstars of her era—Gloria Swanson, Bebe Daniels, and the Talmadge sisters—appeared on screen, in the fan magazines, and on the backs of screen goddesses at parties. Her fabulous outfits included the patent leather swimsuit in *Saturday Night* (1922) and the octopus dress and cape seen in *The Affairs of Anatol* (1921) (which may be considered a forerunner of Adrian's infamous Zeppelin Ball gown in *Madam Satan* [1930]). These and many other creations made West famous. She devised personal clothes for special star clients (as did many costume designers after her, including Adrian, Howard Greer, Irene, and, later, Patricia Field; they also opened retail salons). Her opinion counted and she was the first to champion American fashion over European. In 1923, *Screen News* quoted West's belief, after a trip to Europe, that U.S. motion picture costumes trumped Paris designs and led the couture world.[29] Less than a decade later, Adrian voiced this same conviction and ratified it in his line of fashion "firsts."

These forceful talents and forceful voices were persuasive, but economic failures and political struggle also slowed Europe's couture lead. By 1915, World War I prevented most French imports from reaching the U.S., and this meant that "American-made" clothing gained prominence and even cachet (campaigns urging buyers to "Buy American" were not uncommon).[30] In the 1910s, many European films enjoyed big U.S. audiences, but by the '20s, as studios, especially Famous Players-Lasky, had

1.3A. The bold Babylonian costumes Clare West designed for *Intolerance* influenced fashion trends. *Courtesy of Jerry Ohlinger's Movie Material Store.*

L367X-2

taken corporate control of the industry and of distribution, European films lost favor and were denigrated as old-fashioned or perversely arty. The fashion trades still were under French hegemony, but American cinema costume design, crazy as it could be, began to beat Parisian fashion at its own game because it had the widest public: the wide-eyed moviegoer. In the '30s, seventy-five million Americans went to the movies weekly, but only a few read the couture magazines.[31]

By this time, the prolific Adrian (designing for over ten films a year) was on his way to becoming the true luminary of the American Look, responsible for more fashion firsts than any other U.S. designer in fashion or in film. He advocated simplicity but he also inventively took that quality to new extremes. He perfected a "V-line" silhouette, which enhanced a trim female figure with elegant, hard lines. He used collarless necklines, tie fasteners, slashes, straps that were only decorative, asymmetrical pockets, and asymmetrical balances between large features and small features. His inner work, such as stitching techniques, could be unique and problem-solving. He was daring in mixing textiles and daring in experimenting with complex tailoring, seeing how far he could take a clean line without making it complicated. These are only a few of his hallmarks.

Oleg Cassini, a costume designer and Jacqueline Kennedy's stylist, cited Adrian as "perhaps the only member of our profession powerful enough to impose his taste on a director."[32] Adrian was able to stride both worlds as no one else, and he was direct in his intentions, stating in 1931, "[w]hat I am trying to create for the screen are ultra modern clothes which will be adaptable for the street."[33] By the 1930s he became a household name and, like West, had an opinion that counted.

In 1932, Adrian changed the garment industry forever when he converted a cinema costume into a ready-to-wear retail dress. With this feat, he became a triumphant force in both the fabric and the clothing trades, major economies of the time. Adrian's ruffled white organdy gown for Joan Crawford in *Letty Lynton* (1932) was the first cinema costume to be mass-marketed and was described by Edith Head as the single most

1.3B. Clare West's famous stark, outré, and elegant Octopus cape for *The Affairs of Anatol. Courtesy of Photofest.*

important fashion influence in film history.[34] This is hardly an exaggeration. The dress became an overnight craze. One Macy's outlet bragged of selling five hundred thousand copies. Whether true or not, the boast indicates the dress's fame. When Adrian began to market his *Letty Lynton* dress, he entered into a swirling maelstrom of radical transformations in the fashion world.

In the 1930s, Paris and New York had been struggling for decades over ready-to-wear, which had eclipsed handmade clothes (previously worn by all parts of the population). Ready-to-wear had been a slowly growing segment of the French industry since the late 1800s, when small dressmaking workrooms, often run by women, and the rich salons for exclusive clients, grouped into larger conglomerates. Men took over the management of these new workrooms. Labor was forced into many strikes. In 1925, though the garment industry (especially *haute couture* patterns and the rights to them, as well as ready-to-wear clothing) was still France's second largest exporter, it was weakening. By the late '20s, ready-to-wear had stormed the U.S. fashion world and was considered a successful base for couturiers such as Hattie Carnegie and Omar Kiam, who were touted in American *Vogue* as creators of "a mode that is definitely American."[35] By the 1930s, France's export–import trade, the basic bread and butter of its garment world, and its ready-to-wear market had been drastically changed by the strikes and the war, and its global reach had diminished.

While an American Look and the ascendance of ready-to-wear clothing were already in the making, it was Adrian's move that definitively brought film and its costume design to a new kind of commercial marketing. By seizing this advantage, he changed the course of the American sense of Americanness forever, sealing a fantastically productive bond between basic artisan crafts like costume design and filmmaking with an economic boom that jettisoned the U.S. from Europe's hold. He was part of the early foundations of a rapidly developing American identity. He adamantly defended an American Look that still exists today with all the Adrian earmarks—clean tailoring, practical elegance with an original and extravagant use of fabric, and an urban sophistication that speaks of a woman on the move. He described this as "the natural kind of American grace for which I strive."[36] These traits were further developed as identifiably American over the decades in the work of designers like Claire McCardell, Bonnie Cashin, James Galanos, Halston, Bill Blass, and Calvin Klein.

No designer is isolated. Some of these design motifs also appeared in Chanel, Schiaparelli, and in the *fashionista zeitgeist* of the early century, but Adrian more than anyone diversified and unified these ideas with an American style in mind. He and West, both film costume designers, saw the grace in the American Look long before Americanism and its culture became acceptable internationally. Remarkably, though still an underappreciated profession, the qualities of film costume design—strange mixtures of *declassé, classé,* wild style, artisanship, and economic and artistic constraints—are part of the roots of American individuation.

NOTES

1. Richard Martin, *Charles James*, 6–7. Martin argues that James's heavy, highly engineered dresses conveyed an eroticism and empowerment unlike any other in the '40s and '50s and that this anomaly was James's greatest achievement.

2. Christian Esquevin, *Adrian*, 36. Though the question of who invented the woman's shoulder pad silhouette, and when, has been much debated, Esquevin places the debut of Adrian's shoulder pad in 1928 and Schiaperelli's and others' in 1931.

3. Charles Baudelaire, *The Painter of Modern Life*, 13. In the 1860 essay, *The Painter of Modern Life,* Baudelaire extols the "ephemeral" and "contingent" found in fashion as the real measure of modernity, in part because the vogues of what people wear embody living in modern time and so are the most representative of it.

4. Stella Bruzzi and Pamela Church Gibson, "Introduction," 2.

5. Francesca Miglietti, *Fashion Statements*, 15.

6. Christopher Breward, *Fashion*, 9.

7. Mira Leihm, *The Most Important Art*, 34. V. I. Lenin in conversation with A. V. Lunacharsky in 1922 said, ". . . film, of all the arts, is the most important. . . ."

8. Jane Mulvagh, *Vogue History of Twentieth Century Fashion*, 123.

9. Hattie Carnegie fostered the great couturiers James Galanos, Claire McCardell, Norman Norell, and Pauline Trigère as well as the great costume designers Travis Banton, Howard Greer, and Jean-Louis.

10. Paul Poiret, *King of Fashion*, 154. Conversely, French couturiers also had trans-Atlantic complaints. Poiret, years before, complained that couture clothes were bastardized by "intermediaries" between the continents who were only interested in what they could sell. He maintained that Americans "were condemned to see nothing of the true Parisian mode except what is without personality, without significance. . . ."

11. Esquevin, 19.

12. NPR Radio, *All Things Considered*, September 10, 2009. In response

to reporter Richard Harris's quoting Elizabeth Barber as saying that "woven clothing developed not so much for comfort as for fashion, especially important fashion," Barber answers, "It's not until you start to get haves and have-nots that people start differentiating themselves by, look what I'm wearing as opposed to what you're wearing or not wearing."

13. Valerie Steele, *Fifty Years of Fashion,* 3.

14. Deborah Landis, *Screencraft,* 7. Many other costume designers describe their profession in this way.

15. Mary Ellen Harrington, *Fifty Designers/ Fifty Costumes,* 26. Interview with Ruth Carter.

16. Landis, 84.

17. After another designer briefly worked on three episodes, the actors demanded that Polsca return, believing their roles were inextricably tied with the costumes and the Look that she created for them. She completed the entire series, seventy-three episodes. (Interview with Juliet Polsca by the author.)

18. In conversation with the author, costume designers Rita Ryack (Academy Award nominee) and Carol Oditz confirmed that Ballard would approach the costume in this manner.

19. Nathaniel West, *Miss Lonelyhearts and Day of the Locust,* 4.

20. Susan Prichard, *Film Costume,* 247. West's first name is variously spelled Clair, Claire or Clare. Pritchard claims that "Clare" is correct.

21. By the 1920s, the budgets for costume design could be enormous. In 1922, West spent $100,000 on furs for one actress in *Manslaughter* (Prichard, 304).

22. One exception is Paul Iribe, graphic artist and designer of theater sets, furniture and more, who had worked for Poiret and Jeanne Paquin. He designed for a number of American films, either solely or in collaboration with other costume designers. He and West worked on *The Affairs of Anatol, Adam's Rib, Manslaughter,* and *The Golden Bed.* But, it is difficult to separate out a single costume designer's silent era work in these kind of collaborations. Each costume designer could make outfits for specific actors or work on specific scenes (vignettes were popular in this era) or one could be responsible for the film overall while another costume designer created for a single actor. Costume designers did not necessarily work together. Many sources still conflict over accreditation. In histories written after the silent era, the names of the men in such collaborations, such as Iribe or Mitchell Leisen, have typically been favored over those of the women, such as West or Natacha Rambova. But it's not always the case. Also, many excellent talents came from France to make careers in Hollywood, and some stayed permanently, including Jean-Louis, known as the French Adrian, and René Hubert. (Madeleine Delpierre et al., *French Elegance in the Cinema,* 45–79.)

23. Prichard, 154. Griffith is known to have conceived some of the costume design.

24. David Chierichetti, *Hollywood Costume Design,* 8.

25. This was such an important achievement that nine years later, in 1925, *Motion Picture* still noted it (Prichard, 109).

26. Lillian Howard, "Back to Babylon for New Fashions," 39–40. West's Babylonian costumes were influential.

27. Cecil B. DeMille, *The Autobiography of Cecil B. DeMille,* 261.

28. Esquevin, 22.

29. Prichard summarizes two newspaper articles from the time. "Say Europe's Designers Using Our Film Ideals," *Screen News* 2, no. 10 (March 10, 1920): 14. "Once

Paris . . . Now Los Angeles," *Grauman's Magazine* 5, no. 36 (September 24, 1922). (Both Prichard, 304.)

30. Mulvagh, 33.

31. Robert McElvaine, *Encyclopedia of the Great Depression,* 576.

32. Oleg Cassini, *In My Own Fashion,* 107.

33. Esquevin, 33.

34. Ibid., 17.

35. Mulvagh, 85–86.

36. Esquevin, 35.

WORKS CITED

Barber, E. J. W. *Prehistoric Textiles: The Development of Cloth in Neolithic and Bronze Ages.* Princeton, N.J.: Princeton University Press, 1991.

Baudelaire, Charles. *The Painter of Modern Life and Other Essays.* Trans. Jonathan Mayne. New York: Da Capo, 1964.

Baudot, François. *Poiret.* New York: Assouline Publishing, 2003.

Breward, Christopher. *Fashion.* Oxford: Oxford University Press, 2003.

Bruzzi, Stella, and Pamela Church Gibson. "Introduction." In *Fashion Cultures Theories, Explorations and Analysis,* ed. Stella Bruzzi and Pamela Church Gibson. London, New York: Routledge, 2000.

Calhoun, Dorothy. "Styles Are Dictated in Hollywood and Paris Designers Follow Them." *Motion Picture* 29 (March 1925): 116–117.

Cassini, Oleg. *In My Own Fashion.* New York: Pocket Books, 1987.

Chierichetti, David. *Hollywood Costume Design.* New York: Harmony Books, 1976.

Delpierre, Madeleine, Marainne de Fleury, and Dominique Lebrun. *French Elegance in the Cinema.* Paris: Musée de la Mode et du Costume Palais Galliera, 1988.

DeMille, Cecil B. *The Autobiography of Cecil B. DeMille.* Englewood Cliffs, N.J.: Prentice-Hall, 1959.

Esquevin, Christian. *Adrian: Silver Screen to Custom Label.* New York: Monacelli Press, 2008.

Green, Nancy L. *Ready-to-Wear, Ready-To-Work, A Century of Industry and Immigrants in Paris and New York.* Durham, N.C.: Duke University Press, 1997.

Gutner, Howard. *Gowns By Adrian: The MGM Years 1928–1941.* New York: Harry N. Abrams, 2001.

Harrington, Mary Ellen, ed. *Fifty Designers/ Fifty Costumes: Concept to Character.* Los Angeles: Academy of Motion Picture Arts and Sciences, 2004.

Howard, Lillian. "Back to Babylon for New Fashions." *Photoplay* 11, no. 5 (April 1917).

Kaplan, Joel, and Shelia Stowell. *Theatre and Fashion: Oscar Wilde to the Suffragettes.* Cambridge: Cambridge University Press, 1994.

Landis, Deborah Nandoolman. *Screencraft: Costume Design.* Burlington, Mass.: Focal Press, 2003.

Leach, William. *Land of Desire: Merchants, Power and the Rise of a New American Culture.* New York: Pantheon, 2003

Leese, Elizabeth. *Costume Design in the Movies.* New York: Dover, 1991.

Liehm, Mira, and Antonin Liehm. *The Most Important Art: Soviet and East European Film After 1945.* Berkeley: University of California Press, 1977.

Martin, Richard. *Charles James.* New York: Assouline, 2006 [reprint:

TWO

What to Wear in a Vampire Film

MARY ANN CAWS

Nothing is more fashionable than the enduring and recurring rituals of fashion. The very fashioning of film itself brings the mind into a heightened ritualistic state. For each genre has a stock tradition out of which the ritual is enacted in film after film. The anticipation of the ceremony rests upon a certain degree of visual sameness that allows us to recognize how the specific example plays into and with or against the fashion that has been built up by tradition over the years.

Now, I am particularly interested by the fashion of the vampire film, about which Michael Wood's column in the *London Review of Books* of May 14, 2009, remarks (in this case, about the recent *Let the Right One In*): "Vampires seem to be making a comeback these days and not just at night and from the grave."[1] On July 1, 2009, we read lots about the vamped-up excitement in a *New York Times* article cleverly called "A Trend With Teeth," written by Ruth La Ferla (and what a great name for the topic!): "Rarely have monsters looked so sultry—or so camera-ready. No small part of this latest vampire mania seems to stem from the ethereal cool and youthful sexiness with which the demons are portrayed. Bela Lugosi they are not."[2] True, but sometimes I wish they were: shows my old-time nature. Sex is nice, and youth is lovely, but Bela Lugosi's costume, ah . . .

Now, that's something to sink your spectator's teeth into.

Some of the best minds in cinema and fashion are involved in these films, as has always been the case. The ritual of the vampire film has its own rules, and the audience delights in it, as do, in appearance at least, the actors, and very certainly the designers. What the perpetrator of the blood-enjoying act wears and what his or her victim wears is a topic worth dwelling on, as it is an act they are always specially dressed up for. The act is a ritual, even, not to shy away from its quasi-religious over-tones, a sacrament. How one dresses the celebrants of that sacrament, sacrificer and sacrificed, is key, for every aspect of appearance points toward the ritual of blood to be accomplished. The point is of the ritual all wrapped up in the custom and costume of the scene; every word brings its own weight with it, as does every item of clothing. The audi-ence has to anticipate the action, and to recognize well beforehand who is the villain and who the victim. In the case of the victim, cinematic portrayal is of course a matter of setting innocence against criminality, naïveté against cunning. The spectacle of the feast has to start with the spilling of a bit of the victim's blood—usually with a scratch or a tiny slash—which lets the vampire reveal the excitement of the red color, the true background for the eroticism so closely entwined with vampirism. In these films, the villain is in fact the hero or heroine: such a criminal, generally dressed in at least semi-erotic garb, has to be (and to want to be) hated and, therefore, according to the code, beloved. And audience recognition of the roles to be played out has to be instant. Thus the central importance of the costume. Everything is high and on a high: spectacle is all.

This is true even when—or perhaps more when—the spectacle is wrapped up. Best of all the costumes of this type is the long black cloak that wraps up even as it reveals the character underneath, which is famil-iar to us from the iconic *Dracula,* Tod Browning's masterpiece of 1931. The great Count Dracula, Bela Lugosi, comes so majestically down the stairs, his pace matching the length of the intensely black cloak: slow and heavy, *something fearful impending.* Things have to move slowly for the proper solemnity of the ritual. And the very idea of the cloak suggests disguise, the cloaking of the fearful fact of our excitement at the blood-sucking, the drawing out of energy from victim to vampire. Ever after, the long black cloak has signified vampiredom, the evil empire of night. It is a glamorous version of the cape, which was common in the Europe of the Middle Ages and then returned to fashion in the nineteenth century,

so the cape-turned-cloak reminds us of Count Dracula's fabled long life as well as his fashion appeal.

The human who can defeat a vampire is rare, and so also specially marked. Only daylight, or a stake in the heart, or a cross can undo that cloaked empire, as Buffy and every other vampire slayer will come to know. Buffy, the modern teenage version of the One Who Spells Death to the Vampire (1997–2003), most famously appears in early seasons dressed in a miniskirt and black boots with perhaps a white two-piece cotton top or a bright-blue jacket, signifying purity and, of course, the color of the sky in daytime, the contrary of the dark night-colored cloak. The brevity of her skirt creates a contrast with the dragging length of the traditional vampiric cloak, as white does with black. Bela Lugosi's garment has, of course, in its and his superb elegance, both colors: the black wing collar of his cloak rises up high on the back of his neck, while his very white vest with its perfect bowtie and V-shaped front, with the cutaway panels at the waist, match the small V-shape of his dark pocket handkerchief. Nothing is unplanned in this image, nor in the way the tails of the cloak rise to suggest bat wings when he shrinks away backwards from the cross Van Helsing shows him. Nor is Buffy's miniskirted, high-booted costume unplanned: each is perfect in its contemporary elegance. We could take these two figures as the ur-figures of the vampire film.

Even before Lugosi, in France, Louis Feuillade's serial *Les Vampires* (1915) was an instant and long-lasting hit. In it we can already see visual icons that become classic: the preening stance of the vampire with front protruding, and the visible bat wings, both alluring and frightening. Here the fabled Musidora as Irma Vep, wearing a tight black bodysuit and mask with holes for the eyes, vamped her way over the screen, making the film an instant cult favorite. Vampires are never timid. Audiences, past and present, long for the fear instilled by the black winged costume.

The hidden violence implied even in the first moment when we see only the costume is what makes vampire films such a raving success, even the recent *Twilight* (2008), which is only watered-down vampire-

2.1. Bela Lugosi as Dracula in Tod Browning's *Dracula*.
Courtesy of Jerry Ohlinger's Movie Material Store.

treated to an elegance befitting the tradition and the ritual. In place of the long black cloak, we are offered a delightful vision of vampire London mod style, with top hat, long curls, blue glasses, grey suit with narrow lapels, stickpin (an early sign of bloodletting to come, the aware observer may note) and, naturally, his perfectly fitting black gloves. His is an appearance with which any self-respecting victim would fall in love. Later, in London, he appears with white hair piled high and a long red cloak dripping behind him: "I am the last of my kind." It certainly makes you hope so. His white collar replies to the good guy Keanu Reeves's white collar in the film. Behind him, a shadow is always cast—suggestion turned into statement. Evil casts a long shadow.

In the famous bed scene, Winona as Mina lounges on her bed in her ravishing nightgown—white, of course—and announces how she wishes to get away from this realm of death. You don't know what you are saying, says Oldman, but he is as wrong as he is right. In another wonderful scene, the victim wears heavily eroticized black leather gloves as she caresses the white fur of an animal, the covering of the hands only intensifying the visceral stroking of the fur; the victim has now also adopted the erotic dynamic of covering up. Costuming here emphasizes that vampirism as a style is contagious: the ritual of blood calls for the heavy accent on dress and dressing up.

Mel Brooks's parody of vampiredom, *Dracula: Dead, And Loving It* (1995), one of the most screamingly funny vampire movies ever made, plays to the hilt the classic costume of Mr. Vampire: a black cape, of course, because that is necessary for the transformation into a bat (he hovers on the ceiling, smashes against the window, shrivels up into a bat costume like Clark Kent into Superman, or Batman himself, only backwards). Again we see high-piled white hair—a touch of Old World wisdom signifying an ancient vampire—along with a white jabot and red insert, and again a stickpin: always a very good touch, the stickpin. This parody has it all, with the slow-speaking naïve and innocent Jonathan, the always hungry Renfield snatching at every insect that comes along and ending with the tail of some forlorn beastie protruding from his mouth, the heavily accented vampire specialist brought in for good counsel, and the lovely Mina turned vulgar redmouth with the jagged teeth we long to recognize, her robe turned seductive, her mind to mayhem.

Then there is the entire tradition of the lesbian vampire, a very low form of which is exhibited in *Vampyrs* (1974). While not the most elegant vampire film, it illustrates the allure of vampiredom over and against sunlit humanity very clearly. The couple is perfectly matched: a blonde (who hides behind trees, with the red for DANGER showing on a part of her black outfit) and a darker, more obviously menacing woman. Her role is to stop the cars with male drivers, say to the driver, a true naïf, of course, that her car has broken down, get in with him and manage to get him to the castle, and thence her bedroom, where he is made to absorb endless quantities of red wine. This singularly unsubtle reference to blood also naturally reminds us of the blood of Jesus and the Christian ritual of which vampirism is a depraved variant. The sacrament is always in the mind of the spectator, who is, vicariously, a participant.

In any case, these lesbian vampires are very repetitive in their fashion: they wear various versions of low-cut black garments, most of which are very décolletée (which means, literally, de-necked). These beings in their low necklines are bloodsuckers down to their garments, completely given over to their ghastly and alluring act. After seducing and drinking the seduced man's blood, they hightail it in their long black cloaks— robes and cloaks flow like blood—across a field to the cemetery, where they will find a coffin to sleep in. Or they may be trapped in the castle and so forced to sleep huddled in the cellars, all curled up like two bats. These loving/slaying heroines so interestingly dressed, in and out of the castle, in their black and red garments, are clearly opposed to the drearily dressed couple who appear, normally outfitted, living in a trailer car, thus setting up the contrast of trailer against castle, dull against elegant, unremarkable against remarkable and unusual. Would one not rather be a chic black-caped vampire with lots of black décolleté dresses than a boring, staid, regular old trailer wife? The normal and therefore victim-ized woman wears boots (no self-respecting vampire would be caught in boots; rather they fit the vampire slayer like Buffy). But she *wants* to be seduced by the strange. So here, as always, it is the well-dressed kill-ers who get to serve and maybe drink the good "Transylvanian wine" (about which vintage no one can guess) and wear the groovy black and red cloaks and hide behind the trees and pounce on the unsuspecting drivers. Who wouldn't opt for that?

But just as the viewer must secretly prefer a fashionable vampire to a drab victim, there is also an undeniable sexiness to the victim's role. John Carpenter's *Vampires* (1998) shows a vampire stretched out on the ceiling like a giant bat, descending in a most erotic fashion onto Cheryl Lee in a very low-cut blue dress. His kiss is planted below her neck, and planted with such vigor that she manifests a delight quite over the top; there's not much difference here between making love and vampire mischief. All vampires seduce, after all, but some do it more quickly than others. Here the act happens in a flash, just as the costumes are more flashy than elegant. Blood from a chalice is served by a cardinal in his robes, stressing the relation between the blood of Christ and the blood served and drunk by the vampire, testing the limits of the profane and the sacred.

For me, the ultimate, ultimate in costume for vampire and victim is to be found displayed in two very great films. First is *The Hunger* (1983), one of the best vampire films of all time, in which David Bowie singing behind a pane of glass sets the initial scene, an incipit in which his fame and his rich elegance of costume work together—seduction already at work behind the glass. But he won't have the last word. As he ages so rapidly, his lover, the chilly Catherine Deneuve in her eternal mature beauty remains her stolidly cool self, marked by the black sunglasses covering her all-seeing blue eyes, her perpetual cigarette showing off her red lips. In one wonderful scene, her extraordinary unnaturalness is highlighted in contrast to some plants that are dying naturally, their yellow against her black. This is elegance personified, drama all the more suggestive for being low-key.

The initial presentation of the vampire is all-powerful. We see her first in her black hat and watch her slow takeoff, before she approaches the piano to play out her seduction, her black earrings dangling from her earlobes, as an ankh dangles between her breasts in her very décolleté black dress. Woof. The ankh, focus of attention, will be the murder weapon.... The music always matches the costume: Lalo here, Schubert there, Vivaldi elsewhere. The supreme Catherine is always supremely tailored: a simple silk blue suit, matching hat, or a Jill Sander–type stark-lined blouse with black slit skirt, mesh stockings, and pearl earrings. For the final sacrifice scene, her short-sleeved black satin robe reveals an inset of ecru satin . . . and the ankh, which will unsheathe a small dagger

2.3. Catherine Deneuve as Miriam in *The Hunger*.
Courtesy of MGM/UA/The Kobal Collection.

tal globe placed over the red-robed groom's face, preparing him for the feast. The final shot, as the two vampires hover over the man robed for sacrifice and splayed out flat on the floor between them, might remind us of post-crucifixion paintings (the Deposition of Medardo Rosso, for instance)—the red, white, and silver showing how baroque vampirism can be.

But finally, it is all about the costume, from the black bat's wing cloak to the white or red robes of the ritual: it is all about what the cloth veils, and what it reveals. And how seductive is all this aggression! Listening to a news program the night after I saw the triumphantly elegant *Les Levres Rouges,* I distinctly heard, instead of someone "violating the applicable laws," this totally convincing phrase: "a violation of applicable jaws." Vampirism gets to you. It is a sublime spectacle.

NOTES

1. Michael Wood, "At the Movies."
2 Ruth La Ferla, "A Trend With Teeth," E1(L).
3. André Breton, first in *Les Vases communicants,* discussing it on pp. 36–37, reproduction facing p. 32, and then in *L'Art magique,* discussion p. 281, reproduction p. 280.

WORKS CITED

Breton, André. *L'Art magique.* Pléiade edition, vol. 1V. Paris: Gallimard, 2008.
———. *Les Vases communicants.* Paris: Gallimard, 1955.
La Ferla, Ruth. "A Trend With Teeth." *New York Times,* July 2, 2009: E1(L).
Stoker, Bram. *Dracula.* Westminster: Archibald Constable and Co., 1897.
Wood, Michael. "At the Movies." *London Review of Books,* May 14, 2009.

FILMOGRAPHY

Bram Stoker's Dracula. Dir. Francis Ford Coppola. Costumes, Eiko Ishioka. Columbia Pictures, 1992.
Daughters of Darkness [*Les levres rouges*]. Dir. Harry Kuemel. Costumes, Bernard Perris. Maron Films, 1971.
Dracula. Dir. Tod Browning. Costumes, Ed Ware and Vera West. Universal, 1931.
Dracula: Dead, And Loving It. Dir. Mel Brooks. Costumes, Dodie Shepard. Castle Rock Entertainment, 1995.
The Hunger. Dir. Tony Scott. Costumes, Milena Canonero. MGM Studios, 1983.
Interview with the Vampire: The Vampire Chronicles. Adapt. by Anne Rice. Dir. Neil Jordan. Costumes, Sandy Powell. Warner Brothers, 1994.

Nosferatu. Dir. F. W. Murnau. Costumes, Albin Grau. 1922. Film Arts Guild, 1929.

Twilight. Dir. Catherine Hardwicke. Costumes, Wendy Chuck. Summit Distribution, 2008.

Vampires. Dir. John Carpenter. Costumes, Michel Robin Bush. Columbia Pictures, 1998.

Vampyres. Dir. José Ramón Larraz. Wardrobe Supervisor, Dulcie Mid

TELEVISION

Buffy the Vampire Slayer. Prod. Joss Whedon. Costumes, Cynthia Bergstrom et al. 20th Century Fox, 1997–2003.

Les Vampires. Dir. Louis Feuillade. Societe des Etablissements L. Gaumont, France, 1915.

THREE

Noir Fashion and Noir *as* Fashion

ULA LUKSZO

The streets are dark and wet, and in the background we see a city skyline. Out from the shadows steps a man in a fedora and trench coat. The audience sits back, aware that it has been transported into the world of film noir. It would be difficult to dispute the fact that the clothes of the noir film—part of the noir Look—are essential to the nostalgia and fascination we associate with these films. Significantly, however, despite the depth and breadth of noir criticism, very little attention has been paid to the semiotics of dress in the noir film. As a concept, movement, or Look, noir has been highly influential in twentieth-century cinema, television, and advertising, yet its costuming has been largely ignored. Given the use of noir as a tool of "cinephilia," as described by James Naremore,[1] we must consider what exactly about the movement or Look of noir lends itself to visual cinephilia as well as to the proliferation of noir pastiche, parody, and imitation that continues well past the classic noir period of the 1940s and '50s. Although many film critics define the Look of noir as relating to techniques of filming (low- and high-angle shots, close-ups, chiaroscuro effect, etc.), few would argue that a fedora and trench coat are any less important or recognizable aspects of the creation of the film noir Look. It is precisely the fact that these elements of dress are overlooked despite their obviousness that makes them conspicuous. In this chapter, I will be examining elements of dress in classic film noir as well as their reinterpretations in retro- and neo-noir films such as *Chinatown* (1974), *Body Heat* (1981), *Miller's Crossing* (1990), and *L.A. Confidential*

(1997), among others. My interests lie in the use of clothing to tell the stories of the characters, how certain elements of dress become symbolic of noir as a whole, and, finally, how noir becomes a kind of "fad" or fashion in and of itself.

One of the reasons for suggesting that noir can be defined by fashion is that film noir was not thought of as a genre during the classic period but only belatedly in subsequent criticism. The term "film noir," coined by film critic Nino Frank in Paris after World War II, was adopted by the French critics *after* many classic noir films of varying plots had already been made, including John Huston's *The Maltese Falcon* (1941), Otto Preminger's *Laura* (1944), and Billy Wilder's *Double Indemnity* (1944). In this sense, the French invented American film noir, for the term was not used in the United States during the war at all.[2] And though we may now think that certain elements of noir are endemic to it, such as the femme fatale, the voice-over narration, flashbacks, a hard-boiled detective, a criminal investigation, or a chiaroscuro visual style, many films of the classic era lack these elements. *Key Largo* (1948) has no femme fatale; neither does *The Big Sleep* (1946); though the title character is initially set up as one in *Gilda* (1946) she is distinguished by being played by a known actress, sharing in the hero's victimization at the hands of the villain, and ultimately by her happy ending.[3] *The Blue Dahlia* (1946) has no voice-over narration and no detective, and *Double Indemnity* is told from the criminal's point of view. In other words, we are dealing with several kinds of film genres within the noir movement: the detective story, the police procedural, the thriller, the crime film, and so forth. Therefore, film noir cannot be considered a genre, as Elizabeth Cowie writes , for it is "at least not a genre in the sense that the term is applied to other cinematic forms such as the western, or the gangster film, which have a specific iconography of objects and milieux as well as a limited set of narrative themes or problematics. . . . [The film noir] has no unique elements, and whilst it has some obligatory elements, notably narrative elements of the suspense mystery or thriller form, it does not have any forbidden elements."[4] Steve Neale, in *Genre and Hollywood*, similarly notes that many elements of the films we might consider noir, such as the femme fatale, can also be found in other Hollywood films from the 1940s.[5] Conversely, though the classic period is considered to extend until Orson Welles's *Touch of Evil* in 1958, 1950s noirs already differentiate themselves from their 1940s forerunners in fashion, characterization, and representations of family. Janey Place suggests that rather than a genre, film noir is best interpreted as a film movement: "Film movements occur in specific historical periods—at times of national stress and focus of energy. They express a consistency of both thematic and formal elements which makes them particularly expressive of those times."[6] Indeed many film critics identify the mood of noir films as expressive of angst, apathy, war-time paranoia, and anxieties about the American man's masculinity during and after World War II. Steve Neale proposes, similarly, "as a concept film noir seeks to homogenize a set of distinct and heterogeneous phenomena; it thus inevitably generates contradictions, exceptions and anomalies and is doomed, in the end, to incoherence. Paradoxically, however, both film noir and neo-noir . . . have, as we shall see, both acquired a much more secure generic status over the past three decades as the term 'noir' itself has become more ubiquitous."[7] I will develop the second half of his argument further in the rest of this chapter.

As a result of the flexibility of this movement, style, or set of conventions, it may appear useless or next to impossible to find patterns in dress and costume in film noir. However, as I have already noted, these films *do* contain common patterns of dress and related signifiers, making noir fashion a significant means of constructing noir into a contemporary genre and a cultural fantasy. As Todd Erickson suggests, the emergence of noir as a distinct genre in the 1980s resulted in recognition among film scholars "that we could understand *film noir* on two distinct planes. First, as an overall cinematic movement which, to some extent, modified most of Hollywood's product during the forties and fifties, and secondly, as a (new) genre that emerged from the overall movement."[8] The early movement, however, was immediately linked to the fashions of the 1940s and '50s, and films of the period were then incorporated into the genre canon after the fact. What has made film noir into a genre since the 1950s is perhaps the simple fact that it is taught and spoken about as one; we now conceive of film noir as a genre regardless of the fact that no one in 1940s Hollywood used the term. The use of the term by scholars and the general public reinforces the perceived reality of noir as a genre, just as its recognizeability reaches a peak in its pastiche form. I argue that the fashions prevalent in the early "noir" movement and the meanings they carry become so overused that they eventually contribute to the recognition and *creation* of noir as a genre. It is therefore worthwhile to look back first on the fashions of the original noir films to see if we may detect any patterns in how this Look was initially crafted out of existing fashions of the time, lending noir its generic status retrospectively.

PART ONE: THE "CLASSIC" NOIR PERIOD, 1941–1958

Because the films we now consider film noir were made in Hollywood studios such as Warner Bros, RKO, and Paramount, they not only had to adhere to the Hayes Production Code of 1934, but they also in many ways reflect certain semiotic conventions of the classic Hollywood style that later became part of the nostalgic quality associated with noir. In particular, the representations of villains and femme fatales become particularly stylized in the film noir, even when there is some improvisation in individual films. Initially, it seems that the styles portrayed in classic noir films are merely reflections of styles popular at the time. Jane Gaines notes that "the motion picture industry in this period . . . represented its product as uplifting entertainment which stood outside time and was never 'dated.' The industry avoided tying in so closely with the woman's fashion trade that it would be required to refer to the seasonal shifts which stimulated the retail clothing business."[9] Though this may be true, a visible shift can be seen in the noir films of the 1940s as compared with those of the '50s, especially in women's hairstyles and men's suits, a reflection of actual changes in styles for men and women. The 1940s men's suit was high-waisted and wide-legged, with the jacket forming the "inverted triangular silhouette—broad shoulders and narrow waist—[that] defined both men's and women's styles" in the '40s.[10] In *Gilda* (1946), Glenn Ford's character Johnny Farrell sports high-waisted trousers and a wide-shouldered jacket; by the time Ford makes *The Big Heat* in 1953, his pants are much narrower and his shoulders much less boxy. It is, perhaps, a logic of small differences, as Gilles Lipovetsky terms it, yet the changes are especially noticeable to a contemporary viewer, for whom the 1940s men's suit appears rather unusual. These small fashion changes, however, have minimal bearing on the plot of the film or the representation of its characters. In *The Maltese Falcon* (1941), Sam Spade appears to own several fedoras of varying colors and shades, yet these changes in shade (or presumably color, though it is difficult to tell in black and white) of headwear have little to no bearing on his characterization; neither does the fact that he wears variously a double-breasted pinstripe suit or a dark three-piecer. In this era, a three-piece suit sometimes seems to offer a picture of someone a little stuffier or older, but not always. A watch-chain glimmering on a character's bulging stomach might signify wealth—or it might not. The trench coat that we so closely associate with the hard-boiled detective and noir films is most often worn, quite logically, in scenes where it is raining. Thus, it might seem that most clothing choices reflect little more than everyday personal choices. As will become apparent, though, when we look at the costumes in the context of comparing protagonist to antagonists, we find that these films *do* in fact have a code that lets the audience know how to read the main characters via their clothing.

It is essential, of course, in many of these films—such as *The Maltese Falcon, The Glass Key* (1942), or *The Blue Dahlia* (1946)—that the hero be dressed sharply, though within the norms of men's fashion at the time. In most noir films a lack of tie simply means the protagonist is at home, relaxing; he wears his hat outdoors or in hotel lobbies (*The Maltese Falcon*) or grocery stores (*Double Indemnity*). He takes it off in the presence of ladies, but never forgets to take it with him. The fedora, as I will explore further a little later, becomes one of the key expressions of noir-ish-ness in later periods. In the classic period, though, the archetype of the hero in the fedora seems to draw on the 1930s precedent of the well-dressed gangster, while simultaneously cleaning him up for his role as the dispenser of "true justice." The hero of the classic Hollywood noir is for the most part well dressed and well put together, the studios of the day preferring a fantasy of sharp new suits rather than using wardrobe to faithfully reflect the rumpled, gin-soaked Dashiell Hammett or Raymond Chandler protagonists that formed the basis for many noir heroes. Erin A. Smith comments that the "everyman" character and his tough-talking are "allegories about workers' control and autonomy. . . . This places hard-boiled pulp fiction squarely in a time characterized by intense struggles over who would control the pace and method of production." The literary noir hero is, consequently, "his own man," tough, not fashion-conscious, and utilitarian in his dress.[11] The fantasy of the Hollywood screen version is that these "everyday Joes" wear custom-fitted suits. However, the suit ensemble becomes, more than a fantasy, a signifier when compared to other forms of male dress. The villains' costumes inevitably signify something other than that of the hero, namely wealth, which by extension also signifies greed, vanity, and cruelty. Probably the most well-known example of these qualities in dress can be found in *The Maltese Falcon,* the 1941 film most often credited as being the first true film noir. In *The Maltese Falcon,* Humphrey Bogart wears the standard double-breasted suit with the handkerchief in the breast pocket, often a pinstriped suit that perhaps signifies professionalism. The male villains of the film, played by Peter Lorre and Sydney Greenstreet, appear, respectively, in a black, short-jacketed tuxedo, plaid bowtie, white gloves, and walking stick; and in a velvety jacket and vest with a braid across the stomach, striped pants, and a boutonnière. They, of course, only care about the recovery of the falcon and the riches it will afford them, though it is evident in the film that Greenstreet's character, Mr. Gutman (a faintly Germanic name), is already wealthy.

The motif of the rich and *ethnicized* villain can be seen in many, if not all, noir films. Edward G. Robinson's gangster character in *Key Largo* (1946), Johnny Rocco, appears in a silk bathrobe and smokes a cigar before dressing smartly in a dark suit with a patterned tie and gold tie clip, a dandyism associated with Europe, not America. He is also marked as foreign by his last name. Similarly, the gangsters in *The Big Heat* and *The Blue Dahlia* (both from 1946) are cast as Italian or Italian-American. The Germans in *Gilda* (1946) are almost always dressed in tuxedos with white bowties, and when they go out in the evening, they wear black top hats and capes. *Out of the Past* (1947) portrays Kirk Douglas's villain character initially in a silk dressing gown / smoking jacket while giving orders to Robert Mitchum's Jeff Bailey, who constantly wears a trench coat and fedora. (Significantly, Bailey does not wear the trench coat during the pastoral initial scenes of the film, which take place in a small town in California where he has been hiding from his criminal past, so the coat stands for the past he cannot escape and links him to the world

Latin American rumba dancer—visual shorthand which depends, like musical typage, on ideological premises lodged in this iconography."[14] In this case, a silk dressing gown lets the audience know this is a wealthy, cruel man and in opposition to him is the tough good guy who wears the trench coat and fedora. Though perhaps these signifiers are not quite as simple or obvious as a turban with bananas, over time they come to fulfill the same function.

Women's clothing in the classic noir period does similar work in setting up the dichotomy between the femme fatale and what Janey Place calls the "nurturing woman." Place argues that "the iconography [of the film noir] is explicitly sexual, and often explicitly violent as well: long hair (blond or dark), make-up, and jewelry. Cigarettes with their wispy trails of smoke . . . and the iconography of violence (primarily guns) is a specific symbol . . . of her 'unnatural' phallic power."[15] I would add to this list any articles of clothing that are conspicuous for their excessive luxury, such as evening gowns, exotic hats, long gloves, high heels, and furs. This last object often signifies a woman of excess, one who is in some way or another dangerous to the male protagonist, such as Kathie Moffat in *Out of the Past,* Gloria Grahame in *The Big Heat,* or Brigid O'Shaughnessy in *The Maltese Falcon.* Beautiful and luxurious gowns, often body-hugging and strapless, similarly define a woman as "trouble." *Gilda* provides the best example of this. Gilda spends much of the film either in fancy silk dressing gowns or pajamas, or dangerously tight strapless gowns, her extravagant clothing emphasizing how she has sold herself to Ballin for his fortune, flirting and dancing with various men to make Johnny jealous, and in general not being true to her feelings for Johnny. It is significant that at the end of the film, when Gilda is finally penitent (or perhaps she has just been punished too many times by Johnny), she is shown wearing a simple pinstripe skirt suit. In *Out of the Past,* Kathie wears long, flowing gowns or tight, body-hugging dresses while seducing Jeff Bailey. At the end of the film, though, directly before her demise, she shows up at Bailey's wearing a modest, high-collared skirt suit with a nun-like habit over her hair. Even more reserved is Ann Miller, in *Out of the Past.* Jeff Bailey's sweetheart in Bridgeport, California (where Jeff lives his double-life), Ann is coded as a "nurturing woman"; her hair is pulled back in a conservative style and she wears

3.2A. Rita Hayworth, in the titular role of Gilda, in her appearance as the fatal woman on stage, famously attired in a slinky gown with long black gloves.

country clothes: jeans, a button-up collared shirt, and sensible shoes. In *The Big Heat,* Jocelyn Brando, in the character of Ann Bannion, is set up as a homemaker and guardian of hearth and home, with friendly polka dots that contrast with the sensuous gowns and tight dresses Grahame wears as the femme fatale Debby, who is a gangster's girl. As Place explains, this nurturing female is the hero's link to an ideal that serves as an alternative to the dangerous women he is surrounded by, even if that alternative is only a dream, an impossibility. Similarly, the nurturing woman "is linked to the pastoral environment of open spaces, light, and safety."[16] The femme fatales, however, are phallic women whose sexuality is dangerous, even at its most alluring. Their extravagant gowns, like the villains' tuxedos, come to bear the weight of villainy, moral looseness, and emotional turmoil.[17]

In many ways, of course, these clothing and narrative conventions were imposed on the classic noir films by the Hayes Code, which speci-

3.2ʙ. At the end of the film, having given up the life of a kept showgirl, Hayworth's Gilda appears as a "penitent" femme fatale in a demure suit.

fied that crime cannot pay and moral looseness must always be punished. At the same time, as Naremore points out, "[noir films] usually depict nightclubs, café society, and the homes of the extremely rich. By their very nature, they are deeply concerned with sleek clothing styles, and they repeatedly give us women who signify what Laura Mulvey describes as 'to-be-looked-at-ness.'"[18] This desire for luxury becomes part of the paradox of the film noir and the beginnings of a cultural fantasy situated in the noir. This is a fantasy that has to do with the rich getting punished and evil-doers receiving true justice, and the protagonist must dress well while avoiding the kind of concern over appearance that connotes homosexuality. Despite the Hayes Codes, though, the films still manage to give a sense of a degenerate society where nothing is as it seems and everyone is corrupt. As John Cawelti writes of the hard-boiled fiction that much film noir is based on, "the hard-boiled detective encounters a linked series of criminal acts and responsibilities; he discovers not a single guilty individual, but a corrupt society in which wealthy and respectable people are linked with gangsters and crooked politicians."[19] At a time when the thrill of winning the war has been superseded by anxieties regarding jobs, women in the workforce, immigrants, and disillusioned GIs back from the front,[20] the noir takes ascendancy for a while. It allows the audience to enjoy the thriller plots of films like *Double Indemnity* or *Gilda,* while at the same time appreciating the clothing the characters wear and the wealth or security they portray, even if ultimately that wealth is coded negatively. One example of popular interest in the noir characters' wardrobes can be seen in the example of "when RKO's *Murder, My Sweet* was released in 1945, [and] it prompted the *Hollywood Citizen News* to run a long article entitled 'It's Murder, but Gowns Are Sweet,' by fashion correspondent Florabel Muir, who spends two full columns lovingly describing the costumes worn by Claire Trevor."[21] Thus, the film noir relies on both the visual pleasure that resides in the costuming and the lighting of the film, and the emotional pleasure of seeing criminals punished and tough protagonists either dispensing "true justice," as Bogart's Sam Spade does in *The Maltese Falcon,* or succumbing to their transgressions, like Fred McMurray's Walter Neff does in *Double Indemnity.*

In fact, I would argue that these films, as varied as they are in plot and portrayals of male protagonists and their female antagonists, converge on the point of fashion. The visual pleasure of the films lies precisely in the gowns and costumes of designers such as Orry-Kelly (*Maltese Falcon*), Edith Head (*Glass Key, Blue Dahlia, Double Indemnity*), and Jean Louis (*Gilda, The Big Heat*). Though many film noirs may have originally been thought of (and some are still considered) as B movies, it is evident that studios recognized their appeal to their audiences and had no scruples about using some of their best designers to create costumes for them. In this way, the fashions of noir and noir's association with the classic Hollywood era; the glamour of stars such as Humphrey Bogart, Alan Ladd, Veronica Lake, Rita Hayworth, and Lauren Bacall; the unique lighting; and the gritty plot lines of its films, together created a powerful cultural memory. Though forgotten for nearly two decades, noir makes its comeback in the seventies—and beyond. It is in the retro- and neo-noir films that the fantasy of the to-be-looked-at-ness of the noir hero and heroine (or anti-heroine, as the case may be) resurface, imbued now with nostalgia for pseudo-toughness and all its various accoutrements, and simultaneously "creating" a now recognizable genre known as film noir.

PART II: RETRO-NOIR, NEO-NOIR,
AND NOIR FOR NOIR'S SAKE

At the present moment, I would argue that the elements of noir are easily recognizable, to the point that noir elements have been appropriated in nearly all media types. Noir elements are used in commercials, cartoons, episodes of television shows, fashion advertising, and, naturally, in contemporary films. In order to differentiate between contemporary noir films that are set in the classic period of noir—the 1930s, '40s, or '50s—and those set in the time period when they were filmed, I have chosen to use the terms most often used by other critics: retro-noir and neo-noir, respectively. I agree with Jans Wager that, "retro-noirs tell primarily reactionary, nostalgic tales about gender and race, stories that confirm white male supremacy while marginalizing women and nonwhites."[22] For these films, more often than not, setting a film in the past gives free rein to use sexist and racist motifs that are explained in the film as inherent to the time period in which it is set. In fact, Wager goes on to argue that "retro-*noirs* have far more in common with non-*noir* films from the classic period than with classic *film noir*,"[23] and he cites *L.A. Confidential* (1997) as an ideal example of this phenomenon. *Chinatown* (1974) is something of an exception among retro-noirs in that, though it is set in the 1930s, Faye Dunaway's character struggles against her powerlessness, trying to protect her daughter/sister, and ultimately her demise becomes part of the film's critique of noir motifs of women as cunning deceivers who deserve death. It is the neo-noirs, however, that span the widest spectrum of gender portrayals, with some, like *Brick* (2005), portraying women as sexually loose and/or powerless deceivers, while others, such as *Bound* (1996) or *Body Heat* (1981), portray women who empower themselves at the cost of men. From the perspective of costume, the neo-noirs are naturally much more varied, while retro-noirs do their best to adhere to the standards of dress in the classic Hollywood era. In fact, retro-noirs are much more likely to suffer from a "noir for noir's sake" syndrome, in which the plot and character development are subsumed by the film's visual obsession with the "look" of noir fashions; that is, the fashions of the 1930s, '40s, and early '50s. Even if originally the fashions of the first noirs were chosen for their contemporaneity, their meaning takes on a false fullness for the films that worshipfully recreate them without considering what the clothes can do for the characterization of the protagonist(s) and antagonist(s), or what kind of work they can do for the film beyond reinforcing setting and mood.

Chinatown deserves its own analysis, since it is one of the first noir revival films of the 1970s. Cawelti argues that "a film like Chinatown deliberately invokes the basic characteristics of a traditional genre in order to bring its audience to see that genre as the embodiment of an inadequate and destructive myth."[24] Though the traditional elements of the film noir are present and the characters strut around in 1930s-inspired clothing (Dunaway even sports pencil-thin eyebrows and Marcel waves), the wise-cracking hard-boiled detective is clumsy in his investigation, the femme fatale turns out to be a victim, and the "bad guys" get away with their horrific crime. Jake Gittes (Jack Nicholson), the protagonist, is unable to navigate the corrupt universe he lives in, and he ends up perpetrating the same mistakes he did in the past when he worked on the police force. As Cawelti points out, "[Gittes's] attempt to be the tough, cynical, and humorous private eye is undercut on all sides; he is terribly inept as a wit, as his attempt to tell his assistants the Chinese joke makes clear."[25] His dandyish appearance in perfectly tailored white suits is undercut quite soon in the film by a large bandage he must wear over his face, disfiguring him in a way inconceivable for either noir heroes of the past, such as the uber-masculine Bogart or boyishly handsome Ladd, or retro-noir film heroes from the end of the millennium, whose suits and fedoras do the work of conveying sex appeal. Gittes is not a ladies' man to begin with, and with the bandage he takes on a monstrous appearance, not unlike Debby in *The Big Heat* after gangster Vince has poured hot coffee over half her face. The bandage makes Gittes a victim as much as supposed femme fatale Evelyn Mulwray (Dunaway), though he doesn't know it at that point in the film. Similarly, Dunaway lacks the glamour and beauty of traditional film noir women, and, as Naremore notes, "her face is powered, her eyes are red, and her teeth are stained from lipstick. Her hair, which she compulsively brushes back from her forehead, is stiffened with permanent waves."[26] This attention to detail is singular among retro-noirs in that the details are not one-to-one signifiers as tuxedos or long satin gloves are in the classic noir, yet they manage to convey characterization even as they subvert the conventions of noir. There is, significantly, very little nostalgia for the time period portrayed in the film. Instead of creating yearning for a bygone time, the film works to expose inequalities present in the 1970s. The corruption of politicians in southern California in the 1930s is code for contemporary corruption. The nostalgic golden light of the film and Jake Gittes's white suits are subverted by his bandaged nose, Dunaway's tired, lined face, and the overall sense of dread that permeates the film. At the same time, the characters' clothes may be the most positive element of the past that the film acknowledges; evocative and well-tailored, the costumes reinforce the notion that while telling a story of social evils, *Chinatown* still revels in the sartorial glory of the past.

In contrast to the importance *Chinatown* gives its plot of political corruption, many other retro-noirs focus on clothes as if the clothing was an end in and of itself. Fredric Jameson, in regards to *Chinatown*, calls it a "nostalgia film," part of a postmodern sensibility of pastiche, which, according to Jameson, "is, like parody, the imitation of a peculiar or unique style, the wearing of a stylistic mask. . . . : but it is a neutral practice of such mimicry, without parody's ulterior motive, without the satirical impulse, without laughter."[27] I would argue, however, that if *Chinatown* or Bertolucci's *The Conformist* (1970) (another film Jameson cites) are "nostalgia films," they at least attempt to comment on both the time period portrayed in the film and the time period of the film's production, while later retro-noirs do neither. Both of those films, in fact, work to expose false notions of nostalgia for bygone eras by portraying the ugly truth underneath the attractive façade of the past. In contrast, the Coen Brothers' *Miller's Crossing* (1990) appears to exist solely to worship Dashiell Hammett–style banter, Prohibition Era violence, and fedoras. The film is particularly concerned, nearly obsessed, with hats. As Naremore writes of the film: "*Miller's Crossing* is 'about' little more than wide-angle lenses, low-level compositions, tracking shots . . . smoking a cigarette in the dark while sitting next to a black telephone, with oriental rugs spread over hardwood floors and gauzy curtains wafting in the night breeze. Perhaps most of all, it is 'about' the glamour of men's hats."[28] The film begins with a surrealistic scene of a fedora flying through the forest at Miller's Crossing, and Tom (Gabriel Byrne) is led back to Verna's (Marcia Gay Harden) apartment to get back his hat. The hat becomes a self-conscious symbol in the film, even figuring in Tom's dream of his hat being blown off his head. When Verna guesses that the dream was about Tom chasing his hat, he responds with the line, "Nothing more foolish than a man chasing his hat," which becomes the catch-phrase of the film. Elizabeth Wilson writes that "the obsession with pastiche, this 'nostalgia mode' is related to the way in which the dictatorship of *haute couture* broke down in the 1960s and 1970s. A single style can no longer dominate in the post-modern period. Instead there is a constant attempt to recreate atmosphere."[29] If we take this to be true, then *Miller's Crossing*, like Ridley Scott's *Blade Runner* or *L.A. Confidential,* are full of atmosphere, perhaps at the cost of other filmic elements.

Blade Runner (1982), though set in the future, consciously channels noir fashions by giving Harrison Ford's Deckard a trench coat and the femme fatale/female victim Sean Young a 1940s-inspired skirt suit, as well as various large and luxurious furs. Deckard's fellow blade runners and his boss sport fedoras as well. As Elois Jenssen explains, "Scott's vision of *Blade Runner* was a 1940s film noir detective story, like Humphrey Bogart's portrayal of Philip Marlowe in *The Big Sleep.* . . . The most obvious touches in the wardrobe are Harrison Ford's Bogart-esque trench coat and Sean Young's broad-shouldered business suit."[30] In this case, a film about the future is able to draw on film noir clothing styles (as well as low lighting and Venetian blind shadows) to create an atmosphere unusual in science fiction, but one still familiar to the audience, especially just a year after the release of *Body Heat,* which, though a neo-noir, also draws heavily on film noir atmosphere and fashion. Although William Hurt may sport a mustache and shaggy tresses, he still wears a suit and tie, and Kathleen Turner's clothing is rarely specifically rooted in early 1980s fashions. In fact, her wardrobe is almost entirely white, as though

3.3A. Sean Young as *Blade Runner*'s fatal woman wearing one of many luxurious fur coats.

alluding to white-garbed Phyllis (Barbara Stanwyk) in *Double Indemnity,* one of the films *Body Heat* consciously remakes. Kathie Moffat of *Out of the Past,* one of the most paradigmatic femme fatales of the classic period, wears white when Jeff Bailey first sees her. The notion of having the femme fatale wear white does a kind of inverted semiotic work, the icon of danger wearing the color of innocence. It is significant that all three characters manage to successfully seduce the male protagonists in their films, while a femme fatale like Brigid in *The Maltese Falcon* never wears white and never succeeds in fully duping Sam Spade. Thus, having Turner wear white in *Body Heat* further conflates the time period of the film, pushing it into the "eternal '30s" suggested by Jameson. The noir atmosphere is only increased by the fact that Turner's character gives Hurt's character a fedora as a gift in the film, explicitly linking *Body*

3.3B. In *Blade Runner,* Deckard's boss Bryant (M. Emmett Walsh) explicitly channels noir fashion in a fedora.

Heat to the perceived genre of the noir. The fedora in *Body Heat,* as in *Miller's Crossing* and *Blade Runner,* becomes the central object through a sense of noir-ishness that is portrayed. It becomes an object imbued with meaning through patterns of nostalgia and, via nostalgia, cultural fetishism and fantasy regarding the noir. Modern culture romanticizes the fedora because it is perceived as saturated with various positive meanings: dashing hero, "golden-era" days, high fashion, etc. Films, naturally predisposed toward conspicuous clothing display, focus on the fedora as an object that comes to signify, in film shorthand, all the fantasies inscribed into film noir by the culture of pastiche.

Though perhaps lacking in fedoras, *L.A. Confidential* (1997) returns to the pattern of obsessively accurate retro-noirs in the style of *Miller's Crossing.* In fact, *L.A. Confidential* goes one step further in playing out

3.4A,B. Jane Greer in *Out of the Past* initially appears in white, a color that Kathleen Turner wears throughout *Body Heat.*

its pastiche of film noir by centering the story on high-class call-girls whose agency promises its patrons that they will be entertained by a prostitute "cut" to look like a famous actress: Rita Hayworth, Jean Harlow, Veronica Lake, etc. The fact that Kim Basinger's character looks nothing like Veronica Lake and is much too tall and too old to reprise the 1940s actress, whose screen career foundered shortly after the end of the decade, rendering her eternally young, is of no consequence to the film. In fact, the film seems to rely on the *unknowing* of the audience: it can use 1940s fashions and refer to 1940s actresses, sure of itself that the fashions will be recognized even if, *especially* if, the actresses referred to are not. Instead, the names of those actresses work in similar ways to the fedora: merely invoking these people or objects becomes symbolic of an entire history of filmmaking and cultural production that is collapsed by the new film and compacted in a small, easy-to-parse package. Expressive of this idea is Jans Wager's notion that Basinger's character

is a "pastiche femme fatale" because "just as she represents Veronica Lake, Lynn also represents the femme fatale of *film noir*. She walks the walk, talks the talk, and certainly dresses the part."[31] This last point is of key importance. Though Basinger may not physically resemble Lake, she sports Lake's signature hairdo, the platinum blonde color, and retro gowns that, even if nothing similar was ever worn by Lake, code Lynn as of her time period. However, accuracy in *L.A. Confidential* in terms of *resemblance* is not nearly as important as accuracy of dress and gender and race relations. As Naremore points out, "unlike *Chinatown*, which it vaguely resembles, *L.A. Confidential* uses the past superficially and hypocritically. On the one hand, it attacks Hollywood of the 1950s, making easy jokes about the 'reality' behind old-style show business; on the other hand, it exploits every convention of the dream factory, turning history into a fashion show. . . . The film's primary appeal seems to be its stylish 'look.'"[32] The very visualness of the film medium, combined with the parody and pastiche that Jameson argues characterizes the postmodern era, turn the film noir into a visual *style,* a certain look or fashion that always resembles something else that came before it. As Lipovetsky writes of the consummate fashion epoch: "fashion is in

charge, because the love of novelty has become general, regular, limit-
less."[33] In films such as *L.A. Confidential* or *Miller's Crossing,* fashion is
most certainly in charge, and the plot and characters become secondary
to their self-conscious channeling of noir fashions. In many respects,
these films betray a sensibility that I term "noir for noir's sake," which
is also evident in more recent films that tanked at the box office, such as
Hollywoodland (2006) and *The Black Dahlia* (2006). There is no questioning of the conventions of noir in these films, as in *Chinatown,* no
extra meaning secured by the clothes the characters wear. The fashions
of noir are imitated for the purely nostalgic pleasure of visuality, to the
point that *Hollywoodland* and *The Black Dahlia* seem to be aping not
classic Hollywood noirs, but rather, in a strangely postmodern twist of
fate, *L.A. Confidential* or *Chinatown.*

Though many neo-noirs have no such respect for the fashions of
the 1930s and '40s, they still play with the conventions of noir, usually in
order to seem marketably chic. *Bound* conflates the gangster film genre
with the conventions of film noir and twists them both by making the
protagonists female and, specifically, lesbians.[34] *Brick* appears to be an
experiment in cleverness to see whether a noir story can be successfully
transposed onto a contemporary Southern California suburban high
school setting. Both films, despite giving their protagonists nominally
contemporary clothing, still manage to evoke noir fashions, as *Body
Heat* does. The gangsters of *Bound* dress in fedoras and pinstripe suits,
while Violet (Jennifer Tilly) is a pastiche femme fatale, imitative of
Debby in *The Big Heat* (who is also a gangster's moll, like Violet), with
her tight black dresses and short, curling hair cut. Even Corky (Gina
Gershon) manages to evoke the 1950s greaser girls portrayed in *Touch
of Evil* (1958), the film that many critics argue was the last true film noir
of the classic period. Similarly, though the hard-boiled teenage protagonist of *Brick,* Brendan, wears a windbreaker rather than a trench
coat, the femme fatale, Laura, wears black throughout the film, a coat
with a faux fur collar, and a black beret, echoing Lauren Bacall in *The
Big Sleep* or, in another postmodern twist, Faye Dunaway in *Bonnie and
Clyde.*[35] The villain of the film, "the Pin," wears all black, with a black
cape and walking stick reminiscent of Ballin and his German associates
in *Gilda.*

The commercial world that uses retro-noir for advertising has further hammered out the codes of noir. A recent Tekserv commercial plays on a scene from *Chinatown*, specifically, one of the most emotionally affecting scenes, when Gittes slaps Evelyn to try to get a straight answer out of her, only to realize that she has been the victim of incestuous rape. The commercial uses chiaroscuro lighting, black and white film, and a detective slapping a thug to get information from him about . . . a computer. Guess Jeans ran a commercial in the 1990s with Juliette Lewis as an undercover spy for a detective (Harry Dean Stanton) who investigates unfaithful spouses. Here the link between noir fashion and commercial fashion is made explicit, for the Guess label attempts to become associated with the sensuality, mystery, and cultural cachet of noir. However, noir has been used to advertise products as banal as ketchup, Colombian coffee, or Hellman's mayonnaise as well as fashionable clothing lines,[36] creating something of a quandary: the codes of noir are now so well-defined, so easy to invoke, that beyond recoding films from the past as "noirs," noir-ishness is now on the one hand fashionable, and, on the other, prosaic and commonplace. The very fashionableness of noir is taken up and transmuted, thus becoming a parody of itself, and perhaps, even a parody of a parody, erasing its historicity and, while creating a genre, simultaneously disengaging it from any particular purpose aside from the pleasures of the atmosphere being evoked as well as of the recognition of the thing being parodied.

CONCLUSION

Hence, though "classic film noir avoids generic status . . . neo-noir achieves it."[37] An episode of the 1980s show *Moonlighting* titled "The Dream Sequence Always Rings Twice" illustrates the new generic requirements perfectly: black and white film, a city apartment, a man (Bruce Willis) playing the trumpet in an undershirt and suspenders, voiceover narration, cigarettes being chain-smoked, and a bombshell femme fatale (Cybil Shepherd). Retro-noir especially, and neo-noir to an extent, rely on these easily recognizable and consumable characteristics of noir to give themselves a history they don't have while accessing a set of conventions that in and of themselves are already perceived as pleasurable. As Gilles Lipovetsky explains, the customs of the past "have the charm of days gone by, a past restored less through respect for ancestors than through a spirit of play and a desire for individualist affiliation with a given group."[38] In the case of modern film directors, producers, studios, and actors, the affiliation of the given group is the film noir "genre" that serves as a charming paradigm, ahistorical in its historicalness, and fashionable precisely because those fashions no longer exist. They have become fragmented, as in the neo-noirs, where a beret or fur collar or fedora stand in synechdocally for the gown or fur coat or three-piece suit that are no longer in vogue. In retro-noir, the viewing pleasure lies in recreating those fashions of the past on actors who are fashionable now. In the words of Lipovetsky, "the axis of the present has become the socially prevalent temporality,"[39] and the preoccupation with the paradigm of noir is an essentially narcissistic one, in which the characters wish to see themselves as part of the noir fantasy, a paradigm that remains static, accessible, and novel with each reiteration. With this static set of conventions, noir has become a genre precisely because contemporary noir films are made self-consciously, evoking what has collectively come to be considered "noir-like." In doing so, they make history "a fashion show," as Naremore has suggested, which colludes with contemporary sensibilities about the fashionableness of vintage and retro clothing. Unfortunately, by doing so, modern noir films do not elaborate on the genre, do nothing new, and in fact, make noir simply like a Halloween costume, to be worn, enjoyed, and discarded once its novelty (the novelty of the past, perhaps) has worn off. It is precisely the fascination of costume that noir fashion holds for contemporary audiences, who yearn for an older definition of glamour that bespeaks both romance and toughness, high emotions and gritty exteriors. The fantasy of noir is an escape from the complications of modern gender roles, an exciting and effortless receding into a story that does not question women's body-hugging dresses and awkwardly large hats. These elements, along with the bygone glamour that is perceived in men who wear suits all the time, elide issues of female subordination, male-on-female violence, and punishment of sexually provocative women into a careless fetish for stylish, if dated, clothing.

Certainly, many neo-noirs, such as *Bound* or *Body Heat,* are able to revise gender roles, expose inequalities, and play with traditional noir conventions.[40] However, other such films, and certainly most retro-noirs, don't. Films like *L.A. Confidential* or *The Black Dahlia* are sometimes even more strident than classic-era noirs in demonizing and punishing powerful, independent women while either beating up or protecting the innocent, nurturing women. *L.A. Confidential* manages to do both to Kim Basinger's Lynn: she works for the villain, so she must deceive her true love, Bud, and seduce his rival, Ed. For this Bud punishes her with a beating; then, as a part of "protecting" her, he goes and beats up Ed. Lynn herself has no power except that of first wooing the audience with her glamour and then eliciting their sympathy for her imposed passivity and inability to act. At every move, Lynn's ability to act for herself and become a phallic woman is circumscribed, and she becomes the prototype for the pastiche femme fatale. Similarly, issues of race are even less acknowledged in retro-noirs, where racist epithets and lack of actors of color are explained away by the idea that "this is how it was in the past." For these reasons and others, Fredric Jameson argues that retro- and neo-noir films are "an alarming and pathological symptom of a society that has become incapable of dealing with time and history."[41] I would also add, incapable of dealing with contemporary gender roles, though this claim might be made for most Hollywood films. The particularly alluring notion inherent in noir, however, is, what Marc Vernet writes, that "on the whole, *film noir* is like a Harley-Davidson: you know right away what it is, the object being only the synecdoche of a continent, a history, and a civilization."[42] Though noir, as I have discussed it here, is evidently neither cohesive nor, in fact, so easily categorizeable upon close consideration as it at first seems, the fantasy of noir evades all these problematic details. And it is this *fantasy* of the film noir that has been adopted: certain single images and stereotypes that become a synecdoche for a fake history and an archetypal civilization that never really existed. The very *fashionableness* of noir attests to the way its elements have been picked up *à la carte by* contemporary filmmakers and advertisers who seek to bring back the glamour and fashions that appear to be the only true constants of film noir.

NOTES

1. James Naremore, *More Than Night,* 39.

2. Todd Erickson writes, *"Film noir* was just a term, which French cineaste Nino Frank reputedly invented it in 1946, when the move houses of post–World War II Paris were deluged with a wave of hard-edged American crime pictures.... Remarkably ... thirteen years passed before an English-language book—*Hollywood in the Forties* by Charles Higham and Joel Greenberg—used the term and formally recognized film noir as a distinct body of films." (Erickson, "Kill Me Again," 309.)

3. This interpretation of Gilda comes from Richard Dyer, "Resistance Through Charisma," 117–119.

4. Elizabeth Cowie, *"Film Noir* and Women," 127. In the Introduction to the 1978 edition of *Women in Film Noir,* E. Ann Kaplan also recognizes the nebulous generic status of film noir: "film noir can perhaps better be seen as a *sub-genre* or a *generic development* emerging from the earlier gangster genre than as a genre by itself" (Kaplan, "Introduction," 16).

5. Steve Neale, *Genre and Hollywood,* 163. See Neale for a more detailed discussion of the crossover between supposedly noir-specific elements and elements of other Hollywood films from the classic noir period.

6. Jane Place, "Women in Film Noir," 49.

7. Neale, 154.

8. Erickson, 308.

9. Jane Gaines, "Costume and Narrative," 198.

10. Tiffany Webber-Hanchett, "The Modern Era: 1910–1960," 54.

11. Erin A. Smith, *Hard-Boiled,* 80.

12. Richard Dyer, "Postscript: Queers and Women in Film Noir," 123.

13. Gaines, 193.

14. Ibid., 204.

15. Place, 54.

16. Ibid., 60.

17. Of course, in the case of *Gilda,* the fact that Gilda has been unreasonably "punished" for her flirting with other men by Johnny, both physically and emotionally, seems to be of no consequence to the film's trajectory, which ends on a happy note with Ballin being killed by the men's room attendant (Argentinean, of course) and Gilda and Johnny going back to America together having happily resolved their turbulent relationship.

18. Naremore, 197.

19. John G. Cawelti, "Chinatown and Generic Transformation," 245.

20. For more information regarding postwar disillusionment in regard to the Hollywood noir, see Sylvia Harvey, "The Absent Family of Film Noir," 35–46; Frank Krutnik, *In A Lonely Street;* and Paul Schrader, "Notes on Film Noir," 153–170.

21. Naremore, 197.

22. Jans B. Wager, *Dames in the Driver's Seat,* 75.

23. Ibid., 76.

24. Cawelti, 254.

25. Ibid., 274.

26. Naremore, 208.

27. Fredric Jameson, "Postmodernism and Consumer Society," 114.

28. Naremore, 215.

29. Elizabeth Wilson, *Adorned in Dreams,* 172.

30. Elois Jenssen, "Vision of the Future," 109.

31. Wager, 84.

32. Naremore, 275.

33. Gilles Lipovetsky, *The Empire of Fashion,* 229.

34. It is possible to read *Bound* as doing positive work to the noir genre, as it rewrites the roles women can play in the genre and challenges portrayals of femme fatales through the character of Violet, who proves herself to Corky as a real lesbian and a trustworthy partner in crime. Chris Straayer expands this argument in "*Femme Fatale* or Lesbian Femme," where he writes that "*Bound* revisits and revises film noir" by inscribing the film with "a lesbian feminist discourse" (151–60).

35. As Wilson notes in *Adorned in Dreams*, "In 1967 *Bonnie and Clyde* set going the thirties look of berets and long, lanky skirts with 'old-fashioned'

jumpers—although Faye Dunaway's hair remained relentlessly straight and sixties" (172).

36. Naremore, 197.

37. Wager, 14.

38. Lipovetsky, 230.

39. Ibid., 229.

40. For a more detailed look at '90s neo-noirs that focus on sexually fatal women in films such as *Basic Instinct*, *The Grifters*, *Mother's Boys*, *Body of Evidence*, *Single White Female*, and *The Last Seduction*, see Kate Stables, "The Postmodern Always Rings Twice," 164–82.

41. Jameson, 117.

42. Marc Vernet, "*Film Noir* on the Edge of Doom," 1.

WORKS CITED

Abbott, Megan E. "'Nothing You Can't Fix': Screening Marlowe's Masculinity." *Studies in the Novel* 35 (2003): 305–24.

Cawelti, John G. "Chinatown and Generic Transformation." In *Film Genre Reader III*, ed. Barry Keith Grant, 243–61. Austin: University of Texas Press, 2003.

Cowie, Elizabeth. "*Film Noir* and Women." In *Shades of Noir: A Reader*, ed. Joan Copjec, 121–66. London: Verso, 1993.

Dyer, Richard. "Postscript: Queers and Women in Film Noir." In Women in Film Noir, ed. E. Ann Kaplan, 35–46. London: British Film Institute, 2000 [1978].

———. "Resistance through Charisma: Rita Hayworth and Gilda." In Women in Film Noir, ed. E. Ann Kaplan, 35–46. London: British Film Institute, 2000 [1978].

Erickson, Todd. "Kill Me Again: Movement becomes Genre." In *Film Noir Reader*, ed. Alain Silver and James Ursini, 307–30. New York: Limelight Editions, 1996.

Gaines, Jane. "Costume and Narrative: How Dress Tells the Woman's Story." In *Fabrications: Costume and the Female Body*, ed. Jane Gaines and Charlotte Herzog, 180–211. New York: Routledge, 1990.

Harvey, Sylvia. "The Absent Family of Film Noir." In *Women in Film Noir*, ed. E. Ann Kaplan, 35–46. London: British Film Institute, 2000 [1978].

Jameson, Fredric. "Postmodernism and Consumer Society." In *The Anti-Aesthetic: Essays on Postmodern Culture*, ed. Hal Foster, 111–25. Port Townsend, Wash.: Bay Press, 1983.

Jenssen, Elois. "Vision of the Future: Costume in Science-Fiction Films." In *Hollywood and History: Costume Design in Film*, ed. Edward Maeder et al., 97–112. New York: Thames and Hudson, 1987.

Kaplan, E. Ann. "Introduction" to 1978 edition of *Women in Film Noir*, ed. E. Ann Kaplan, 15–19. London: British Film Institute, 2000 [1978].

Krutnik, Frank. *In A Lonely Street: Film Noir, Genre, Masculinity.* London: Routledge, 1991.

Lipovetsky, Gilles. *The Empire of Fashion: Dressing Modern Democracy.* Trans. Catherine Porter. Princeton, N.J.: Princeton University Press, 1994 [1987].

Naremore, James. *More Than Night: Film Noir in Its Contexts.* Berkeley: University of California Press, 1998.

Neale, Steve. *Genre and Hollywood.* London: Routledge, 2000.

Place, Janey. "Women in Film Noir." In *Women in Film Noir,* ed. E. Ann Kaplan, 47–68. London: British Film Institute, 2000 [1978].

Schrader, Paul. "Notes on Film Noir." In *Movies and Mass Culture,* ed. John Belton, 153–70. New Brunswick, N.J.: Rutgers University Press, 1996 [1971].

Smith, Erin A. *Hard-Boiled: Working-Class Readers and Pulp Magazines.* Philadelphia, Pa.: Temple University Press, 2000.

Stables, Kate. "The Postmodern Always Rings Twice: Constructing the *Femme Fatale* in 90s Cinema." In *Women in Film Noir,* ed. E. Ann Kaplan, 164–82. London: British Film Institute, 2000 [1978].

Straayer, Chris. "*Femme Fatale* or Lesbian Femme: *Bound* in Sexual *Différence.*" In *Women in Film Noir,* ed. E. Ann Kaplan, 151–63. London: British Film Institute, 2000 [1978].

Vernet, Marc. "*Film Noir* on the Edge of Doom." In *Shades of Noir: A Reader,* ed. Joan Copjec, 1–32. London: Verso, 1993.

Wager, Jans B. *Dames in the Driver's Seat.* Austin: University of Texas Press, 2005.

Webber-Hanchett, Tiffany. "The Modern Era: 1910–1960." In *The Fashion Reader,* ed. Linda Welters and Abby Lillethun, 46–58. New York: Berg, 2007.

Wilson, Elizabeth. *Adorned in Dreams: Fashion and Modernity.* Berkeley: University of California Press, 1985.

FILMOGRAPHY

The Big Heat. Dir. Fritz Lang. Costumes (gowns), Jean Louis. Columbia, 1953.

The Big Sleep. Dir. Howard Hawks. Perf. Humphrey Bogart, Lauren Bacall, and Martha Vickers. Costumes, Leah Rhodes. Warner Bros., 1946.

The Black Dahlia. Dir. Brian DePalma. Costumes, Jenny Beavan. Universal, 2006.

Blade Runner. Dir. Ridley Scott. Costumes, Michael Kaplan and Charles Knode. Warner Bros., 1982.

The Blue Dahlia. Dir. George Marshall. Costumes, Edith Head. Paramount, 1946.

Body Heat. Dir. Lawrence Kasdan. Costumes, Renié. Warner Bros., 1981.

Bonnie and Clyde. Dir. Arthur Penn. Costumes, Theadora van Runkle. Warner Bros., 1967.

Bound. Dir. Andy and Larry Wachowski. Costumes, Lizzy Gardiner. Gramercy, 1996.

Brick. Dir. Rian Johnson. Costumes, Michele Posch. Focus Features, 2005.

Chinatown. Dir. Roman Polanski. Costumes, Anthea Sylbert. Paramount, 1974.

The Conformist [Il Conformista]. Dir. Bernardo Bertolucci. Costumes, Gitt Magrini. Paramount, 1970.

Double Indemnity. Dir. Billy Wilder. Costumes, Edith Head. Paramount, 1944.

Gilda. Dir. Charles Vidor. Costumes (gowns), Jean Louis. Columbia, 1946.

The Glass Key. Dir. Stuart Heisler. Costumes, Edith Head. Paramount, 1942.

Hollywoodland. Dir. Allen Coulter. Costumes, Julie Weiss. Focus Features, 2006.

Key Largo. Dir. John Huston. Costumes, Leah Rhodes. Warner Bros., 1948

L.A. Confidential. Dir. Curtin Hanson. Costumes, Ruth Myers. Warner Bros., 1997.

Laura. Dir. Otto Preminger. Costumes, Bonnie Cashin. 20th Century Fox, 1944.

The Maltese Falcon. Dir. John Huston. Costumes (gowns), Orry-Kelly. Warner Bros., 1941.

Miller's Crossing. Dir. Joel Coen. Costumes, Richard Hornung. 20th Century Fox, 1990.

Out of the Past. Dir. Jacques Tourneur. Costumes (gowns), Edward Stevenson. RKO, 1947.

Touch of Evil. Dir. Orson Welles. Costumes (gowns), Bill Thomas. Universal, 1958.

TELEVISION

"The Dream Sequence Always Rings Twice." *Moonlighting.* Dir. Peter Werner. Costumes, Susan Cohoon-Swain. ABC, Los Angeles, Calif. 15 Oct. 1985.

4.1. Fashion creates intimate contact in the hands of Wong Kar-wai's characters. *The Hand.* Segment from the omnibus film *Eros.*
Courtesy of Warner Independent Pictures, Photofest.

FOUR

Surface, Fabric, Weave: The Fashioned World of Wong Kar-wai

GIULIANA BRUNO

It is all in *The Hand,* in that expert tailor's hand. Shaping her dresses, he lovingly fabricates her image. She, in return, has taught him the feel of fashion by the touch of her hand. This woman can mold herself to a cheongsam, turning the enveloping fabric into her second skin. For these two, fashion is a permeable, erotic bond, a play of hands. Although they cannot be together, the garments connect them. Haptically threaded between bodies, clothes are, indeed, transitive matter, and fashion is a form of intimate contact. It can ferry much across bodies and spaces and carry the very scent of being in its cloth.

The tailor knows this secret story of fashion. When he stitches her dress, he can get close to the texture of her being. She, in turn, can trust him to hold her in the threads of the fabric. And so he lovingly handles the cloth, caressing that inner sense of her, embracing the trace of her fleeting existence stitched in the fabric of her dress. Life, like fashion, is not only transitive but transitory. She may die of her illness, but her clothes will remain, a loving trace. Like a shroud, stained by her presence, her garments will endure as a residue, imbued with the energy they absorbed as she moved through the space of her life. Through this continuing fiction of fashion, in the transitive motion of clothes, the story itself will continue, as if following an invisible thread. By now we may be in *2046,* but he still dreams of her, elegantly clad in her retro cheongsam and still, unrequitedly, *In the Mood for Love.*

A MATTER OF TAILORING

In the world of Wong Kar-wai, tailoring rules. In his films, the living fabrics of being and memory are endlessly fabricated in sartorial ways, held in the texture of clothes. Unfolding as a tapestry on the screen, fashion, as we will see, creates many forms of "wearing" the image and activating surface, which are woven across the textured filaments of time. Images are fabricated as if they were textiles. Time itself moves in folds, as if it were cloth, suspended between pleats of narrative fabric, veiled in opaque transparency. It is layered in "sheets" of a future past and interlaced with clothes, in and out of films. A sartorial world unfolds in tessellated form here, stitched in patterns on the fibrous surface of intersecting screens. Ultimately, in this form of "fashioning," the fabric of the visual comes alive. For, after all, as the story of the tailor shows, everything in film is designed, tailored.

Film itself can be said to be a form of tailoring. It is stitched together in strands of celluloid, or now even virtually, woven into patterns, designed and assembled like a customized garment. The filmmaking process has been linked in this intimate way to the pattern of tailoring since its inception. When speaking of fashion and film, we should first observe that cinema, historically, has been literally manufactured: in the silent era and beyond, film was worked on largely by women editors, who labored on strips of film in production houses that resembled fashion houses, where they cut and stitched together materials, mimicking the very process of clothing construction. The language of cinema thus can be said to have developed out of the mode and model of tailoring.

Film language is "fashioned" in many ways. Not only the pattern of editing but also the movement of film can be said to issue from the undulation of cloth. The motion of motion pictures is, in fact, inextricably linked to a modernist variant of the "skirt dance" born of the vaudeville stage. At the origin of film, Loïe Fuller's Serpentine Dance was transferred into cinematic rhythm as film production companies imitated her stage creations, creating numerous filmic versions of her performances.[1] Fuller's elaborate, modern version of the skirt dance, a sort of fashionable dance of veils, had the potential to activate a kinesthetic sense as the motion of her garb, folding and unfolding, made for shifting figures and patterns, whirling in spirals. When we watch an electric rendering of the whirling clothes in Thomas Edison's versions of the Serpentine Dance as performed by Annabelle Whitford Moore (1894, 1895, 1897) and in the many others of the era, including the Lumière brothers' *Danse serpentine* (1897), we can see how fashion activated film. The translucent folds of a woman's dress, dancing across the frame, tangibly animated the surface of the film screen and gave it moving texture. The folds of the clothing, rippling through luminous projections, brought the wave of painted fabric and the fabric of painted light into the language of film. As Loïe Fuller's Serpentine Dance thus was translated into cinema at the very inception of the medium, fashion was charged with becoming the living fabric of film.

FILM, FASHION, AND VISUAL DESIGN

In a sense, Wong Kar-wai has picked up the cinematic paintbrush where Loïe Fuller put it down. He has used it to expand the practice of filmic tailoring and drive it forward, into the realm of the visual arts. The artistic nature of this work urges us to consider style in cinema within the large and growing field of intersections between art and fashion, to which it makes an important contribution.[2] Fashion is here an art form in the sense that it is a form of imaging, as much as visual art is. As Ann Hollander has pointed out, fashion can in fact work as art, for it has the potential to be a "visual fiction, like figurative art itself."[3] Its creations, as she suggests, should therefore be viewed "as paintings are seen and studied—not primarily as cultural by-products or personal expressions . . . but as connected links in a creative tradition of image-making."[4] Wong Kar-wai conceives of fashion precisely in these terms, as an expression of visual representation and an interactive form of image-making. In his films, fashion is an aesthetic form of visual fabrication that is aligned with the history of art and the language of visual culture.

Wong's artistic sensibility for fashion reflects a vision of cinema itself conceived as an art of visual tailoring. In some way, he aims to stand in the place of the tailor-designer as a maker of visual dressing, montage, and collage. While Wim Wenders fantasized about the relationship

4.2. The art of visual fabrication: tailoring as imaging. *2046.*
Courtesy of Sony Pictures Classics, Photofest.

between fashion designer and film director in *Notebook on Cities and Clothes* (1989),[5] Wong has actually made it into a practice. He conceives of filmmaking as a total work of visual design, laboring on fashion not only as an art but as an architecture. Refusing to distinguish between costume and set design but rather treating them jointly, he tailors them together in filmic assemblage. For *In the Mood for Love* (2000), *2046* (2004), and *The Hand*, the segment he directed for the omnibus film *Eros* (2005), he worked with William Chang Suk-ping, who in each case assumed the triple role of costume designer, production designer, and editor, and has been essential in creating the visual texture of the films. His work has enabled a rhythmic form of fashioning that results from the fluid visual intersection between clothes and settings. Costume design is redefined in this view of filmmaking. Fields of vision, art forms, and professions that are usually considered separate, and kept apart in both film production and criticism, are here put into aesthetic dialogue on spatio-visual grounds.

FASHIONING FILM SPACE

The cinema of Wong Kar-wai configures a world out of clothes and reveals all that is layered in the intimate creases of fashion. *In the Mood for Love* is emblematic of this vision, fashioning a filmic world in which our gaze wanders freely from the shape of clothing to the configuration of sets and locations and we are made aware of the permeable spaces that reside in between them. An exquisite cheongsam continually enwraps the actress Maggie Cheung as she plays the fashionable Su Li-zhen, and we are equally enveloped in the city's fabric. In this film, attire is carefully constructed as if it were a tangible form of architecture, while lived space, in turn, is fashioned as if it were an enveloping dress, a second skin.

Tailored in the guise of one of Maggie Cheung's cheongsams, the city of Hong Kong appears itself encased. It is wrapped tightly in time and sheathed in space, somewhere in the 1960s. Fashion is a marker of time period, for the cheongsam represented the trend of the moment, as popular in Hong Kong throughout the 1960s as it was in Shanghai or

4.3. Design sets a mood, fashioning lived space as an enveloping dress. *In the Mood for Love. Courtesy of Universal Studios Licensing LLLP.*

Taiwan.[6] Women in the vanguard of fashion paraded the tightly fitted one-piece garment in multicolored forms and fancy patterns. Su Li-zhen, also known as Mrs. Chan, is no exception. This leading lady is defined by her passion for adorning herself. Always fashionably attired, she needs no special occasion to flaunt her exquisite wardrobe of variously patterned dresses. She knows the inner rules of fashion and wears her best outfit even when going out for noodles. The street, as she walks down it, turns into a catwalk. As she sashays around the apartment, clothes suit her as comfortably as skin. In her cheongsam, she is always, as the French say, *bien dans sa peau.*[7]

In this film the self is fashioned, and so are relationships. Fashion is shown to be a dermal, haptic affair as well as a subjective experience, and, in this tangible sense, it is also revealed to be a connective thread between persons and things. Our trendy Mrs. Chan and the equally married Chow Mo-wan, played by a dapper Tony Leung, enact an erotic dance of missed encounters across hallways and alleyways, which are designed to match the tone of their attire. At some point, this ballet turns into a swapping of identities and objects of design. As Mr. Chow notices that his wife possesses a handbag similar to the one Mrs. Chan received from her husband, and she notices that her husband has a tie that Mr. Chow also wears, the two conclude that their respective spouses are having an affair. The transfer of accessories creates an uncanny link between the pair, which, ultimately, becomes a transmission of affects. Mrs. Chan and Mr. Chow are drawn to each other and become hooked on a game of exchange themselves. In a play of mimicry rather than mimesis, each makes use of fashion to act out the character of the other's spouse, performing these roles until each is able to enter the skin of the "other." She tries out what it would feel like to be the other woman who carries that handbag and likes meat; and he enacts a similar game. In the process, the two end up "suiting" themselves to each other and falling in love. Fashion here acts in performative ways as a connector, becoming a vehicle for putting oneself in the place and taking the affective space of a loved one. And thus, in the erotic fold of object relations, a new relationship is born.

Over the course of *In the Mood for Love,* fashion unfolds as a transitive matter that conveys the "transport" of affects. When the fashionably attired bodies draped in exquisite textures travel through an equally designed space, seamlessly set against the surface of the urban fabric, this fashioning makes mood. Apparel intersects with the settings in creating the affect of the place, fabricating not only the tone but also the tenor of the city. Veiled by a rain that coats its surface like gauze, its inhabitants shrouded in delicate fabrics, Hong Kong emits the epidermic feeling of an inner space. The architecture of the clothes and the architectonics of the space become ever more permeable and connected as the film progresses. Together, they end up casting a mental image of the city, exuding an atmosphere of longing and creating a hopelessly melancholic mood for love.

FASHION THEORY AND SARTORIAL PHILOSOPHY

In the hands of the filmmaker-tailor, fashion emerges as a way of fashioning space. This is achieved via atmospheric forms of imaging that are stitched together in filmic assemblage, across costume, production, and editing design. It is a process that calls into question what fashion usually means in the language of cinema, and the restrictive way in which the term is used. It asks us to revise a common understanding that fashion in film is simply costume design. Here fashion goes beyond costume and becomes an altogether different object of circulation of meaning. What is at stake in Wong Kar-wai's work is a form of desire that is not simply attached to the costume as an object or commodity but concerns the larger sense of the fabrication of an affect-space. An agent of imaging and a maker of worlds, fashion is akin to architecture as a form of visual design that can convey mental atmospheres. As it tailors this world of fiction in film, fashion does not dwell exclusively or separately in clothing but resides in the architectonics of the film language, contributing to the shaping of its aesthetic texture.

This use of fashion as a form of fashioning urges us to rethink not only the object of fashion but also the methods of fashion studies. As fashion goes beyond the mere use of costumes, it exceeds a strict concern with personal, social, gender, or national identities; it cannot be explained as only a question of identity and identification or as a function of voyeurism, exhibitionism, and fetishism—topics that have traditionally been the focus of much fashion theory. It is time to propose a different "model" for the theorization of fashion, able to account for the way fashion works as a fabric of the visual in a larger field of spatio-visual fabrications.[8] In thinking of fashion in this new way, we need to move beyond issues of spectacle and commodity and elaborate a playful form of sartorial theorization, less concerned with sociology or the semiotics of clothing per se and more connected to the history of art and the design of space, and their theorization. This sartorial theory should be able to address forms of fashioning that include the relation of clothes to the production of (mental) space; the clothing of space and the layering of time; and the tailoring of visual fabrics and the dressing of surface.

In order to further theorize this kind of fashioning and grasp how it materializes in the cinema of Wong Kar-wai, I suggest a turn to Gilles Deleuze's philosophy of the fold.[9] Inspired by baroque architecture and Leibniz's concept of the monad, *The Fold* can be interpreted as a form of sartorial philosophy. In this book that treats pleats of matter and folds of the soul, the world emerges as a body of infinite folds, a set of in-between spaces. It is fabricated as a canvas of interlaced textures and layered as an interwoven surface, ultimately becoming a screen of pliable materials. As in the cinematic world of Wong Kar-wai, this sartorial world is full of connective threads: it holds folds of space, movement, and time. Here, motion and duration go hand in hand to create not only a textural language but also a language for texture. In fact, the philosophy of the fold can account for the way cinema is fashioned, for it contains an understanding of, and a feeling for, moving images. Ultimately, the fold is itself a moving image, for it is an image of thought. It projects that inner sense of motion that the act of thinking contains, as a feeling of being alive. In this sense, the fold finally represents the unfolding of experience. It can thus render the way we actually experience the world—in life as in film—as "fashioned," indeed.

FOLDS OF TIME, CONNECTIVE THREADS

Constantly unfolding upon itself, *In the Mood for Love* engrains the rhythm of the fold. In this work of moving images, all is pleated. Space and motion appear to unfold as an emotion, and so does the sense of time. The film reminds us that the fold issues from the material of clothes and from their function as timepieces, and it shares their quality of being objects activated by the motion of the body in the air. Here, time ripples like the folds of clothing or waves in the wind. It moves rhythmically, drifting across narrative space in undulating patterns. Knit to the fabric of the city, this kind of time is an experiential matter. A way to sense an atmosphere, time here is more a tonality, a rhythm, than a specific moment. One never really knows what time it is in this city, despite the ever-present clocks. Time is endlessly unfolding as a form of infinite duration or pervasive ambience.

Clothes punctuate this repetitive folding of duration. We are mesmerized by what Mrs. Chan wears, and through her outfits we become aware of the existence of time. We sense that time is passing, that hours or even days might have gone by, because of a change of clothes. Just as we seem forever wrapped in an endless feeling of temporal drift, a new cheongsam appears, marking time. In this film, then, the cheongsam, more than just a period piece, becomes a real matter of temporality.

'overcome' and precisely through the sex appeal of the inorganic, which is something generated by fashion."[17] When interpreted beyond fetishism, this affirmation of the relationship between organic and inorganic matter reveals the profound sense in which fashion is closely bound to a form of psychic severing and joining. This binding is a folding form of in-betweenness, and it can stand for the bridge of remembrance—the type of material separation and connectivity that creates the process of mourning. For Benjamin, in fact, a theory of fashion eventually unfolds as a form of historical remembering; in his philosophy, fashion becomes the material of time and history, a passage that is a temporal fold. And when fashion ends up embracing memory in its folds, it can weave it within its texture. Benjamin constructs a fragmentary text of passages, itself redolent with folds and moving like pleats of fabric, while making fashion a central metaphor for the weaving of mnemonic time. In such a way, a sartorial, material philosophy is born that can ultimately convey in the folds of its fabric the capacity to fabricate the texture of cultural memory.

Benjamin's mnemonic twist on the fold reveals an important aspect of Wong Kar-wai's material way of fashioning the image, for the Benjaminian idea of fashion foreshadows the filmmaker's own fascination with mnemonic textures as expressed in visual form. This is a matter of the "wearing" of images, for as Siegfried Kracauer also noted, "photography is bound to time in precisely the same way as *fashion*."[18] Over the course of *In the Mood for Love,* clothes in many ways absorb time, and the city of Hong Kong itself becomes lived in, consumed, and worn as if it were cloth. Here, cloth is used as in the folds of Baroque architecture and sculpture: as both erotic and funerary drape. At the hotel where Mrs. Chan and Mr. Chow might have made love, the fabric of the red curtains holds the memory of an affair that couldn't materialize. The red curtains, matched by her red coat, move in the wind, becoming the emblem of mourning for an impossible, unrequited love, and recalling that "the fold is inseparable from wind" and the wave of time.[19] In the end, the whole film unfolds in this way, like a memory fabric, sensuously joined to mourning and melancholia. It moves as if it were retroactively told to us in folded mnemonic form, from the conclusive moment when Mr. Chow whispers the secret of their story and deposits

its memory in a hole in the wall at Angkor Wat, thus fashioning a process
of mourning.

In the sartorial world of Wong Kar-wai, fashion embraces the folds of
time as its very model insofar as it shows how the fold of cloth embodies
the actual pattern of memory: its iterative way of returning in repetitive
pattern, like undulating pleats. The iterative matter of folding stories
characterizes Wong's cinema in a way that goes beyond intertextuality
to reach into a space that we may call "intertexturality." In a way, *In the
Mood for Love* is a souvenir of the events that occurred in his earlier film
Days of Being Wild (1991). And in retroactive fashion, Mr. Chow's love for
Mrs. Chan is mourned in the future time of *2046*, knit into the memory
of a cheongsam, as also occurs in *The Hand*. As the cheongsam reappears
in *2046*, framed and worn in the same fashion, on the street or in a car,
it turns the object into a remnant and all women into the Su Li-zhen of
In the Mood for Love. As the train of the future of *2046* travels back from
the memory land of lost loves, narrative elements are threaded between
films and interwoven between them. It is not by chance that the hotel
room of the red curtain that matches her red coat is numbered 2046 in
In the Mood for Love. This space held in its fabric an anticipated memory
and unfolded, in Benjaminian ways, a future remembrance. Ultimately,
then, it is the folding texture of the editing that is at play here, tailored
by the director, in collaboration with William Chang Suk-ping, to be as
mnemonic as fashion. They have even created intervals of the future, em-
bedding them in the past and foreshadowing them in mnemonic folds, as
in the case of a pair of pink slippers in *In the Mood for Love,* a cherished
souvenir that disappears before it can be taken away. In the cinema of
Wong Kar-wai, we could be offered no better testimony that objects of
clothing are indeed, à la Benjamin, the melancholic form of collection
that is our future recollection.

DRESSING THE SURFACE

In Wong's cinema, the fashioning and wearing of the image takes shape
in folding forms, in a moving aesthetic of visual fabrication. Here, as a
theoretical sartorial concept, the fold appears not only as a mobile, iterative, temporal structure, as we have shown, but also as a pliable surface

4.5. Inside out: exterior and interior dressed as permeable fabrics. *In the Mood for Love.*
Courtesy of Universal Studios Licensing LLLP.

that can sustain a play of reversibility. In folds of cloth, as in folds of paper, there is no real distinction between exterior and interior surface. The fold is, literally, a reversible construction. As a surface, pleats of matter can be said to stand for both an inside and an outside.

Wong fashions his visual world in such a pleated manner. He uses fashion as an architectonics and in relation to architecture, employing the structure of the fold to create a fluid relationship between inside and outside. The atmosphere of *In the Mood for Love* is especially fashioned as an "inside out." The exterior of the city feels internal, and at the same time, the interiors are permeated by exterior motifs. Su Li-zhen often wears floral patterns on her dresses that match curtain folds and wallpaper textures. The natural motifs and variously shaped flowers that decorate both her lavish cheongsams and the interiors turn things inside out.

This wearing of an exterior surface in the interiors creates affect in the film. Atmosphere issues from the haptic quality of cloth, as permeable and intimate as skin. After all, folds of cloth are transitive matter, for they create a surface that lies in between inside and outside and thus is potentially reversible. As Hélène Cixous put it, reversibility is a quality of fashion, for "the dress does not separate the inside from the outside, it translates. . . . In this way, the dress, like the dream . . . hides in its folds the great voyage in proximity and intimacy."[20] Because it relies on foldable structures, fashion—an agent of the transmission of affects—is able to create permeable, reversible, intimately emotive atmospheres that can be transformative.

Every time Mrs. Chan puts on another cheongsam an atmospheric shift occurs, a subtle change of disposition. The mood of the space changes as the geometry that sculpts her figure gives way to vibrant patterns and colorful blurs. Her dresses seem to exteriorize her inner world, and, reversibly, to make it come to the surface. The design of the pattern adorning her body interprets the way she seeks privacy in the crowded apartment or, conversely, shows how she tries to open herself up. Matters turn inside out most explicitly in an iterative, moody scene that rhythmically flows to the sound of melancholic music. As Su Li-zhen drifts away into a reflective state of mind, the floral pattern of her dress blends into the flowery folds of the curtains, the vase of flowers, and the lampshade, equally decorated with floral motifs. Enveloped in this pleated environment, she is folded into textured atmospheres. As she weaves her way into this interior world representing external space, she ends up by a window, framed in a tessellated shot against an outdoor plant, with all the natural interior scenery visible in the background. In the permeable fabric of exteriors that turn into interiors, and vice versa, we sense her yearning for an exit from her own enclosure, and from the constraints of her marriage, into the space of desire. In this enveloping surface, we are able to access her inner state of mind—the fabric of her inner landscape, itself adorned with its own tapestry of affects.

TEXTUROLOGY: TAPESTRY, TEXTURE, WEAVE

In the sartorial atmospheres of Wong Kar-wai, visual text is actual textile. Here we have what Deleuze calls a "texturology": a philosophical and artistic conception of matter in which "matter is clothed, with 'clothed' signifying . . . the very fabric or clothing, the texture enveloping."[21] The filmmaker's use of fashion reflects this enveloping design, consistently

4.6A. Visual tapestry: ornament and depth of surface create a sartorial aesthetic. *2046.*
Courtesy of Sony Pictures Classics, Photofest.

4.6B. The texture of the city: clothing environments as woven, worn-out fabrics. *In the*
Mood for Love. Courtesy of Universal Studios Licensing LLLP.

figuring a fibrous form of visual representation. This is most evident
when Su Li-zhen is seen outdoors in Hong Kong, clad and framed against
the ruinous texture of the dilapidated city walls. In a scene dense as a
tapestry, the peeling layers of paint, rendered even more textural by the
peeling fabric of the posters attached to their surface, are set against, and
threaded to, the fabric of her cheongsam.

The same tessellated pattern, almost like a form of braiding, is repeated in the interiors, beyond floral motifs. If Su Li-zhen's patterned cheongsam is woven in an undulated form, you can be sure that the curtains behind her will reprise the wave. If she reads a magazine, the graphic design is transferred onto the design of her dress. The crimson brocade of her dress gives volume and surface thickness to the ornate wallpaper she stands against. And, finally, the geometry of the cheongsam enhances minimal figures and minimalist shapes, as when the light that shines on the gray wall matches a translucent, splendidly monochromatic cheongsam design. In collaborating closely with William Chang Suk-ping, the director has created a real visual tapestry: a filmic canvas that is actually "textural" as it emerges out of overdressed, saturated surfaces, where clothes are turned into walls and walls into fabric.

The sartorial surface of this cinema joins dress to address in ways that engage the fundamental meaning of decoration. In dressing lived space while dwelling in clothes as modes of inhabitation, this cinema finally reminds us of the origin of fashion as a form of architecture. As the nineteenth-century German art and architectural historian Gottfried Semper showed, walls have an origin in textiles, as hanging cloth or woven mats.[22] In speaking of dressing walls, Semper fashioned a textural theory of space, activating the vital connection between surface and ornament.[23] And in establishing a relationship between ornament and mobility, he considered the wall *wand,* that is, partition or screen, and put it in relation to *gewand,* meaning garment or clothing. When Wong fashions a world of ornaments and décor, Semper's theory becomes materialized in film. We experience precisely this textural form of space: the activation of a sartorial surface. In these films, as clothes turn into wallpaper, walls become partition. They are never tectonic but rather lightly built as panels, and often function as if they were screens. Walls breathe, as fabric does. They are dressed in clothes and act as fashion does, as connective thread between people. Their surfaces are enhanced by a play of light and shadow, in the same way that the fabric of the cheongsam is activated. Decorated in a luminous manner, walls become as enveloping and riveting a canvas as the fabric of dresses, in a play of surfaces that elegantly fuses ornament and adornment.

SURFACE TENSION: SCREENING AND VEILING

In the interlacing of wall, garment, and screen, a material depth is visualized, for, when luminously dressed, surface has materiality. In the activation of ornament, we can experience another aspect of Deleuze's "texturology": folds of matter characterized by the fact that "matter is a buoyant surface."[24] A flowing depth of surfaces comes into being in this sartorial philosophy as it does in the sartorial aesthetic that practices fashioning as wearing. In the fashioned world of Wong Kar-wai, the fold works at producing a dense, floating surface in which one senses the material of light and the fabric of color in a rich play of hues and shift of shades. Visual pleating and folding create volume and depth, grain and granularity. Residue and sedimentation appear retained in the saturated surface. This practice of folding is a layering of the image that ultimately makes for the thickness of surface.

As fashion folds fluidly into architectural veneer, an aesthetic of coating is activated on the screen. In the connective thread between the patterned cheongsam and the textured walls, the screen becomes as layered as painted walls and as condensed as wallpaper. The textural materiality that issues from the latticed quality of the image eventually turns the surface of the screen into actual wallpaper. We almost never see clearly through the fabric of this screen. Several coatings and planar surfaces are constructed out of different materials, and all are folded together. To enhance the effect of partition, the frame is often obscured on one side. Door or window frames are also used to create an opacity of surface. Cigarette smoke accentuates the density. Glass and mirrors create reflective material, and curtains veil the space. There are always so many layers to traverse on the surface of this screen that its apparent flatness is defied. The screen itself, layered like cloth, takes on volume and becomes a space of real dimension.

The screen is activated in such a way that the play of surface can also appear to show coats of paint, as occurs often in painting. Like Loïe Fuller's cinematic version of the skirt dance, fashion is indeed for Wong

4.7. The screen as canvas: surface tension in the projected image. *2046. Courtesy of Sony Pictures Classics, Photofest.*

Kar-wai an electric way of creating dense, luminous surfaces by painting with light. As in her Serpentine Dance of whirling, transparent, shining folds of cloth, this sartorial surface is characterized by reflections and iridescence, which become space and fill the planar surface of the screen. This pervasive technique of fashioning the image finds full expression in *Ashes of Time* (1994), which was rereleased in 2008 after a digital visual remastering that enhanced color effects. Here, the textural materiality of the surface is pushed to the limit. Scintillation and translucency enhance the compositional luminosity of the screen. In drafting an almost abstracted play of hues, the camera acts like an actual painterly tool, turning into a paintbrush that glides across the screen surface. As the camera sweeps across the frame, there are no longer definite shapes or contours but only blurs on the screen. It is as if we can feel the motion, the texture of the brush strokes. As we become aware of motion resembling the tension of the brush against the grain of the canvas, we sense the deep working of the surface and, in the end, can even perceive a set of finishes and patinas. Thick with visual residues that resemble deposits of pigment, this surface is, literally, "coated."

The depth of the surface is the result not only of coating but also of veiling, for the layers of partition through which we see can be as light as a veil in Wong's cinema. This veiling of surface can be usefully interpreted in light of Semper's view of the architecture of the screen as partition and shelter, a reading that can help theorize the film screen. Such play of surface shows that the film screen itself can act as a veil. Here, screening is understood as a form of shielding and concealing, utilizing a property that belongs not only to the fabric of the veil but to the function of veiling. The surface of the screen is "dressed" as if shrouded in an actual "serpentine dance" of translucent collisions between dress surface and veiling. In this sense, the use of fashion in Wong Kar-wai's cinema can make one feel the presence of the screen, rendering it not only visible but as palpable as tissue. After all, the screen is itself a material made of reflective surface. Historically, it was even an actual sheet of cloth, hung on walls to receive projected images of light. No wonder the screen can now act like a real canvas. In this dressing and veiling of surfaces, cinema joins fashion as a way to project imaging on canvas—activating that textile support that is shared by painting, clothes, and screen.

The sinuous dance of film's origin thus materializes in a sartorial filmic aesthetic that shares a fashioning of surface with painting and architecture. In this fashioned world, we finally experience the material of the screen in surface tension. The effect of the surface dressing and the visual tapestry of *In the Mood for Love* is further enhanced in *2046*, where, as in *Ashes of Time*, swipes and superimpositions create additional effects of textural depth and tension, like striation and distress in the projected image. The surface of the screen becomes a stretched-out canvas, elastic and tensile and thus, in the end, appears really "worn."

Such wearing of surface is an important phenomenon that cinema shares with architecture and art: today, surface tension has emerged as a concept in the visual and spatial arts and is shaping their aesthetic development.[25] In the contemporary fashion of architecture, the facades of buildings have become lighter and more tensile, energized by luminous play, texturally decorated as if they were canvas, and treated increasingly as envelopes.[26] When a surface condition is activated in this way on visual planes, it turns facade and picture frame into something resembling a screen. But this filmic screen is no longer a window. It is configured like a canvas in which distinctions between inside and outside temporally dissolve into the depth of surface. Hence, the screen itself is becoming a fold. And thus, in this contemporary fashioned world, all can fold back into screen surface—that reflective, fibrous canvas spectacularly dressed by luminous projections.

NOTES

1. On this subject, see Rhonda Garelick, *Electric Salome*; and, Tom Gunning, "Loïe Fuller and the Art of Motion."

2. Cinema and its use of fashion are not often considered in relation to the spatio-visual arts, and should be repositioned in this field of intersections. For an overview of the relation of fashion to art and architecture, see, among others, Hayward Gallery, *Addressing the Century*; and Brooke Hodge, ed., *Skin + Bones*.

3. Ann Hollander, *Seeing Through Clothes*, xv.

4. Ibid., xvi. Other studies considering fashion and art include Nancy Troy, *Couture Culture*; and Peter Wollen, "Art and Fashion."

5. In this documentary film about Yohji Yamamoto, Wenders explores the world of fashion design as seen by the Japanese designer and ultimately compares the process of designing fashion to that of making films.

6. For a history of this attire, see Naomi Yin-yin Szeto, "Cheungsam"; and Hazel Clark, "The Cheung Sam."

7. For a hint to this way of theorizing fashion, see the short text by Marshall McLuhan, "Clothing, Our Extended Skin."

8. This essay represents part of a larger project on fabrics of the visual that I began with such writings as Giuliana Bruno, "Pleats of Matter, Folds of the Soul."

9. See Gilles Deleuze, *The Fold.*

10. Ulrich Lehmann, *Tigersprung,* 91. "Skirting the Memory" is the title of the section of this book devoted to "Mode and Metaphor" (206).

11. Georg Simmel, "Fashion." This text was first published in English in 1904, then in German as *Philosophie der Mode* (Berlin: Pan-Verlag, 1905), and subsequently in slightly revised and enlarged form in 1911.

12. Ibid., 322.

13. Simmel, "The Metropolis and Mental Life."

14. Simmel, "Fashion," 320.

15. Walter Benjamin, "Fashion," 79.

16. Ibid., 69.

17. Ibid., 79.

18. Siegfried Kracauer, "Photography," 55.

19. Deleuze, 31.

20. Hélène Cixous, "Sonia Rykiel in Translation," 98–99.

21. Deleuze, 115.

22. See Gottfried Semper, *The Four Elements of Architecture.*

23. On this subject, see Mark Wigley, *White Walls, Designer Dresses.*

24. Deleuze, 115.

25. See, for example, Chrissie Isles, "Surface Tension."

26. See, among others, Bradley Quinn, *The Fashion of Architecture.*1. On this subject, see Rhonda Garelick, *Electric Salome;* and, Tom Gunning, "Loïe Fuller and the Art of Motion."

WORKS CITED

Benjamin, Walter. "Fashion." In *The Arcades Project,* trans. Howard Eiland and Kevin McLaughlin, 62–81. Cambridge, Mass.: Belknap Press of Harvard University Press, 1999.

Bruno, Giuliana. "Pleats of Matter, Folds of the Soul." In *Afterimages of Gilles Deleuze's Film Philosophy,* ed. D. N. Rodowick, 213–33. Minneapolis: University of Minnesota Press, 2009.

Cixous, Hélène. "Sonia Rykiel in Translation." In *On Fashion,* ed. Shari Benstock and Suzanne Ferris, 95–99. New Brunswick, N.J.: Rutgers, 1994.

Clark, Hazel. "The Cheung Sam: Issues of Fashion and Cultural Identity." In *China Chic: East Meets West,* ed. Valerie Steele and John S. Major, 155–65. New Haven, Conn.: Yale University Press, 1999.

Deleuze, Gilles. *The Fold: Leibniz and the Baroque,* trans. with a foreword by Tom Conley. Minneapolis: University of Minnesota Press, 1993.

Garelick, Rhonda K. *Electric Salome: Loie Fuller's Performance of Modernism.* Princeton, N.J.: Princeton University Press, 2007.

Gunning, Tom. "Loïe Fuller and the Art of Motion: Body, Light, Electricity and the Origins of Cinema." In *Camera Obscura, Camera Lucida,* ed. Richard Allen and Malcolm Turvey, 75–89. Amsterdam: Amsterdam University Press, 2003.

Hayward Gallery. *Addressing the Century: 100 Years of Art & Fashion.* Exhibition catalog. London: Hayward Gallery Publishing, 1998.

Hodge, Brooke, ed. *Skin + Bones: Parallel Practices in Fashion and Architecture.* Exhibition catalog. Los Angeles: Museum of Contemporary Art / New York: Thames & Hudson, 2006.

Hollander, Ann. *Seeing Through Clothes.*
Berkeley: University of California
Press, 1993.

Isles, Chrissie. "Surface Tension." In *Rudolph Stingel,* ed. Francesco Bonami,
23–29. Exhibition catalog. New Haven, Conn.: Yale University Press,
2007.

Kracauer, Siegfried. "Photography." In
The Mass Ornament: Weimar Essays,
trans. and ed. Thomas Y. Levin, 47–63.
Cambridge, Mass.: Harvard University
Press, 1995.

Lehmann, Ulrich. *Tigersprung: Fashion
in Modernity.* Cambridge, Mass.: MIT
Press, 2000.

McLuhan, Marshall. "Clothing, Our Extended Skin." In *Understanding Media:
The Extensions of Man,* 119–22. Cambridge, Mass.: MIT Press, 1994.

Quinn, Bradley. *The Fashion of Architecture.* Oxford: Berg, 2003.

Semper, Gottfried. *The Four Elements of
Architecture and Other Writings.* Trans.
Harry Francis Mallgrave and Wolfgang

Herrmann. Cambridge: Cambridge
University Press, 1989.

Simmel, Georg. "Fashion." In *On Individuality and Social Forms,* ed. Donald N.
Levine, 294–323. Chicago: University
of Chicago Press, 1971.

———. "The Metropolis and Mental
Life." In *On Individuality and Social
Forms,* ed. Donald N. Levine, 324–39.
Chicago: University of Chicago Press,
1971.

Szeto, Naomi Yin-yin. "Cheungsam:
Fashion, Culture and Gender." In
*Evolution and Revolution: Chinese Dress
1700s–1990s,* ed. Claire Roberts, 54–64.
Sydney: Powerhouse Publishing, 2002.

Troy, Nancy. *Couture Culture: A Study in
Modern Art and Fashion.* Cambridge,
Mass.: MIT Press, 2002.

Wigley, Mark. *White Walls, Designer Dresses.* Cambridge, Mass.: MIT Press, 1995.

Wollen, Peter. "Art and Fashion: Friends
or Enemies?" In *Paris/Manhattan:
Writings on Art,* 161–81. London: Verso,
2004.

FILMOGRAPHY

2046. Dir. Wong Kar-wai. Costumes, William Chang Suk-ping. Block 2 Pictures.
2004.

Annabelle Serpentine Dance films. Edison
Manufacturing Company. 1894, 1895,
and 1897.

Ashes of Time. Dir. Wong Kar-wai. Costumes, William Chang Suk-ping. Block
2 Pictures. 1994. Rereleased as *Ashes of
Time Redux.* 2008.

Danse serpentine. The Lumière Company,
1897.

Days of Being Wild. Dir. Wong Kar-wai.

Costumes, William Chang Suk-ping.
In-Gear Film. 1991.

The Hand. Dir. Wong Kar-wai. Costumes,
William Chang Suk-ping. Segment from
the omnibus film *Eros;* dir. Wong Karwai, Michelangelo Antonioni, and Steven Soderbergh. Block 2 Pictures. 2005.

In the Mood for Love. Dir. Wong Kar-wai.
Costumes, William Chang Suk-ping.
Block 2 Pictures. 2000.

Notebook on Cities and Clothes. Dir. Wim
Wenders. Road Movies Filmproduktion. 1989.

PART TWO

Filming Fashion

From the earliest film era, Fashion appreciated its affinity with Film as a means to enhance its visibility. This affinity extended beyond aesthetics to encompass a connection between mutually advantageous industries. Cinema seemed to offer even more possibilities for promoting fashion than fashion's earlier ally, drama, had. This section explores ways that filming fashion stimulated fashion desire, reflected and enforced cultural values, and yet also undermined those values.

Caroline Evans in "The Walkies: Early French Fashion Shows as a Cinema of Attractions" makes a point that applies to all moving pictures and fashion shows: both concern "images of women in motion." Early silent films of fashion shows join other silent films as part of a "cinema of attractions" rather than the "cinema of narrative integration." Fashion show films can be understood as participating in a modern language of visuality. Evans regards fashion language as a new way of seeing: "the visual language of film," she points out, "began to percolate into fashion journalism, suggesting that the viewing competences of fashion writers were structured at least partly by cinema." She traces the parallel development of fashion shows and films to their convergence and then considers implications of their partnership in such modes as the fashion newsreel, originating in France and promulgating an image of Paris as a world fashion center.

Jane Gaines in "Wanting to Wear Seeing: Gilbert Adrian at MGM" focuses on a Hollywood film costume designer and fashion couturier to

FIVE

The Walkies:
Early French Fashion Shows
as a Cinema of Attractions

CAROLINE EVANS

Fashion shows and films came into being almost simultaneously. In France, the first film shown to a paying audience was in 1895; in London and Paris the first fashion shows were staged in the late 1890s. This chapter looks at the sometimes uneven chronological development of fashion shows in French film, particularly newsreel, in the silent period. Starting, paradoxically, with the relative absence of fashion modeling from early film, it identifies some structural similarities between the two, in terms of a common concern with images of women in motion. It discusses why fashion modeling went unrepresented in the first films by distinguishing the audiences for the first fashion shows from those for film shows in the period up to 1910. After that date, the audiences for fashion shows and film began to converge, as both fashion journalism and newsreel began to show scenes of Paris mannequins—as fashion models were called— at work. The chapter goes on to argue that the French fashion show as it developed in the early twentieth century had many affinities with the "cinema of attractions," in particular with the féeries and trick films of Georges Méliès from around 1903. While, however, cinema developed at a rapid pace in the early 1900s, the fashion show in the same period soon settled into a relatively static format. It continued to exhibit the characteristics of an "attraction" long after cinema itself had moved away from an attractions-based format toward a "cinema of narrative integration." The chapter looks at the early marketing devices of the couturier Paul Poiret as a form of attraction, in particular at his use of film from

1910–1913 to show his mannequins modeling. It then surveys the continuing, if varied, types of coverage of fashion shows in newsreel, also a relatively static genre, from the 1910s into the 1920s as a continuation of the attractions tradition. It concludes by suggesting that film footage of fashion shows and fashion modeling in the 1910s and 1920s mixes fact and fiction in such a way as to challenge—as many film theorists have—any simple distinction between attraction and narrative in film.

FASHION IN MOTION IN THE 1900S

Although fashion modeling was not widely filmed until the 1910s and 1920s, fashion shows and film nevertheless shared some characteristics from the outset. The sense that cinema was introducing new ways of seeing and thinking about the world was articulated in 1900 by Henri Bergson in a lecture at the Collège de France on the "Cinematographic Mechanism of Thought."[1] He further developed the theme in *Creative Evolution* (1907), using the example of soldiers walking to explain his ideas about visual perception and consciousness: "we take snapshots, as it were, of the passing reality, we have only to string them on a becoming . . . we hardly do anything else than set going a kind of cinematograph inside us."[2] The French word for a military parade, *défilé*, also meant mannequin parade, or fashion show, and Bergson's cinematic description of watching soldiers marching preceded fashion journalists' descriptions of fashion models at work by only a few years. Soon, the visual language of film began to percolate into fashion journalism, suggesting that the viewing competences of fashion writers were structured at least partly by cinema. In 1910, *Femina* magazine called the forthcoming autumn fashions "un véritable cinématographe de la mode de demain" ("a veritable cinematograph of tomorrow's fashion"),[3] and the *Chicago Daily Tribune* described French fashion as a "rapid film rush," epitomized by the photographs in American department stores of Parisian mannequins "striding along a wind blown walk" on the boulevards or at the races.[4]

In the early 1900s, both fashion and film evidenced a fascination with, among other things, human movement and female display. In 1902, a Parisian couturier commented "une robe est une chose qui marche" ("a dress is a thing that walks") and "nous faisons de la sculpture qui bouge" the 1910s, and it is from then onwards that one finds many more instances of fashion modeling on film.

Before then, the audiences for fashion shows and film remained distinct. In the first decade of the century, the visual language of pose, gesture, and attitude developed separately in the different spheres of fashion modeling and film acting, even though, in their creation of a language of bodily expression appropriate to these new forms of display, both film actresses and fashion mannequins drew on many of the same historical antecedents (stage actresses' gestures, tableaux vivants, and *poses plastiques*).[13] The fashion mannequin, like the silent film actress, was mute, except when the client asked her a question. Descriptions of mannequins at work contrasted the lively chatter of their *cabine* backstage with their silent presentation when modeling to clients in the salon.[14] There, the mannequin had to work with her body to develop a repertoire of movements, gestures, and poses. The cinema, too, required a new acting style akin to mime that used the whole body expressively, a style exemplified by the Danish film actress Asta Neilsen. In 1911, the French actress Mistinguett described the physicality of film acting, and wrote, "Par tempérament, j'ai le gout de la gesticulation ... ces qualités devaient me mener tout droit au cinéma" ("By temperament, I've a taste for gesticulation ... these qualities must have led me directly to the cinema.")[15] She described two, apparently contradictory, styles of acting that the cinema required: vivid movement for long shots, and relative immobility for close-ups. Both these elements featured in the fashion show, where the mannequins' fluid and expressive walk would periodically freeze, momentarily, into static poses, before flowing back into life as they moved on through the salons and disappeared backstage into the dressing rooms. Their static poses, like the cinema actresses' bodily gestures, invoke Bergson's description of the perception of movement through a series of poses or "privileged moments" akin to a series of film stills, and Gilles Deleuze's observation that "cinema appeared at the very time philosophy was trying to think of motion" applies no less to the fashion show than it does to cinema.[16]

The parallel development of film acting and fashion modeling in different spheres in the 1900s provides evidence of how comparable elements of visual culture can become visible at different moments to diverse audiences. Film was shown to a wide public of differing social groups, initially in a variety format in café concerts, music halls and travelling fairground theatres across France, and later in custom-built cinemas.[17] The earliest fashion shows, by contrast, were limited to invited audiences in upmarket Parisian couture houses. It is therefore perhaps not surprising that, in that first period of filmmaking, when the French film production companies, in particular Pathé-Frères (formed in 1902), were developing a range of genres,[18] and despite the fact that many of these genres foregrounded women as spectacle, fashion modeling was not among them. Instead the film genre that disseminated images of women in motion and of swirling fabric and seductive costume was that of dance; between 1900–1902, over half of Gaumont's production consisted of dance films, many of which used dancers from Paris theatres.[19]

THE FASHION SHOW AS ATTRACTION

It is, however, not in only dance films but also in another French genre, féeries and trick films, known at the time as "transformation scenes," that further affinities with the fashion show can be traced. A fantasy genre derived from the "fairy plays" of nineteenth-century French revue theatre, féeries combined a strong element of burlesque with visual trickery. The tradition was given a spectacular contemporary update by its principal exponent, the filmmaker Georges Méliès, a stage magician who adapted the visual motifs of his trade to the cinema.[20] In his féeries and trick films, as in the earliest fashion shows, costume and scenography took precedence over narrative and plot. Méliès's studio, built in 1897, housed a vast store of costumes which, he claimed, eventually numbered 20,000.[21] In planning his films, Méliès began with the decor and costumes before working out the details of the scenario, "using the thread of the story to assemble what was really significant, the trick effects and tableaux of spectacle."[22] Similarly, in his fashion shows around 1908, the couturier Paul Poiret chose to have his mannequins appear, not through the main doorway to his principal salon, but, as if by magic, from a small invisible doorway to one side. In this way the couturier used stagecraft and showmanship to present his fashions, just as the filmmaker used stop-frame photography and other tricks to create the effect of women suddenly appearing out of nowhere.

By carefully choreographing and lining up his shots, then stopping the film to change the actors or props before starting it again, Méliès achieved startling transformations within the camera's field of vision. As well as this stop-motion technique, Méliès used reverse motion and multiple exposures. By means of such "*trucs*," or tricks, Méliès made women appear, multiply, transform, and disappear at breakneck pace.[23] In *La Parapluie fantastique* (1903), he conjures up a group of ten neo-classically clad women who subsequently transform into modern fashionable dress and exit off screen like a row of fashion mannequins. Like the genre to which it belongs, the film points to the inherently unstable and transformative potential of fashion, with its capacity for disguise, masquerade, and deception. And in his *La Lanterne magique* (1903), ten identical ballerinas dance out of an enlarged magic lantern. Linda Williams argues that their identical bodies spewing out of the machine call attention to their status as "totally mastered, infinitely reproducible *images*,"[24] not unlike the way that Arsène Alexandre, the art critic of *Le Figaro,* worried in 1902 that the fashion mannequin was reduced by her job to the status of "un objet matériel, un meuble commun et banal" ("a material object, a common and banal piece of furniture").[25]

In purely formal terms then, early film, in particular the magical transformations of the féeries, has several features in common with the early fashion show and its lines of young women appearing, disappearing, and reappearing in different costumes, sometimes replicated confusingly in the mirrored interiors of the salons. The first period of cinema, from 1895 to approximately 1906 or 1908, is commonly referred to as the "cinema of attractions." First coined in 1986 by André Gaudreault and Tom Gunning, the term refers to a type of film that shocks, astonishes, and directly addresses the spectator instead of using narrative to draw the spectator into a "diegetic universe."[26] Rather than understanding the way people watched these very short pieces of early film in terms of narrative, Gunning tried to relate film to other forces, such as the changing experience of time and modernity, and thereby to explain how the effect of motion, rather than storytelling, might be the defining feature of the experience of watching very early film. In particular, he analyzed

5.1A,B. Scenes of ladies multiplied, from *La Parapluie fantastique*, directed by Georges Méliès.

these early films as a form of spectacle, drawing on the ideas of the film director Sergei Eisenstein from the 1920s about cinema as a "montage of attractions." Although many historians and theorists have challenged, modified or extended Gunning's original periodization and formulation,[27] the term "attractions" has become established, replacing its predecessor "primitive cinema." It has, furthermore, provided a useful model to think about different forms of cinematic address within mainstream Hollywood cinema, such as special effects or stage numbers in musicals. Wanda Strauven argues that "despite the fact that the cinema of attractions was clearly thought of as a time-specific category of film practice (and more specifically of spectatorship), its real attraction consists of its applicability to other periods of film history, to other similar practices beyond early cinema (and even beyond cinema)."[28] It is in this sense that the concept might provide a framework to think about the experience of watching early fashion shows from approximately 1900.

The four characteristics of the cinema of attractions that Richard Abel identifies, following Gunning, can be applied equally to the fashion show.[29] First, both film and fashion show were presentational rather than narrative; their female protagonists, be they fashion mannequins or revue actresses, appeared as "attractions," rather than as personalities with character and individuality. In films like Le Voyage dans la lune (1902) Méliès used showgirls and female acrobats from the Châtelet Theatre; their synchronized movements and uniform appearance was also a characteristic of couture house mannequins, with their robotic, repetitive performance—often modeling the same dress ten times a day to ten different clients—and their standardized, house styles of modeling. Even the word mannequin, derived from the word for an inanimate dummy, suggested their uniformity. Further, the cinema of attractions often addressed the spectator directly, as the actors looked directly to camera, much as the mute mannequins might make a visual appeal to the clients by gazing at them as they modeled. Second, cinema of attractions presented its action in a series of homogenous spaces, or tableaux, that did not alter for the duration of the scene, very like the range of couture salons through which the fashion mannequin would walk, modeling to clients who remained seated within that room. The mannequins were thus, as Gunning describes early films, "enframed rather than emplotted."[30] Third, the fixed viewpoint of the spectator in the couture salon mirrors the single, unified viewpoint of the camera in the cinema of attractions. The use of the long shot in cinema "was to make human figures primarily performers of physical action rather than 'characters' with psychological motivations,"[31] and this also describes the impersonal role of the fashion mannequin. Fourth, early films were "semi-finished products" which the purchaser "finished" by choosing how to present them, with music or sound effects, perhaps a *bonimenteur* or commentator to explain the action,[32] and the choice of varying the projection speed by hand-cranking the film.[33] Similar effects were manifest in the couture houses, where clients could specify that mannequins come closer to give a better view of the dress, and where the couturier decreed how fast or slowly the mute mannequins walked, and performed the role of *bonimenteur* by talking the client through the dresses as they were being modeled. The role of the couturier as scenographer in the show, directing the appearance of the models in groups or singly, was akin to that of the director in the film.

PAUL POIRET AS SHOWMAN

No early-twentieth-century French couturier more resembled an impresario of attractions in the way he directed and managed his own business than Paul Poiret, who opened his first house on the rue Auber in 1903, and who was one of the principal exponents of the fashion show. Poiret's promotion, marketing, and publicity stratagems—of which the fashion show was an important element—mixed media, performances, and audiences. Charles Musser has argued that in the cinema of attractions it was film exhibitors rather than filmmakers who determined how films were seen, because they controlled and directed the multifarious forms of film presentation by adding music or lectures, and by editing or recoloring the film prints they bought.[34] Like them, but a few years later, Poiret marshaled a series of interconnecting attractions intended to create an aura of excitement and expectation, adapting the strategies of popular visual culture to high-end consumer culture. In the years leading up to World War I, besides running his couture house and staging fashion shows, he produced a perfume, he designed for the stage, he opened an interior design studio and school, he cultivated the press, and he threw spectacular themed parties.[35] He took his mannequins to London to model for the Prime Minister's wife in 1909 and on a whistlestop tour of eight European countries in 1911. He commissioned illustrators to make luxury albums of his fashion designs, and in 1911, he was the first to use both photography and film to promote them, modeled by his house mannequins.[36]

In July 1910, the illustrated paper *L'Illustration* published a long article on Poiret with several photographs of his mannequins parading in the formal gardens of his fashion house. It described Poiret's command of the *défilé* (the mannequin parade) in filmic terms, highlighting how he stopped, started, and even reversed it on command, exactly like the stop-action effects, dissolves, and superimpositions of Méliès, whose trick effects made women appear, multiply, and disappear on screen as if by magic.

> D'un mot, d'un geste . . . il dirige le cortège . . . Un signe de lui, une syllabe les lance en avant, les arrête, puis les fait repartir, aller, revenir sur leurs pas, se croiser, mêler, au gré de sa fantasie, ainsi qu'en un ballet aux mouvements paresseux, . . . et se retourner, subitement, toutes, pour faire admirer un moment le galbe de leurs hanches.
>
> (With a word, a gesture . . . he directs the cortege . . . a sign from him, a syllable, throws them forward, halts them, then makes them start again, go, come back on themselves, cross over, mix, according to his fantasy, as if it were a ballet with lazy movements, . . . and return, suddenly, all of them, to show off for a moment the curve of their hips.)[37]

Méliès had made fifteen short publicity films in 1900, including one for Mystère corsets and another for Delion hats, which were projected at night in the street outside his magic theatre, the Théâtre Robert-Houdin.[38] Poiret, who was an enthusiastic amateur photographer, was the first haute couturier (as opposed to corsetier or milliner) to recognize the promotional possibilities of film. In July 1911 he filmed his mannequins parading in his garden on the occasion of his "The Thousand and Second Night" party, with the mannequins and saleswomen brilliantly lit by the light of "un projecteur puisant destiné a remplacer la lune" ("a powerful projector destined to replace the moon").[39] The footage became part of a completed film, now lost, covering the full history of his designs. He showed it in August 1911 to an audience of overseas buyers and customers for his new fall collection as part of "an elaborate reception" which included "oriental dances," a live fashion show, and "*recherché* refreshments and much merriment."[40]

Shortly afterwards, Poiret set off on his European mannequin tour. Two years later, in September 1913, he embarked on a second marketing tour, this time of America. The Paris correspondent of the *New York Times* reported that, instead of living mannequins, he planned to take

> a specially colored cinematographic film representing the dress display in his showrooms here. The film will show all his creations, even those dating a few years back. They will in fact be a review of the fashions of the last twenty years. The films represent a departure from M. Poiret's original intention to take with him a corps of mannequins to show the dresses at his lectures. Consultation with American authorities disclosed the fact that such gowns were dutiable, so the couturier decided not to take them. Instead he had his showrooms specially fitted up for the purposes of taking colored film of the different costumes.[41]

In this way, fashion film had a commercial role to play, as well as a cultural one, in demonstrating Poiret's modernity to his customers. On his lecture tour, Poiret intended to show the film, with himself in the role of lecturer who explained the film, similar to the lecturers of the cinema of attractions in the early 1900s (although by 1913 lecturers were no longer used in the cinema).[42] Prior to his departure, he held a "cinematograph dinner" for thirty guests in the walled garden of his house, where he showed the new film. One of the guests was the Paris correspondent of the *New York Times,* who described his filmed mannequins as "Goddesses from the Machine" and wrote:

> The guests sat on the marble steps that run across half the front of the house, and suddenly, into their vision, came a dramatic parade of pictured mannequins who moved in and out of the garden trees, and sauntered on the graveled garden paths, wearing the very newest clothes that had been invented by Poiret that week. Here was Andrée, famous as the queen of mannequins in Paris, and who indulges in a touch that "gets over the footlights" and never ceases to have its effect, when she saunters across the room wrapped in a costly coat which, with a superb gesture, she unfastens, lifts from her shoulders, and throws to the floor without even a backward look, then saunters on, disclosing an equally costly robe. There is no putting into words the effect she produces by throwing one coat after another onto the floor as she parades up and down the salon. Poiret taught her this touch. She does it in the cinematograph as she does it in the salon, and Americans will see it in the moving pictures with which Poiret will illustrate his lecture here. But back to the supper: it was difficult to believe that these visions of lovely women and costly robes moving among the trees were produced by a machine.[43]

Another journalist corroborated this account in his description of how Poiret taught his mannequin Andrée most of her modeling gestures, one being "to enter a room in a gorgeous wrap. This she unfastens at the throat and lifts from the shoulders, letting it slip carelessly to the floor as she walks on without a backward look. The one principle which Poiret instills is disdain and contempt of the clothes which are being exhibited."[44] Andrée's actions exemplified the exhibitionist side of fashion modeling that constituted it as pure "attraction," on- or off-screen. The mannequin's motion is, is in this sense, inherently "filmic"; it is also "staged" in the acting out of disdain, by 1913 one of the tools of the mannequin's trade.

Poiret's film, which does not survive, was, according to Leese, impounded on arrival by the New York customs on grounds of obscenity.[45] American press reports, however, suggest otherwise. The *New York Times* reported that Poiret arrived with "a set of motion picture films showing models dressed in various gowns designed by him, promenading in the courtyards of [Poiret's] establishments at 26 avenue d'Antin and 107 Faubourg St Honoré, in Paris. He will use the films to illustrate lectures he will give at the Plaza, where he has a suite, and at hotels in Philadelphia, Chicago and Boston."[46] Four days later, it reported that on September 25 Poiret lectured on fashion to an audience of "buyers and men and women interested in women's dress in a business way" who filled the ballroom of the Plaza Hotel. The talk was followed by a four-reel film of his mannequins modeling in his Paris gardens and shop. The *New York Times* reported "many gowns of original and startling color and cut were shown. As each model stepped on to the screen, the lecturer [Poiret] described the colors of the gown she wore and often told where he obtained the idea for it."[47]

A fortnight later, the *Chicago Daily Tribune* described a Poiret screening to an audience of 700 women at the Blackstone Hotel on October 6, 1913. The film showed a mannequin in Poiret's "lampshade [or minaret] gown, whose 'hoop' swayed with the motion of her body," while "another model preened herself before a mirror and showed the basic principle of the trouser skirt."[48] In addition, a few colored slides were projected to illustrate Poiret's orientalist color combinations of blue and green, scarlet and black, purple and white. Unlike fashion newsreels, which were very short, Poiret's film consisted of four reels, and some gowns were shown more than once.

It is unclear if this was Poiret's original 1913 film made in Paris, or a new one shot in the United States. Two weeks later he was supervising the making of a new one, according to the film journal *Motography* which reported that "Kinemacolor is taking natural pictures of the latest creations of Paul Poiret, the Parisian designer, including a number of radiant and diaphanous garments. . . . M. Poiret is in this country at present, lecturing on women's styles, and is personally watching the production."[49] In his discussion of color fashion newsreels, Eirik Frisvold Hanssen has pointed out how Kinemacolor films differed from contemporary film practices, having "more in common with earlier film conventions, specifically the cinema of attractions' mode of presentation which was based on 'showing' rather than 'telling' in order to demonstrate the powers of the photographic process."[50] Kinemacolor technology might therefore be argued to have a natural affinity with the fashion show, itself a form of "attraction," an affinity found in both Kinemacolor's film productions (such as *Paris Fashions*, 1913) and its 1913 "cinemagazine" the *Kinemacolor Fashion Gazette,* a newsreel format showing fashion alone rather than next to "hard" news subjects.[51]

FASHION NEWSREELS FROM THE 1910S TO THE 1920S

At the same time that Poiret began to exploit film for publicity purposes in his fashion business, a significant quantity of newsreel footage showing fashion modeling began to be shown in cinema programs. It was internationally disseminated in a weekly newsreel format by Pathé-Frères from 1909 (*Pathé Revue*) and by Gaumont from 1910 (*Gaumont Journal*).[52] Early newsreels were short, with only two or three items on each reel, and the footage of Paris fashion was especially short. In 1911, however, Pathé expanded its fashion coverage by producing a series of short films entirely devoted to coming fashions for *Pathé Animated Gazette*.[53] That year, an American journalist commented "A growing feature of the imported films is the display in colors of the newest styles in gowns and hats in Paris. 'Mannequins' of the smartest Paris shops glide up and down for the camera operators, and in a brief time the latest fashion hints are

presented to the women of America."[54] The increase in newsreel footage
of Paris fashion was matched in this period by the increasing publicity
given to mannequins in novels, in the fashion press, at the races, and
on stage. From 1912, Gaumont began to use named actresses as well as
professional mannequins to model clothes in couture houses.[55]

In the theatre, the genre of fashion plays had existed since the 1890s,
to which were added two touring plays about mannequins in the 1910s.
In January 1912, *La rue de la Paix* by Abel Hermant and Marc de Toledo
opened at the Vaudeville Theatre in Paris. With approximately fifty costumes designed by the fashion illustrator Paul Iribe and executed by
the couture house of Paquin, the play, which satirized both Lucile and
Poiret, was a glorified fashion show masquerading as a melodrama. Two
years later, Paul Gavault's four-act comedy *Le Mannequin* opened at the
Comédie-Marigny on February 5, 1914. Set in "Maison Augusta" in the
rue de la Paix, the curtain rises on a scene of mannequins modeling for
clients. Mme. Augusta instructs the mannequin on how to walk in this
season's gowns: "Please walk, mademoiselle Julia. Look: with the bust
held back, you understand, as for all our models this season."[56]

Just as Charles Musser has argued that American cinema audiences'
viewing competences were structured by the vaudeville tableaux vivants
and "living pictures" of the 1890s,[57] so these popular French touring stage
plays brought the fashion mannequin's repertoire to a wider audience.
Following them, a considerable number of fashion-related silent feature
films began to be made in France between 1915 and 1929, set in fashion
houses or department stores, some concerned with models and modeling, some featuring actual fashion shows. Most of these do not survive,
and the task of comprehensively researching and cataloguing them from
contextual sources remains to be done.[58]

In parallel with the development of fiction films with fashion-related
themes, fashion newsreel continued to be produced, but remained, as
Hanssen argues, "a remarkably static genre" that changed less than any
other film genre from the 1910s–1930s.[59] Hanssen makes the case for
fashion newsreel as a form of attractions-based film. Just as Poiret's marketing stratagems, which included both film and fashion shows, constituted an arrière-garde attraction at a time when cinema had moved into
a period of "narrative integration," so too did newsreel retain some of the

features of attractions-based cinema. Paradoxically, it is no accident that three of the designers with Paris studios who were most innovative in developing the fashion show, Poiret, Lucile, and Patou, were also among the most open to the new medium of film in promoting their designs.[60] Distributed worldwide, French fashion newsreels promulgated the idea of exclusive Paris fashion, the earliest ones being set in intimate couture salons with scenes of two or three mannequins modeling to equally small groups of clients. Many of the surviving *Gaumont Journaux* have English language intertitles and feature the Paris couturiers who were particularly successful with American buyers.[61]

Fashion newsreel was addressed specifically to a female audience, as Hanssen has shown. He has also argued that the use of color in fashion newsreels in the 1910s and 1920s was derived and adapted from earlier attractions-based film practices and then integrated with more recent narrative cinema conventions. Newsreels reveal how much modeling styles varied between the houses, from the well-known gliding walk of the Paris mannequins to a more theatrical and flamboyant prance. Although the genre was relatively static, as Hanssen argues, there were variations within it in both modeling and directing styles. Photographs of Poiret's mannequins modeling in 1910 suggest that his first film of 1911 featured a line of mannequins walking across the screen. By contrast, Gaumont footage from the house of Boué in 1913 shows a single mannequin who revolves on the spot so smoothly that she might be on a turntable.[62] She does not walk anywhere, and the camera too remains static, a feature of the earlier cinema of attractions which by 1910 had largely been replaced by more complex ways of filming and editing. The short piece of Boué footage is most interesting for its close-up of the mannequin's right arm and hand (showing her wedding ring), during which she revolves alternately clockwise and counter-clockwise, so that the detailing on the sleeve is very well displayed.

In the newsreel footage from the 1910s, some mannequins simply model as they would have done professionally to clients in the salon, but others play the role of society women, chatting and taking tea together in narrative scenarios that thinly veil the point of displaying the latest fashionable costumes, introducing a note of fiction into real-life modeling. They suggest that the editing techniques, modeling styles, and scenography of fashion newsreel have the potential to add a further layer of complexity to debates about the origins, chronology, and development of both the cinema of attractions and narrative cinema, particularly since attractions-based techniques continued to inform some types of fashion newsreel well into the 1920s.[63]

In the 1920s the Manuel Frères studio still used static cameras to film mannequins who revolved on the spot like the Boué manne-quin, their upper bodies motionless, smiling glassily at the camera,[64] whereas in other newsreel footage from the 1920s both camera and man-nequins are animated and mobile.[65] They walk in a lively and springy way through parks and gardens, constantly turning, gesticulating, chat-ting, and shooting the occasional sly glance at the spectator as if to check that they are still watching, while the camera, too, is in constant movement, circling them, first coming in close, then drawing back, so that its actions too seem flirtatious and dynamic. Whereas the former exemplifies Gunning's arguments about the direct frontal appeal of attractions-based film that shows rather than tells, the latter tends to support Musser's argument that even actualities footage creates a "di-egetic universe."[66]

One apparently documentary fashion film from c.1926 or later shows a couture house fashion show, juxtaposing scenes of a real couturier (who may be Jean-Charles Worth)[67] talking a journalist or buyer through the collection with scenes of a glamorous fictional client whose older male companion exhibits a roving eye for the mannequins to add comedy to the scene. The film exemplifies Judith Mayne's argument that the mode of address of the cinema of attractions was inevitably gendered in that it employed "human figures to embody both the visual fascination and the rudimentary narrative structures of early film."[68] All eyes are on the mannequins. The look of the female client's male companion forms a counterpoint to the touch of the male couturier who, in talking the female buyer or journalist through the collection, seems unable to take his hands off the mannequin, whom he manipulates and revolves like a living doll on a turntable. This short film shows the visual seduction of modeling luxury clothing in an elite setting; but it also reveals, as the camera follows the mannequins through the salons in alternating close-ups and long shots, a complex set of gender, economic, and class relations

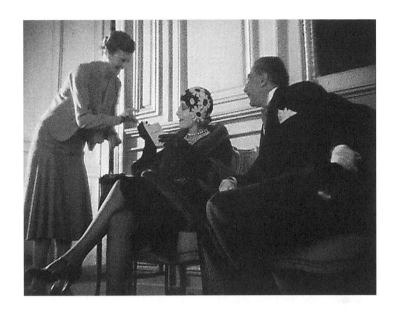

5.2A. Fashion Show in French couture house, possibly Worth, late 1920s. *Courtesy of Lobster Films, Paris.*

5.2B. Couture client at fashion show, possibly Worth, late 1920s. *Courtesy of Lobster Films, Paris.*

between the couturier, his mannequins, his saleswoman, and his two types of female customer, the private client and the professional buyer or journalist. These scenes, be they actualities or fictional reconstruction, highlight the class and gender masquerade that is a structural part of fashion as both industry and image.

The juxtaposition of the client's roving eye with the professional's roving hands in this admixture of fiction and factual film undercuts any simple distinction between attraction and narrative. It seems, in fashion, to be a case of "both/and" rather than "either/or," much as Charles Musser suggests when he argues that, for example, close-ups in narrative cinema do not just forward a film's story but also give the audience an opportunity to look at the stars. Musser concludes that attractions and narrative integration stand in a dialectical relationship to each other, and Elsaesser suggests that it is impossible—as well as conceptually and methodologically problematic—to separate them.[69] Nowhere is this more so than in the French fashion show and the fashion newsreel, for as both Williams and Balides have argued, "women become a certain kind of attraction in the cinema of attractions,"[70] and are "already fictionalised," their bodies invested with "a diegetic surplus of meaning."[71] Lucy Fischer makes the same point about Busby Berkeley's films from the early 1930s when she argues that, in cinema history, "certain myths concerning women are inscribed in the seemingly value-free level of plastic composition," so that female stereotypes amassed on screen constitute "an ongoing fashion show of popular female 'styles.'"[72] From the earliest actualities films portraying fashion in the 1900s to the visually more sophisticated footage of the 1920s where both camera and mannequins have begun to move together in a seductive duet, the fashion newsreel's direct address, like that of the mannequins who model in it, is to the spectator. Both fashion shows and fashion newsreel remained relatively static genres in the period of rapid style and technological change in which they came of age; and, as Mila Ganeva has argued in relation to German fiction films in the Weimar period, fashion modeling scenes disrupt the narrative flow of cinema and provide fragmented glimpses of earlier cinematic forms that reflect the fragmented experience of modernity in the early twentieth century.

NOTES

1. Siegfried Giedion, *Mechanization Takes Command*, 28.

2. Henri Bergson, *Creative Evolution*, 323.

3. Marie-Anne L'Heureux, "Nouveautés d'Automne," 514.

4. Gene Morgan, "Revue de la Ville." Cinematic metaphors, both pictorial and verbal, continued to be used in fashion writing and magazine layouts throughout the 1910s and 1920s.

5. Arsène Alexandre, *Les Reines de l'aiguille*, 61 and 72. The couturier cited is anonymous.

6. Anne Hollander, *Seeing Through Clothes*, 331 and 332.

7. Stephen Kern, *The Culture of Time and Space 1880–1918*.

8. Ghenya, "La Journée d'un Mannequin," 15.

9. Constance Balides, "Scenarios of Exposure in the Practice of Everyday Life," 63–80. See too Richard Abel, *The Ciné Goes to Town*, 219–20.

10. See Balides, 68 and 74.

11. Stills can be can be viewed free of charge online at www.gaumontpathearchives.com. *Modes, Coiffures, défilés de mannequins présentant leurs coiffeurs* (1900, Gaumont), Gaumont-Pathé Archive reference number (hereafter GP ref) 0000GB 00097. *Métiers à tisser, mode, costumes en laine sofil. Plan sur des mannequins de mode* (1900, Gaumont), GP ref 0000GB 00348. *La mode. Aviation. Course cycliste Paris Roubais* (1900, Gaumont Actualité), GP ref 0000GB 00138 BOB1. *Ballet Serge Lifar. Festival de Cannes. Danseur et choréographe* (1900, Gaumont), GP ref 0000GB 007744 BOB 3.

12. Susan Hayward argues that from 1908 Gaumont, closely followed by Pathé, sought to widen its appeal to more middle-class audiences, and Abel argues that by approximately 1912 the high pro-

portion of female characters in contemporary melodrama and spectacle "seems to assume a high percentage of women in certain French cinema audiences" (*French National Cinema*, 354).

13. On cinema acting, see Roberta E. Pearson, *Eloquent Gestures*; and Jean-Philippe Tesse, "Les Gestes qui sauvent," 82. On the influence of stage mannerisms on fashion modeling in early-twentieth-century German fashion photographs, see Susanne Holschbach, *Vom Ausdruck zur Pose*. On the historical precedents for the pose in fashion modeling, see Gabriele Brandstetter, "Pose—Posa—Posing—Between Image and Movement," 248–64.

14. L. Roger-Milès, *Les Créateurs de la Mode*, 68.

15. "Mistinguett fait du ciné," 356–58.

16. Bergson, *Creative Evolution*; Gilles Deleuze, *Negotiations 1972–1990*, 57.

17. Richard Abel, *The Ciné Goes to Town*, 7 and 59.

18. According to Abel, from 1902 to 1904 the Pathé catalogues contain up to a dozen genres or *scènes:* "pleine air films, comic films, trick films, sports films, historical films and actualities, erotic films, dance films, dramatic and realist films, féeries, religious or biblical films, and synchronised-phonograph films" (60).

19. Ibid., 78.

20. On Méliès's féeries, and the genre in general, see Abel, 61–87.

21. David Robinson, *Georges Méliès*, 24.

22. Abel, 62.

23. Lucy Fischer, "The Lady Vanishes," 30–40.

24. Linda Williams, "Film Body," 19–35, quoted in Abel, 67.

25. Alexandre, 105.

26. Tom Gunning and André Gaudreault, "Early Cinema as a Challenge to Film History," 384.

27. Gunning argued that the cinema
of attractions was followed by a period
of transition to "narrative integration,"
from c. 1907 to c. 1913, thus setting up a
binary opposition between attraction
and narrative (although he argued the
two could, and did, coexist in the same
films). Charles Musser has both challenged and modified his periodization
(see Wanda Strauven, *The Cinema of Attractions Reloaded,* 389–416). Musser, like
Thomas Elsaesser (see Strauven, 205–23)
has also queried Gunning's binarism, and
Gunning himself has participated in the
ensuing debates and redefinitions. For an
encapsulation of the principal definitions,
arguments and revisions to the debate
twenty years after its inception, see Strauven's volume, which also reprints four important early papers, by Donald Crafton
[1987, revised 1994], André Gaudreault
and Tom Gunning [Japanese version
1986, French version 1989], Tom Gunning
[1986, revised 1990], and Charles Musser
[1994].

28. Strauven, 20.

29. Abel, 60–61.

30. Ibid., 60, quoting from Tom Gunning, "'Primitive' Cinema," 10.

31. Abel, 61, quoting Noel Burch,
"Primitivism and the Avant-Gardes," 487.

32. See Germain Lacasse, "The Lecturer and the Attraction," 181–91.

33. Abel, 61, quoting Thomas Elsaesser, "Comparative Style Analysis for
European Films, 1910–1918."

34. Abel, 61, citing Charles Musser,
"The Eden Musée," 73–83; Musser, "The
Nickelodeon Era Begins," 4–11.

35. On Poiret's life and work, see *Paul
Poiret et Nicole Groult;* Palmer White,
Poiret; and Nancy J. Troy, *Couture Culture.*

36. In the 1920s Poiret went on to act
with Colette in a touring play, *la Vaga-
bonde,* to design costumes for several
French films and, while on a promotional
tour with his mannequins in 1923, to star

with them in a Czech comedy film, *The
Kidnapping of Fux the Banker,* in which
Poiret played himself, credited as "Leon"
Poiret, presenting his collection to a
young debutante. See Marketa Uhlirova,
"Scandal, Satire and Vampirism."

37. Gustave Babin, "Une Leçon
d'élégance dans un parc."

38. Robinson, 45.

39. Montoison, "La fête chez Paul
Poiret," 829.

40. "Poiret's Elaborate Reception," 42.

41. "To Bring 100 Gowns."

42. Lacasse, 181–91.

43. "Poiret, Creator of Fashion Here."

44. E. M. Newman, "Nothing to Do
but Wear Fine Clothes!"

45. Elizabeth Leese, *Costume Design
in the Movies,* 10. From the late 1900s,
many French films, in particular those of
Pathé-Frères, came under attack in the
American trade press as "morbid, grue-
some, indecent or simply 'in bad taste'"
compared to "'good, clean, wholesome,
national, patriotic, educational' American films," according to Abel, 45, who
cites *Variety* and *Moving Picture World*
from 1908. Abel describes how, from 1909,
when the American National Board of
Film Censorship came into being, Pathé's
films were either rejected or forced to
be cut or retitled in disproportionate
numbers.

46. *New York Times,* "Paul Poiret Here
to Tell of His Art."

47. *New York Times,* "Wants Women to
be Audacious in Dress."

48. *New York Times,* "Poiret Startles
Chicago Women."

49. *Motography,* "Poiret Creations Pictured," 296.

50. Eirik Hanssen, "Symptoms of
desire," 107–108. "Poiret Creations Pictured," 296.

51. "Kino Starts New Series" (*Variety,*
October 17, 1913), cited in Hanssen "Symptoms of Desire," 114.

52. Many examples can be found on the French Gaumont-Pathé website, some under "*défilé*" and many more simply under "*mode.*" See www.gaumontpathearchives.com. The earliest is *Mode à Paris et au Bois* (1909, Pathé), GP ref 1909 1. From 1910 there is *Belle époque. Mode 1910. La mode dans un salon* (1910, Gaumont), GP ref 0000GB 02046. From 1911, the volume increases significantly, with thirty-eight fashion items from that year, and thereafter the volume remains steady throughout the 1910s and 1920s. Coverage is divided between modeling in couture salons and in the fashionable parading grounds of the Bois de Boulogne and at the Paris races. The earliest salon shows, from 1911, are: *Paris, la mode, robes et manteaux Elise Porot* (1911, Gaumont), GP ref 1150GJ 0000; *La Mode à Paris, défilé dans le salon d'un couturier* (1911, Gaumont), GP ref 1113GT 00010; *Mode: les créations de mode Carlier, robe à transformation, robe kimono* (1911, Gaumont), GP ref 1112GJ 00007; *Paris: la mode des fourrures présentée dans un salon* (1911 Gaumont), GP ref 1143GJ 00011; *Paris: la mode feminine du couturier Henrie et Cie présentée dans un salon* (1911 Gaumont), GP ref 1134GJ 00010; *Présentation de mode dans un salon Parisien* (1911 Gaumont), GP ref 1111GJ 00008. An unusual variation showing modeling on a curtained stage is *France, deux mannequins présentent la mode Parisienne pour la camera Gaumont* (1911, Gaumont), GP ref 1121GJ 00017. Fashion in the Bois de Boulogne in 1911 can be seen in *Paris: la mode présenté au lac du Bois de Boulogne* (1911, Gaumont), GP ref 1129GJ 00015; *Paris, présentation de la mode au pavillon d'Armenoville* (1911, Gaumont), GP ref 1149GJ 00015; *France, mode féminine au lac du Bois de Boulogne: accéssoires, sacs et ombrelles* (1911, Gaumont), GP ref 1128GJ 00014. Fashion at the Auteuil racetrack in 1910 is featured in *Grand Steeple Chase en 1910* (1910 Gaumont) GP ref 1000GD

00149, and at Longchamp in 1912 in *Paris, Grand Prix à Longchamp* (1912, Gaumont), GP ref 1227GJ 00020.

53. Leese, 9.

54. Reel Observer, "In the Moving Picture World," 26.

55. The earliest in the Gaumont Pathé archives is *Paris. L'actrice Lucie Hamard présente la mode Laferrière dans un salon* (1912, Journal Gaumont), GP ref 1214GJ 00009, followed by *Arlette Dorgère, chez Drecoll* (1913, Gaumont), GP ref 1309GJ 00003.

56. Paul Gavault, *Le Mannequin*, 3.

57. Musser in Strauven (ed.), 164.

58. They would include *La poupée brisée* (1922), *Métamorphose* (1923), *On demande un mannequin* (1923) and *Faubourg Montmartre* (1924). Mila Ganeva has comprehensively covered fiction films with fashion shows and modeling from the 1910s in German cinema. See Ganeva, *Women in Weimar Fashion.* For America, see Barbara Naomi Cohen-Stratyner, "Fashion Fillers." Fashion in film in Britain in the 1910s–1920s has been covered by Leese, and also by Jenny Hammerton in *For Ladies Only?* For discussions of the ways in which, from the 1930s, narrative cinema incorporated the fashion show in American film, see Charlotte Herzog, "Powder Puff Promotion"; and, Sarah Berry, *Screen Style*, 47–93. On the silent period, see Sumiko Higashi, *Cecil B. DeMille and American Culture*, 87–100.

59. Hanssen, 107.

60. In 1915, Lucile, whose mannequins had featured in two Gaumont newsreels in 1913 and 1914, allowed her New York salon and her mannequins to be used Walter Edwin's *The Spendthrift* (U.S., 1915), a fiction film that integrated scenes of live modeling. On Patou, see the Gaumont-Pathé Archive which contains one newsreel feature, *Paris à la Mode: robes et manteaux, création Parry* (1912, Gaumont), GP ref 1210GJ 00011, that shows the very

first salon of Jean Patou, who opened it as "Parry" in early 1912. To launch Parry, Patou organized an afternoon event at the Théâtre Femina which included a debate on fashion ("une charmante causerie") and a fashion show, "presented on ravishing mannequins" who were illustrated in a lineup in the fashion magazine *Femina*. The printed program identified two schools of fashion, an eighteenth-century one and a more streamlined, neo-classical one—Parry's choice—that prefigured Patou's streamlined modernism of the 1920s. (See *Femina*, 157.) From the 1920s, many newsreels feature Patou fashions, and can be seen on the Gaumont-Pathé website.

61. They include: Parry (1912), later to become Jean Patou; Martial et Armand (1913); Boué (1913 and 1914), later to have a New York branch; Lucile (1913 and 1914), who had American branches in New York and Chicago by 1914; Paquin (1914), who also had a New York fur branch; Drecoll (1913 and 1914); Beer, and Buzenet (both 1916). Pathé's *Aspects de la vie en 1914* (1914 Pathé) has some footage of a Paquin mannequin modeling.

62. "Mannequin à Boué Sœurs en 1913," *Gaumont: Actualités diverses sur Paris 1900 à 1915*, 1915, Archives Françaises du Film (hereafter AFF) ref 50825. This standard modeling technique remained in use

for decades. It features in Tony Lekain's *On demande un mannequin* (France 1923, restored Cinémathèque Française 2006) and is demonstrated in Julien Duvivier's *Au bonheur des dames* (France, 1931, restored Cinémathèque Française and Lobster Films, 2008) in a scene where the heroine Denise is taught to model, including close-ups of mannequins' feet turning on the spot.

63. See Hanssen.

64. Lobster Films, Paris, ref. no. NUM 92, France, documentary, 1929. The shots illustrated in this chapter are at: 01-55-24-24 and 02-54-39-01.

65. Philippe et Gaston, *Créations de Jeanne Lanvin: Vers la mode d'hiver*, 1920, AFF, ref 157153. Quatre mannequins dans un jardin, *Actualités*, 1927, AFF ref 3752.

66. Musser, in Strauven (ed.), 404.

67. I am indebted to Molly Sorkin at FIT, New York, who suggested this possible identification.

68. Judith Mayne, *The Woman at the Keyhole*, 166.

69. Musser in Strauven (ed.), 411–12; and, Elsaesser in Strauven (ed.), 215–16.

70. Balides, 65.

71. Linda Williams, "Film body," 26, 24.

72. Lucy Fischer, "The Image of Woman as Image," 4.

WORKS CITED

Abel, Richard. *The Ciné Goes to Town: French Cinema 1896–1914*. Updated and expanded edition. Berkeley: University of California Press, 1998.

Alexandre, Arsène. *Les Reines de l'aiguille*. Paris: Théophile Belin, 1902.

Babin, Gustave. "Une Leçon d'élégance dans un parc." *L'Illustration*, July 9, 1910.

Balides, Constance, "Scenarios of Exposure in the Practice of Everyday Life: Women in the Cinema of Attractions"

[1993]. In *Screen Histories: An Introduction*, ed. Annette Kuhn and Jackie Stacey, 63–80. Oxford: Oxford University Press, 1998.

Bergson, Henri. *Creative Evolution* [*L'Evolution Créatrice*, 1907] Trans. Arthur Mitchell. London: Macmillan, 1911.

Berry, Sarah. *Screen Style: Fashion and Femininity in 1930s Hollywood*. Minneapolis: University of Minnesota Press, 2000.

Brandstetter, Gabriele. "Pose—Posa—Posing—Between Image and Movement." In *Fashion Body Cult,* ed. Elke Bippus and Dorothea Mink, 248–64. Stuttgart, Germany: Arnoldsche Publishers with the University of the Arts Bremen, 2007.

Burch, Noel. "Primitivism and the Avant-Gardes." In *Narrative, Apparatus, Ideology: A Film Theory Reader,* ed. Philip Rosen, 483–506. New York: Columbia University Press, 1986.

Chicago Daily Tribune. "Poiret Startles Chicago Women." October 7, 1913.

Cohen-Stratyner, Barbara Naomi. "Fashion Fillers in Silent Film Periodicals." In *Performing Arts Resources,* vol. 14, *Performances in Periodicals,* ed. Barbara Naomi Cohen-Stratyner, 127–42. New York: Theatre Library Assoc., 1989.

Deleuze, Gilles. *Negotiations 1972–1990.* New York: Columbia University Press, 1995.

Dry Goods Economist. "Poiret's Elaborate Reception." September 23, 1911.

Elsaesser, Thomas. "Comparative Style Analysis for European Films, 1910–1918." *Deuxième Colloque International de Domitor,* Lausanne, France, July 1, 1999.

Femina. 268, March 15, 1912.

Fischer, Lucy. "The Image of Woman as Image: The Optical Politics of *Dames.*" *Film Quarterly* 30 (Fall 1976): 2–11.

———. "The Lady Vanishes: Women, Magic and the Movies." *Film Quarterly* 22 (Fall 1979): 30–40.

Gaines, Jane, and Charlotte Herzog, eds. *Fabrications: Costume and the Female Body.* New York: Routledge, 1990.

Ganeva, Mila. *Women in Weimar Fashion: Discourses and Displays in German Culture, 1918–1933.* Rochester, N.Y.: Camden House, 2008.

Gaumont-Pathé Archive. http://www.gaumontpathearchives.com/.

Gavault, Paul. *Le Mannequin. Comédie en quatre actes.* Paris: Editions la Petite Illustration, 1914.

Ghenya. "La Journée d'un Mannequin." *Le Figaro-Modes,* no. 14, February 1904.

Giedion, Siegfried. *Mechanization Takes Command.* New York: W. W. Norton & Co., 1969 [1948].

Gunning, Tom. "'Primitive' Cinema—A Frame Up? Or the Trick's on Us." *Cinema Journal* 28 (Winter 1989): 10.

Gunning, Tom, and André Gaudreault. "Early Cinema as a Challenge to Film History." [1986]. Reprinted in *The Cinema of Attractions Reloaded,* ed. Wanda Strauven. Amsterdam: Amsterdam University Press, 2006.

Hammerton, Jenny. *For Ladies Only? Eve's Film Review, Pathé Cinemagazine 1921–33.* Hastings, U.K.: The Projection Box, 2001.

Hanssen, Eirik Frisvold. "Symptoms of Desire: Colour, Costume, and Commodities in Fashion Newsreels of the 1910s and 1920s." *Film History: An International Journal* 21, no. 2 (July 2009): 107–21.

Hayward, Susan. *French National Cinema.* London: Routledge, 1993.

Herzog, Charlotte. "Powder Puff Promotion: The Fashion Show-in-the-Film." In *Fabrications: Costume and the Female Body,* ed. Jane Gaines and Charlotte Herzog, 134–59. New York: Routledge, 1990.

Higashi, Sumiko. *Cecil B. DeMille and American Culture: the Silent Era.* Berkeley: University of California Press, 1994.

Hollander, Anne. *Seeing Through Clothes.* Berkeley: University of California Press, 1993 [1978].

Holschbach, Susanne. *Vom Ausdruck zur Pose: Theatralität und Weiblichkeit in der Fotografie des 19. Jahrhunderts.* Berlin: Reimer, 2006.

most practically understood as the question of costume translatability into both commercial ready-to-wear "knock-offs" and women's dress practice, that I want to concentrate. But as you will see, translatability is not a simple question of stylistic modification. What I want to argue is that Adrian had a productive and creative relationship with what I am calling "unwearability."

To begin with the problem of translation calls attention to a discourse that is fascinatingly yet at times irritatingly inconsistent. This is the discourse or discussion of what modern women should do with the costume Looks articulated in the pages of *Screenland, Photoplay,* and *Vogue,* as well as in local newspaper fashion sections. Interestingly, these publications efficiently achieve three goals with the concept of untranslatability or irreplicability: untranslatability first adores and enshrines the artist designer; second, it discourages knock-offs, and, third, it dispenses style advice to the fashion novice. But the inconsistent wisdom thus imparted to the young woman contains the old double-standard message that springs from the sexual and social mores that applied to working girls in the earlier decades of the twentieth century. This contradictory advice is always what we could call "do–don't advice," such as "Do copy this dress but don't be caught wearing it." Such advice has historically been premised on the assumption that young girls yearned to become other than what they were. Motion picture scholars have found this cultural attitude throughout the first decades of the twentieth century. Shelley Stamp's "movie-struck" girls, filmgoers in the 1910s, for instance, were characterized at the time she says, as "hopelessly caught between their fascination with stories on the screen and a narcissistic desire to appear there themselves."[2] So significant and successful has been the work on the historical female spectator that it is now difficult to recall a time when no such work existed.

However, some years before feminists took up the historical study of consumer culture, Charles Eckert opened the door to this work in his study of 1930s Hollywood, central to which is the classic essay "The Carole Lombard in Macy's Window." In it, he fictionalizes an ideal nineteen-year-old single girl, the same one effectively "fictionalized" by the culture industries. An exquisite advertising model (constructed by each of her consumption choices), she sees in Macy's window a copy of Travis

Banton's design for Carole Lombard in *Rumba* (1935). The girl rushes into Macy's Cinema Fashions Shop to find the dress on the rack for $40 and from there rushes to the matinee screening of the film. Eckert imagines what she sees:

> Three dresses and a fur coat later, the gown entered. Back-lit, descending a stair, vivified by motion and music, it whispered and sighed its way into George Raft's roguish arms. Through the alchemy of his caresses it became libidinous, haunted. It slipped from Carole Lombard's shoulder and had to be lifted back again. It snaked its way across one knee, cascaded from the stairs to the floor like liquid light.[3]

In pursuing my own questions I take my inspiration from Eckert's satire in its assumption that no empirical study can deliver such a girl, nineteen years old in 1935, to the contemporary researcher. We cannot know her and she may never have known herself anyway, as Eckert's fiction of the culture industry's fiction suggests. Thus I propose to locate her here hypothetically—as part of a triangle—between the designer and the consumer culture, both of which we have studied with more success. It has been well established that the motion picture studios, reaching a new height of consumer targeting, in the 1930s launched cooperative advertising arrangements with local merchants as well as national companies, triumphantly taking up women's daily wear as a marketing strategy. But the motion picture studio designer may at times have been the weak link in this imaginary chain.

To begin thinking about the relationship between extravagant screen costume and ordinary women, I want to stress the distance between them, as visualized in Figure 6.1. It is the same as the distance between these women working in a secretarial typing pool and the dream costumes seen in a backstage melodrama such as *Ziegfeld Girl* (1941), the film advertised in a poster on their office wall. One of the last films designed by Gilbert Adrian before he left the Metro-Goldwyn-Mayer studio (MGM), *Ziegfeld Girl* features both wildly fanciful and outrageous stage costumes as well as everyday wear. To ask about the distance between the Ziegfeld success story and these working women today, however, is neither to revive the critique of the culture industries nor to complain about women's unrealizable fantasies. The office in this 1941 photograph must have been a modern one and these women, so intent

6.1. Office typing pool with poster of Ziegfeld Girl.
Courtesy of Academy of Motion Picture Arts and Sciences.

on their typing they are oblivious of the poster, may have been pleased to have found a paying job and may have wished for only somewhat more or for much more. We do not know. We are struck, however, by the incongruity between the ordinariness of these working girls and Lana Turner, the paradoxical "ordinary girl" who becomes a Ziegfeld Girl in the film. We wonder how the studio could be so confident that they could bridge this distance.[4] How, then, do we get around the problematic third aspect of translatability, the style advice corollary—in this case, specifically, the attitude that thinks of women spectators as copycat consumers and the screen as a shop window? As I will argue, there is a way in which Adrian's untranslatable designs throw up a barrier against this very reductiveness. But meanwhile in the background, the forces of commerce, working together with (and formulating) the aspirations of young women, produced the ongoing women's magazine debate: "to wear or not to wear the film."

The question of fashion and film in the 1930s and 1940s requires its own theory of female spectatorship, the fulcrum of which may be the motion picture star designer as much as the star herself. And here the best example may be Adrian, about whose designs the studio publicity was so unabashedly contradictory. During the height of his career at MGM, the publicist discourse effectively encouraged adoring emulation of Adrian designs—but emulation without exact copying. Here the contradictoriness of the message to young women overlaps with the studio discourse around the designer who was, after all, expected to design not just to design, but to design to inspire emulation. Relevant to these competing dicta is a larger world of possibility tucked inside the historical concept of emulation, a concept in need of significant rehabilitation, especially in this case. What we need in order to think fruitfully about emulation is an explanation of the diffusion function of mass culture. Michel Foucault, quite usefully, has discussed the historical term *aemulatio* as a similitude that goes beyond mirroring or the "means whereby things scattered throughout the universe can answer one another."[5] As Foucault theorizes this scale of mirroring, it is as though "Like envelops like, which in turn surrounds the other, perhaps to be enveloped once more in a duplication which can continue *ad infinitum*."[6] So the utility here is in enveloping as a way around communication theory's old one-way sender–receiver model, the model perhaps implied in a typical notion of emulation that is too easily translated into marketing's terms. What is needed in a new theory of emulation is an explanation of the all-consuming divorced from the judgment against consumption.[7] There could be in emulation both the "everywhere-you-go-you-see aspect" and the comfort of a commodity culture which anticipates our every sense need. Like this question of emulation, the wearability–unwearability problematic needs further complicating, so I want to divide it into what I call "five theses on unwearability." These theses I will then discuss in terms of Gilbert Adrian's work with Joan Crawford at MGM, 1932–1938.

THESIS 1) *DECLASSIFICATION OF UPPER-CLASS STYLE*

Sarah Berry relies on this principle in her argument that in the 1930s luxury as a Look was extracted from the upper class and disconnected from economic means as well as from the "breeding" that the class system has historically required. "Glamour," by definition, was developed in popular motion pictures as within reach of all, regardless of social standing.[8] In *Sadie McKee* (1934), for instance, the narrative brings Joan Crawford up from her status as the maid to the wife of the head of the household. Since social class is now only a matter of appearances, Adrian's exquisite detailing can make style-as-class highly visible, appropriating upper-class sumptuousness for the former maid who steps so effortlessly into elegance. Consider, for instance, the asymmetrical placement of the large half-moon rhinestone buttons on her three-quarter length black velvet coat. We cannot help but feel that the rhinestones on velvet, though they may be perfectly set design-wise, are ever so slightly askew. Here, also exemplifying the play with conventional design expectations, Adrian cuts Loretta Young's wonderful neckline out over the shoulder in a detail that is both necklace and collar, and renders her mutton sleeves in velvet. In two designs, old money fabrics and accessories have been de-monied (that is, the stuffy sense of old money has been removed) and repurposed in a youthful, defiant, and ever-so-slightly iconoclastic mode. In this new American mode, Adrian develops a highly reversible principle that if class is style, style is class.

THESIS 2) *UNWEARABILITY AS THE STARTING POINT FOR FASHION FANTASY*

During the 1930s craze for ready-wear, stimulated by cooperative advertising or "tie-ups" and fanned by the popular print media, Gilbert Adrian stood alone. Instead of hopping on the bandwagon, Adrian produced what might be called "never-wear." Fashion detractors thought Adrian's work was too *outré*, certainly for ordinary women who were cautioned never to attempt to wear the Looks he designed; some even thought that Adrian was too *outré* for screen actresses whose scenes did not necessarily require either his modernist experiments or his historical baroque.[9] What we might call the wearability problematic was concentrated, certainly between 1932 and 1938, on the modern dress aesthetic that Adrian

6.2A. *Sadie McKee. Courtesy of Academy of Motion Picture Arts and Sciences.*

6.2B. Loretta Young. *Courtesy of Academy of Motion Picture Arts and Sciences.*

worked out in a particular run of MGM films, a run of run-of-the mill films, really. These are films in which Adrian's designs, in particular for Joan Crawford, are scene stealers, offering visual attraction that exceeds narrative necessity. Recent scholars such as Robert Gutman, Sarah Berry, and Stella Bruzzi confirm as well the importance of the "smashing" dress, which, in Bruzzi's terms can work as an "interjection" with the capacity to undermine the "normative reality" of the film, and this is our opening for considering how the spectacular costume makes imaginative appeals to women.[10]

Here we see the contradictory message in all of its confusion. While the discourse of fan and women's magazines on motion picture screen fashion held that for the ordinary woman, these clothes were virtually unwearable, such costumes seen on screen could encourage imagined wearings. In this regard, Sarah Berry has argued that women *did not* take "unwearability" as a dictate as to what they could and couldn't wear.

Rather, she says, the motion picture extreme inspired new expression and even reinvention of the self through what one chose to wear.[11] The best 1930s test of the wearability/unwearability problematic is still the famous case of the *Letty Lynton* dress. It is well known that first Macy's and then other department stores across the country sold an extraordinary number of copies of the white *mousseline de soi* puffed-sleeve evening dress that Adrian created for Crawford in the 1932 film. The story was circulated that the studio designer was surprised at the extremes to which women took the mutton sleeve, making the voluminous dress sleeves of the screen original, in contrast, seem relatively modest. Intriguingly, Howard Gutner reports that Adrian was surprised by the rage that the dress produced, commenting that "In the studio we thought it a trifle extreme."[12] Adrian, of course, never had any idea which of his designs would be picked up by whom in the relay between studio publicist and fans. Fans, however, were ready to take these improbable clothes to new heights, to expand upon them and to incorporate them into their fantasy lives. So what we can take from the Letty Lynton dress example is that in the 1930s unwearability may be less a prohibition than a starting point for fashion practice, and even an invitation to fashion fantasy. As further support for this I would cite Andy Warhol, who once said that "Fantasy and clothes go together a lot." Now we wouldn't want his flat-footed definition to stand in place of all of the theories of fantasy advanced by feminist theorists in recent decades.[13] But there is a way in which Warhol's reduction of a complicated relation also appears as a penetrating insight insofar as it allows fantasy and clothes to exist together in fantasy space. In other words, we often have "fantasy clothes" whether we wear them or not.

To further test the wearability/unwearability hypothesis, we need to ask about the possibility of a disconnect between the viewer/consumer, the studio publicist, and the retailer, the consequence of the designer's unbridled screen work. Let us not forget those designs that the market rejected, either censored by retailers or the studio or snubbed by female consumers (I have considered in this regard the queerness of the *Queen Christina* (1933) fashions and other merchandising tie-ups[14]). The best example is *Marie Antoinette* (1938), the film Adrian designed

611

for Norma Shearer on what began as the most gargantuan budget of his entire MGM career. By 1938, MGM had given up on the idea of marketing tie-ups for the Adrian designs, and no publicity campaign was mounted for *Marie Antoinette* fashions. One of the problems, in addition to the shear extravagant enormity of the designs, may have been the connotation of "ridiculousness" the period costume inherited from the excesses of the eighteenth-century French court.[15] In particular, note the three foot high coiffure from the late 1780s, and the oblong hoop that defines the complex pannier skirt—two feet on each side of the waist and a third behind. Although costume historian Satch LaValley reports that Hattie Carnegie thought her clients might be interested in "modest little hoops," my contention is that since they apparently weren't, the unadaptable hoop exemplifies literal unwearability for us. Let us say that *Marie Antoinette* stands as Adrian's supreme achievement of the unwearable—clothes as furniture and animal shelter, among other things.[16]

THESIS 3) *SPECTACULARIZATION OF THE FAMILIAR*

Costume historians remind us that relative to Paris design, Hollywood costume in the Golden Era of the 1930s and '40s was seldom avant-garde. Hollywood designers explain that they were constrained to work with recognizable silhouettes because of motion picture release dates, a constraint that implicitly admits a market mindset. Working within these limits, designers knew that they could neither innovate nor anticipate because the appearance of their work was dependent upon the studio's release date timetable, a date set sometimes more than a year after production was complete. To get around this problem, the more adventuresome designers began with a familiar shape and produced the extravagantly spectacular out of it. In other words, the design challenge was to be both familiar and outrageous, a combination exemplified, perhaps, by Adrian's design for what I call the Letty Lynton poisoning suit. Here he begins with a belted afternoon suit, recognizable by its cut as a 1930s classic, but renders it not in wool but in *silver lamé*.[17] Another Letty Lynton

6.3. *Letty Lynton. Courtesy of Academy of Motion Picture Arts and Sciences.*

costume that provides a rendition of ordinariness spectacularized is an evening gown marked by the interestingly incongruous use of sequined faux bandanas. Often, Adrian's designing included unconventional or irreverent uses of fabric. So we have in this evening dress a signature moment of iconoclasm—the mixture of elegance and tawdriness, formal and casual wear—bandana-knots done in black half-sequins on white crepe at the neck and hips. Here, the bandana-knots also work out the film's scandal motif, carrying the idea that this well-bred young girl is having a sleazy affair with a callous playboy (Nils Asther), the man whom she will inadvertently poison. Again, we also see Adrian's characteristic asymmetry deployed between the hip and bodice treatment as well as between the sides of the body itself produced by the duality of the hip sash—half crepe fabric, half sequined.

THESIS 4) *ENVELOPMENT OR WEARING THE FILM*

Recall again Foucault's theorization of emulation: "Like envelops like, which in turn surrounds the other, perhaps to be enveloped once more in a duplication which can continue *ad infinitum*."[18] Let us say that the goal of the studios was to envelop the female consumer, but this envelopment is only part of what I mean by "wearing the film." There are ways of wearing the film and ways of *wearing* the film. I mean not only the sensorial engulfment of the spectator, a kind of commodity immersion, but also a more comprehensive engulfment. I also see in some cases an engulfment of the film by the dress, and perhaps even a rivalry between the dress and the film culminating in the victory of the dress that is the film.

This theory of the emulative with its tendency toward engulfment would rely upon the concept of synesthetic aesthetics, an adaptation of Vivian Sobchack's phenomenological approach to cinema. Synesthesia, the confusion of one sense with another, is of course a clinical disorder as well as a more general human tendency, and only following Sobchack an approach to cinema aesthetics. As an aesthetic, synesthesia begins with the principle of confusion between the senses and, as I see it, can

6.4. *Marie Antoinette. Courtesy of Academy of Motion Picture Arts and Sciences.*

6.5. *Dinner at Eight. Courtesy of Academy of Motion Picture Arts and Sciences.*

crescendo to a profusion of senses. Sobchack's synesthetic body, as I have discussed elsewhere, is a body that knows one sense in terms of another, a body "wrapped up in seeing and viewed in touching."[19] Theoretically, this confusion/profusion could extends to the experience of taste as well, and is suggested by the image of Jean Harlow's gold digger in *Dinner at Eight* (1933) where Adrian's visual literalization of a "concoction" was capitalized on by the MGM publicity department in a widely used production still (Figure 6.5). The synesthetic aesthetic exemplifies what I like to call the "much too much" aesthetic, a concept that figures the social into the sensorial. One principle of the "much too much" synesethetic aesthetic is this: when you run out of extreme signs in one semiotic system you draw from another. Conversely, something "over the top" involves a spilling from one sign system into another. Engulfed in so many ruffles, Jean Harlow here taxes the eye; at the exhaustion of the eye we are referred to another sense, taking a cue from her character's penchant for eating chocolates in bed.

Again, the philosophy of Andy Warhol explains something both obvious and impenetrable, filling out the dimensions of this crucial "felt" component. "It's the movies," he says, "that have really been running things in America. . . . They show you what to do, how to do it, how to feel about it, and how to *look* how you feel about it." The synesthetic principle, then, is in the invitation to "*look* how you feel about things" as well as to "feel how you look about things," and is easily extended to the suggestion that you might also "taste how you feel about things." Yet sensorial engulfment and its concomitant sensorial confusion accrue to theories of the female spectator, the weakest side of the triangle, the other sides of which are the designer and the culture industry. She is the most unknowable.

Here the relative knowability of the designer's screen work picks up where the female spectator question leaves off and takes theoretical flight. Adrian's designs epitomized the film itself, going beyond the mere wearing of the costume within the film. His designs aspire to the condition of the film itself; they are designs that, even today in retrospective viewing, produce the effect of *wanting to wear the film.*

Adrian was interested in the architecture of the dress that glitters as much as the dress that billows, but he also knew that light-catchers and sparklers were scene-stealers. At least two of his most dazzling designs never appear on screen, their relegation to publicity an admission of their threat to the film. I refer to the famous bugle-beaded dress from *The Bride Wore Red* (1937) and a less familiar cape from *Sadie McKee* (1934). Sadie's full-length cape replicates aspects of the technological process, being itself a pro-filmic light source generating patterns on the wall without the aid of the projection apparatus. The motion picture star is here illuminated by her own costume. Daring to put light shows within the light show, Adrian organized his own sartorial discourse within and sometimes against the mise-en-scène, and sometimes against the characters, as we will see. Who other than Adrian would have decided to render a dress and matching cape in red bugle beads? Let us not forget, however, that bugle beads, sequins, and rhinestones have a long history of signifying the side-show and burlesque side of sexualized entertainment, relying on a stabilized caricature of money and finery. Undeniably, Adrian's bugle-beaded matching cape and gown for *The Bride Wore Red* is cast in the narrative with this aesthetic history in mind. For when she chooses to wear this gown (against the protests of her maid), the Crawford character fatally reveals her gold-digger's motives to her fiancee's artistocratic parents. But more important, we need to consider what Adrian was attempting to do in the context of the latter half of the thirties. In both the *Bride Wore Red* dress and the *Sadie McKee* cape he created a sheet of light that can be seen to be worn—not worn, but *seen to be worn,* that is, not exactly seen as *wearable* in the practical, translatable sense, but only worn insofar as it is seen. And yes, I do mean, with reference to cinematic illusionism, that the phenomenal mountain of bugle beads may only "seem to be worn."

THESIS 5) ARTISTIC AVERSION TO ADAPTATION EXPRESSED AS SOCIAL BARB

I have already suggested that Gilbert Adrian had an aversion to adaptation. A hallmark of his MGM work could be seen as the development of clever barriers to copying, defiant designs that ready-wear manufacturers could not easily follow. It has also been noted that his detail and use of shapes, in their extremity, undercut a crucial premise of women's fashion—flattery. The most evident example of this unflattering fashionability would be the gowns and hats for *The Women* (1939), which appear in some scenes to mock the characters who wear them by playing on comic incongruity. Here, a large woman wears a small perky hat (see Figure 6.7a). Or, consider the famous kite lapel which he used on Crawford in several films, and which, when featured in *No More Ladies* (1935), was called an upside down nun's cap in one fan magazine article (see Figure 6.7b).[20] Rather than attributing this troublesome design to either misogyny or wit, I want to suggest that the dissonant detail is a double knot: a social barb as well as a defiant resistance to adaptation. Let's concentrate on the social barb for a moment. What I mean by the social barb capacity of the design features is the way they are tucked into the social situation as comment on the absurdity of current protocols of dress and demeanor. The barb is "hidden in plain sight," as we might say,

6.6. *Sadie McKee. Courtesy of Academy of Motion Picture Arts and Sciences.*

unseen by the straight (male) view of the world. Who else would miss
the fact that in 1935 Adrian was beginning to satirize Joan Crawford's
Joan Crawford? Certainly the unwearability features of his clothes take
on a certain attractive danger whose confusing message to the ordinary
woman was: "Wear at your own peril," but do as Joan Crawford does.

6.7A. *The Women. Courtesy of Academy of Motion Picture Arts and Sciences.*

With these theses in mind, I would like to argue for yet deeper insight, stepping back momentarily from particular designs. The problem with the term "fashion," of course, is that it has come to stand for both the particular stylistic features of dress and the recurrent change of these features. And this changeableness is thought to be as fickle as an unfaithful lover. There is something of the cruelty of the fashion system in Walter Benjamin's profound analysis of fashion culture in which he says that "Every fashion is to some extent a bitter satire on love; in every fashion, perversities are suggested by the most ruthless means."[21] In relation to the "bitter satire on love" I want to consider an example of Adrian's work in the ready-wear business that he started in 1941 after leaving MGM. Here I find the signature anti-copying device

6.7B. *No More Ladies. Courtesy of Museum of Modern Art Stills Archive.*

as well as the barb. His mode has an edge, its extravagance concentrated in the jacket that juts out into an asymmetrical triangle, the severity of the Crawford-Look wide shoulders turned upside-down and sideways. Was he now more free to send up the Crawford silhouette after having left MGM? The wonderfully unwearable but nevertheless to-be-worn jacket tells us that its details are perversely unfunctional and that dress in this mode is both absurd and phenomenally fantastic. Finally, this tailored suit epitomizes the flow of glamour into daily life. We have always known that glamorous fashions are in some way about love, especially if love is the reverse side of money. Perhaps Adrian's fashions are unwearable because we don't always want to know their underside, let alone wear such a sly commentary on yearning. As for the bitter satire, seen in the extremity and severity, really the ferocity, the angularity of his designing: to wear the film is to wear the unwearable, anyway.

6.9. *Dream of Love. Courtesy of Academy of Motion Picture Arts and Sciences.*

6.8. (*facing page*) Adrian, Ready-Wear Suit. *Private Collection.*

CODA: *DREAM OF LOVE* (1928)

But wanting to wear seeing? Isn't that the ultimate in unrequited yearning? Consider the last of our examples of costumes that strive to rival or
exceed the film in which they appear. Consider Joan Crawford in a lost
film titled *Dream of Love* (1928), framed in white fox fur and wearing an
Adrian design hemmed in glittering icicles. Consider how our appetite
for wearing seeing is like our appetite for love. Ask, will our appetite for
wearing seeing ever be satiated?

NOTES

1. See Jane Gaines, "On Wearing the Film," for illustrations of the Madam Satan dress.

2. Shelley Stamp, "Movie-Struck Girls," 198–199. She further explains that experts in those years characterized these girls as so distracted by themselves, others, and their own daydreams, that they were never exactly "absorbed" by the image on screen. See also Gaylyn Studlar, "The Perils of Pleasure?" 6–33, on how fan magazines in the 1920s worked to direct readers toward approved and "appropriate" interests.

3. Charles Eckert, "The Carole Lombard in Macy's Window," 110. First published in *Quarterly Review of Film Studies* 3(1) (1978), this was one of the earliest articles to open up the serious study of cinema and consumer culture.

4. Dyer's main idea of in "Four Films of Lana Turner" is that Turner is quite remarkably constructed as both sexy and ordinary. Despite Dyer, I remain unconvinced that this actress ever stood for "ordinariness" very successfully.

5. Michel Foucault, *The Order of Things*, 19, is describing the way the now discredited notion of resemblance as a way of knowing had in the sixteenth century a nuance and richness that allowed for the kinds of distinctions we may have forgotten.

6. Ibid., 21.

7. See Jane Gaines, "On Wearing the Film," 167, where I suggest that following Merleau-Ponty (*The Visible and the Invisible*, 146) we get around a mechanistic understanding of emulative dress with the reciprocity of the bodily that "sees itself, touches itself seeing and touching."

8. Sarah Berry, *Screen Style*, xix, answers the question of class envy and fashion emulation quite complexly. She urges an understanding of dress in the 1930s that goes beyond the question of economics, especially as it "acquired social protocols." Further, the "implication that upper-class glamour [was] a matter of appearances rather than 'breeding' (and therefore could be emulated) does not imply that viewers were interested in adopting the *values* of the upper class." The opposite would be the case, as both Hollywood films and popular fashion discourses "demystified" upper-class glamour in ways that em-phasized economics, not upper-class moral superiority. Joan Crawford, for instance, who always moved up from working class to middle class, was "most likely admired and imitated for

her characters' determination not to be trapped in predetermined social rules," suggesting that she represented more than mere "escape" from working class situations.

9. See Howard Gutner, *Gowns by Adrian*, 160, on this charge against Adrian.

10. Stella Bruzzi, *Undressing Cinema*, 17. But to suggest how this dress breaks the code, consider director George Cuckor's comment that if the costume "knocked your eye out" it was not good for either the scene or the film (as quoted in Gaines, "Costume and Narrative," 195, which see also for how Hollywood creative personnel gave lip service to the idea that costume posed a threat to the narrative).

11. Berry, 87, argues against seeing a contradiction between fashion marketing's insistence on wearability and the apparent unwearability of screen fashions: "Far from contradicting consumer fashion marketing and its emphasis on 'wearable' costumes and star emulation, these stylistically excessive modes of costuming can be seen to represent the apotheosis of both costume and fashion as agents of self-invention and the malleability of social identity."

12. Gutner, 119. Berry, 88, references the *Fortune Magazine* article that reports the Modern Merchandising bureau's claim that Macy's sold 500,000 copies of the Letty Lynton dress, also states that fans created even more exaggerated sleeves, and concludes that the American woman is much more "dramatic" as well as more "courageous" than Adrian ever imagined that her to be. These claims could be true, but we should also consider that the news story may have originated as a press release written by MGM publicists or an interview with Modern Merchandising Bureau's founder Bernard Waldman. For more on the

Letty Lynton dress, see Jane Gaines and Charlotte Herzog, *Fabrications*, 1985.

13. For a feminist theory of fantasy that is perennially productive see chapter 4 ("Fantasia") of Elizabeth Cowie's *Representing the Woman*, 123–165.

14. See Gaines, "The Queen Christina Tie-Ups," especially 53, on the subversion of gender assumptions. On Adrian as gay male designer see Gaines, "Dorothy Azner's Trousers." Satch LaValley, "Hollywood and Seventh Avenue," 81–82, says that the *Queen Christina* collars were successfully adapted and sold at Macy's, Saks Fifth Avenue, and Gimbel's. I am still looking for evidence of women wearing this collar that comes close to the evidence of women wearing the Letty Lynton puffed sleeve.

15. Gaines and Herzog, *Fabrications*, 21.

16. The reference here is to the vermin that reportedly infested eighteenth-century wigs, attracted to the four-paste used in their construction. See Gaines and Herzog, *Fabrications*, 21–22.

17. For further discussion of the scene and illustration see Gaines, "Costume and Narrative," 207.

18. Foucault, 21.

19. Gaines, "On Wearing the Film," 167. This would begin with Vivian Sobchack, *The Address of the Eye*, 76, where she refers to the "cooperation" of the senses. Sobchack's earlier notion of cinematic synesthesia is based on her use of Merleau-Ponty. Less indebted to him is the more recent concept of "cinesthetic" in Sobchack, "What My Fingers Knew," 53–84, which doesn't develop the feature of reciprocity that I am relying on here.

20. Gaines, "Costume and Narrative," 192.

21. Walter Benjamin, *The Arcades Project*, 79.

WORKS CITED

Benjamin, Walter. *The Arcades Project.* Trans. Howard Eiland and Kevin McLaughlin. Cambridge, Mass.: Harvard University Press, 1999.

Berry, Sarah. *Screen Style: Fashion and Femininity in 1930s Hollywood.* Minneapolis: University of Minnesota Press, 2000.

Bruzzi, Stella. *Undressing Cinema: Clothing and Identity in the Movies.* London: Routledge, 1997.

Cowie, Elizabeth. *Representing the Woman: Cinema and Psychoanalysis.* Minneapolis: University of Minnesota Press, 1997.

Dyer, Richard. "Four Films of Lana Turner." In *Only Entertainment,* ed. Richard Dyer, 65–98. London: Routledge, 2002.

Eckert, Charles. "The Carole Lombard in Macy's Window." In *Fabrications: Costume and the Female Body,* ed. Jane Gaines and Charlotte Herzog, 100–121. New York: Routledge, 1990.

Foucault, Michel. *The Order of Things: An Archaeology of the Human Sciences.* New York: Vintage Books, 1973.

Gaines, Jane. "Costume and Narrative: How Dress Tells the Woman's Story." In *Fabrications: Costume and the Female Body,* ed. Jane Gaines and Charlotte Herzog, 180–211. New York: Routledge, 1990.

———. "Dorothy Arzner's Trousers." *Jump Cut,* no. 37 (1992): 88–98. http://www.ejumpcut.org/archive/onlinessays/JC37folder/ArznersTrousers.html.

———. "On Wearing the Film: *Madam Satan.*" In *Fashion Cultures: Theories, Explorations, and Analysis,* ed. Stella Bruzzi and Pamela Church Gibson, 159–177. London: Routledge, 2000.

———. "The Queen Christina Tie-Ups: Convergence of Show Window and Screen." *Quarterly Review of Film and Video,* no. 11 (1989): 35–60.

Gaines, Jane, and Charlotte Herzog, eds. *Fabrications: Costume and the Female Body.* London: Routledge, 1990.

———. "Norma Shearer as Marie Antoinette: Which Body Too Much?" In *Fashioning Film Stars: Dress, Culture, Identity,* ed. Rachel Moseley, 11–26. London: British Film Institute, 2005.

———. "'Puffed Sleeves Before Tea-Time': Joan Crawford, Adrian, and Women Audiences." *Wide Angle* 6, no. 4 (Spring 1985). Repr. in *Stardom: Industries of Desire,* ed. Christine Gledhill, 74–91. London: Routledge/British Film Institute, 1991.

Gutner, Howard. *Gowns by Adrian: the MGM Years 1928–1941.* New York: Harry N. Abrams, 2001.

LaValley, Satch. "Hollywood and Seventh Avenue: The Impact of Period Films on Fashion." In *History and Hollywood: Costume Design in Film,* ed. Edward Maeder, 78–96. New York: Thames and Hudson/Los Angeles County Museum of Art, 1987.

Merleau-Ponty, Maurice. *The Visible and the Invisible.* Trans. Alphonso Lingis. Evanston, Ill.: Northwestern University Press, 1968.

Sobchack, Vivian. *The Address of the Eye.* Princeton, N.J.: Princeton University Press, 1992.

———. "What My Fingers Knew: The Cinesthetic Subject, or Vision in the Flesh." In *Carnal Thoughts: Embodiment and Moving Image Culture,* ed. Vivian Sobcack, 53–84. Berkeley: University of California Press, 2004.

Stamp, Shelley. *Movie-Struck Girls: Women and Motion Picture Culture after the*

Nickelodeon. Princeton, N.J.: Princeton
   University Press, 2000.
Studlar, Gaylyn. "The Perils of Pleasure?
   Fan Magazine Discourse as Women's

Commodified Culture in the 1920s."
   Wide Angle 13, no. 1 (1991): 6–33.
Warhol, Andy. *Style, Style, Style*. New
   York: Bulfinch, 1997.

FILMOGRAPHY

The Bride Wore Red. Dir. Dorothy Arzner.
   Costumes, Gilbert Adrian. Metro-
   Goldwyn-Mayer, 1938.
Dinner at Eight. Dir. George Cukor. Cos-
   tumes, Gilbert Adrian. Metro-Gold-
   wyn-Mayer, 1933.
Dream of Love. Dir. Fred Niblo. Cos-
   tumes, Gilbert Adrian. Metro-Gold-
   wyn-Mayer, 1928.
Letty Lynton. Dir. Clarence Brown. Cos-
   tumes, Gilbert Adrian. Metro-Gold-
   wyn-Mayer, 1932.
Madam Satan. Dir. Cecil B. DeMille.
   Costumes, Gilbert Adrian. Metro-
   Goldwyn-Mayer, 1930.
Marie Antoinette. Dir. W. S. Van Dyke.
   Costumes, Gilbert Adrian. Metro-
   Goldwyn-Mayer, 1938.

No More Ladies. Dir. Edward H. Griffith.
   Costumes, Gilbert Adrian. Metro-
   Goldwyn-Mayer, 1935.
Queen Christina. Dir. Rouben
   Mamoulian. Costumes, Gilbert Adri-
   an. Metro-Goldwyn-Mayer, 1933.
Rumba. Dir. Marion Gering. Costumes,
   Travis Banton. Paramount Pictures,
   1935.
Sadie McKee. Dir. Clarence Brown. Cos-
   tumes, Gilbert Adrian. Metro-Gold-
   wyn-Mayer, 1934.
The Women. Dir. George Cukor. Cos-
   tumes, Gilbert Adrian. Metro-Gold-
   wyn-Mayer, 1939.
Ziegfeld Girl. Dir. Robert Z. Leonard.
   Costumes, Gilbert Adrian. Metro-
   Goldwyn-Mayer, 1941.

in the studio era especially, influenced and affected off-screen fashions quite noticeably.

Dior needed Hollywood as much as he influenced it; although he designed relatively few film costumes (including *Les enfants terribles* [1952], *Stage Fright* [1950, uncredited] and Jennifer Jones's costumes for *Stazione Termini* [1954]) stars of Hollywood's classical era—including Olivia de Havilland, Rita Hayworth, Marlene Dietrich (who starred in *Stage Fright*), and Ava Gardner—were among his most high-profile clients.[5] The proliferation of the New Look brought high fashion to ordinary women, and it is perhaps this that also led to the style's interestingly contradictory connotations: that, as Maynard observes, it was exaggerated and stylized but also emphasized features "supposedly 'natural' to all women (very tight waists and wide skirts, full bosoms and high heels."[6] The New Look brought back not just femininity but pleasure in fashion. The twinned issues of female pleasure and empowerment through overtly feminine fashion is something to which I will return, linking it to a number of films in which feminine passivity, while assumed by many of the male characters for instance, is contradicted by the female characters' far more nuanced and authoritative adoption of the New Look and its accompanying pleasures.

James Laver, Colin McDowell, and others note the equivocal reactions to the New Look's arrival in 1947, and McDowell quotes several British women remarking about the New Look that these are not clothes for "today's active and restless life" and that a woman "will be fortunate if coupons run to one coat or suit"; then there's the female MP who sees the new fashions as attempts to curtail women's freedom,[7] while another comments in *Picture Post* in 1947 that the New Look is likely to move women "back to the indolent and wealthy years before the 1914 war."[8] Although it was supposed to be hyper-feminine (and these women are reacting negatively to this femininity), the New Look had further ambiguous connotations; as Elizabeth Wilson suggests in *Adorned in Dreams*: "although the New Look was supposed to be so feminine, there was a weird masculinity about it all. The models were tall as guardsmen, and their street clothes resembled those of guardsmen in mufti, or City men leaning against furled umbrellas."[9] (This masculinity is also noted by Pam Cook in *Fashioning the Nation*.) At another point in *Adorned in*

Dreams, Wilson returns to the connotations of the New Look, citing Simone de Beauvoir's exploration of the idea of "elegance as bondage," placing this orthodox feminist judgment of elegance against the backdrop of the late 1940s, when *The Second Sex* was published: that de Beauvoir was "writing at a time when fashions, with Dior's New Look, had become unusually nostalgic, backward-looking and shackling."[10] This notion of elegance as retrogressive nostalgia and McDowell's argument that the New Look was a consolidation of late 1940s trends as opposed to an innovative break with them (he quotes *Vogue* from March 1947, saying "Paris develops current trends; makes no revolutionary breakaways")[11] have significant implications for what happened in Hollywood in the 1950s in terms of its use of the New Look.

Hollywood championed the New Look in a particular way: the full-skirted and tight-bodied shape became synonymous through the late 1940s and into the 1950s with a romantic, romanticized femininity, a means quite often of differentiating the romantic woman from her working, professional counterpart. While the professional female character in Hollywood (Lauren Bacall in *Designing Woman,* for example) more often adopts the pencil skirt look—although it is not necessarily at all more functional—the woman with time on her hands was frequently clad in the swishy and indulgent New Look. As Pamela Church Gibson observes, the New Look was "enormously popular with Hollywood costume designers because of its inherently spectacular qualities."[12]

As it became a Hollywood staple, the New Look also came to reflect the dominant attitude at the time to costume design: that it shouldn't be too daring, too risqué, but should stay safe and middle of the road. Hollywood's most renowned and revered costume designer Edith Head linked this tendency within her profession directly to the New Look. She commented once that she had learned the need to keep her designs "very middle of the road in terms of current fashion trends . . . the hard way": . . . "Just after Dior brought out the New Look, every film that I had done in the past few months looked like something from the bread lines. With each screening, I was reminded. I vowed that I would never get caught by a fashion trend again."[13]

In keeping with Head's sentiment here of wanting to play safe with fashions (even if she herself cut a more contemporary figure), the New

Look became an essential part of the lexicon of Hollywood costume and, as in fashion terms it became old hat, came to stand for the tendency to create designs that could not be caught out so easily by the capricious evolution of fashion. Church Gibson is correct when observing that the New Look initially leant itself to Hollywood because of its inherent spectacularity and romanticism; however, as it became a familiar—perhaps overly familiar—fashion style, it also became linked to less glamorous, more maternal, and domestic forms of femininity as well. The inherent eroticism of the New Look, as indicated by many of the original critiques of it, became compromised or complicated by its affiliation to that other 1950s ideal: the devoted mother and housewife. The women I am about to discuss are both devoted—and so in many respects de-eroticized—and sexual; their frequent frustration and sexual disappointment is represented by and linked to their adoption of the New Look. As I indicated above, Hollywood adapted and used the New Look in a certain way; although Grace Kelly in *Rear Window* (1954) is the height of feminine glamour, on the whole by the mid-1950s the New Look was used to reflect safe, not particularly sexual, and quite matronly forms of femininity. Full-skirted, small-waisted outfits were often worn by female characters who were unthreatening, at times stodgy. In the contemporary television show *Mad Men* (the first season of which is set at the very end of the 1950s turning into 1960), it is housewife Betty who still sports exaggeratedly full-skirted styles, while the fashion-forward secretaries wear pencil skirts and one-piece shifts, a distinction that probably references Hollywood costume antecedents as much as the fashions of the times. As Jane Gaines argues in *Fabrications,* the New Look silhouette is readily used to "tells the woman's story" and reveals key aspects of her character. In this sense it can be linked also to Geoffrey Nowell-Smith's influential interpretation of 1950s Hollywood melodramas as examples of conversion hysteria, expressing through the elements of mise-en-scène the heightened emotions that cannot be directly voiced through narrative and character.[14]

The spectacular use of costume—and *haute couture* in particular— which I argue for in my *Undressing Cinema: Clothing and Identity in the Movies* was a means of developing an alternative idea of how costumes could be used. I termed costumes "spectacular" if, rather than function as costumes were conventionally meant to do and blend into the character and background, they "intrude on, dominate the scenes they are couched in."[15] Departing somewhat from Pamela Church Gibson defining "spectacularity" for onscreen costume, I do not argue that only the most extravagant costumes can be spectacular; Catherine Deneuve's Yves Saint Laurent costumes in *Belle de Jour* (1967), for example, are perversely *un*spectacular as sartorial specimens, but nevertheless function in a spectacular way in that they are not neatly assimilated into narrative and character and instead call attention to themselves so that they intrude on and interrupt the straightforward flow of Buñuel's narrative. Yves Saint Laurent's costumes are almost masochistically understated, befitting a film that centers on a character, Severine (played by Deneuve) who is a bored, masochistic housewife. One particularly unspectacular outfit—a beige, shift-shaped, light jersey dress—is treated in a spectacular way by having attention drawn to it when Severine (the "belle de jour" of the title) arrives at the brothel in which she works during the day. The other prostitutes—much more conventionally clad in frilly, feminine, and revealing clothes—heap admiration on the ostensibly dull dress, fondling it, glancing at the label, and complimenting Severine on her sense of style. In terms of the styling and framing of femininity, the spectacular costume allowed for—and indeed invited in many instances—a more radical conceptualization of the feminine as spectacle. The woman, in film studies' adaptation of feminist writings of the 1970s, was argued to be the object of the gaze; the broad aim of my earlier arguments around clothes in film was to problematize this view, that is *not* to see clothes as merely reflective of a *woman's* beauty and a means of enhancing *her* spectacularity, but as a means of interrupting that objectifying relationship altogether by drawing attention to themselves. In Alfred Hitchcock's *Rear Window*, Lisa Freemont (played by Grace Kelly) makes her first appearance in the film's third scene, arriving at her partner Jeff's apartment (James Stewart) with dinner from the exclusive New York restaurant 21. Jeff is trapped in his apartment due to a broken leg in a full cast; in the early evening darkness he has fallen asleep and Lisa wakes him with a kiss, sensuously filmed in soft, slow motion close-up. Jeff asks dreamily "Who are you?" to which Lisa replies, "From top to bottom: Lisa . . . Carol . . . Freemont" as she turns

melodrama Kerr plays the frustrated and unhappy wife of a boys' school-master. She attracts and is attracted to Tom Lee, one of the older boys in her husband's house, whose effeminacy also renders him sexually am-biguous (Tom is often interpreted as one of Hollywood's many closeted gay characters). Minnelli, who had been a window dresser, was especially particular about costume and production design. In an early scene, Laura (Kerr) is fitting Tom's costume for an imminent production of Richard Brinsley Sheridan's comedy of manners, *School for Scandal,* in which he— in an all boys' school—is due to play Lady Teazle. Kerr is wearing a New Look ensemble, rather than a full dress: a golden yellow blouse with a darker brown skirt, divided by a brown belt. This full-skirted outfit is worryingly coordinated with the décor of her kitchen and living room as well as complementing Kerr's striking red hair. The coordination is wor-rying because, in this domestic context, it connotes a lack of individuality, a need to blend in or a tendency to be swallowed up by her surroundings. Particularly, as she sets about making tea for herself and Tom, the fact that she is coordinated with the yellow curtains behind her and several prominent items of dark wood furniture suggests domestic entrapment. Throughout *Tea and Sympathy* the New Look resonates with a different form of tension than Lisa's longer and more opulent gown in *Rear Win-dow.* This scene in *Tea and Sympathy* is the first time we encounter Laura, and so, like Lisa's entrance in *Rear Window,* it demonstrates how, by the mid-1950s, the New Look serves to cement a particular view of the film's female characters. Here, Deborah Kerr's look is inextricably linked to her marital unhappiness, the fact that she is, from early on, clearly rejected by her husband Bill (who, oblivious to how this might undermine his masculinity, is far keener on homosocial bonding with his pupils) and finds herself attracted to the much younger Tom Lee. Tom's repressed homosexuality becomes a hugely significant factor in how we are invited to interpret Laura's look. Tom's feminization and repressed homosexual-ity couple with the sexual disappointment felt by Laura herself at being marginalized by Bill in favor of pupils like Tom, and it all feeds into the full-skirted dress style they are both at this moment wearing.

Kerr's version of the New Look is mumsy and maternal, connota-tions that stem from not only the warm, golden colors and the merging into the background but from the styling of the garments. The shirt is neatly and not extravagantly cut and made from crisp and unglamorous cotton; the skirt is made using a relatively generous amount of fabric, but is not puffed out with voluminous underskirts. The belt—as opposed to Dior's subtle silk jacket with its cinched in waist—adds a functional touch. Here, the symbolic matronliness of the classic mid-50s Hollywood New Look is especially ambiguous. Laura, the "older woman," is far removed from the Dior model of the early New Look photo shoots recalled by Grace Kelly in *Rear Window;* she represents not only a potential lover but also a mother substitute for a young man brought up by his father and, because of the unconventionality of their coupling—the older woman and the teenager—an externalization of Tom's repressed sexuality as well as her own.

Kerr represents one end, as it were, of the Hollywood New Look spectrum. The style's ambivalence is more definitively exemplified by the roles played by Jane Wyman in her two Douglas Sirk melodramas, *Magnificent Obsession* (1954) and *All That Heaven Allows* (1955). The costumes for both these melodramas were designed by Bill Thomas. The sometimes contradictory confluences encapsulated by the New Look silhouette as the style lingers into the 1950s are brought to the fore in that most characteristic of the decade's genres—the melodrama. These "women's films" have, despite their ostensible attachment to a reactionary and conservative ideology, been understood (since the late 1960s) "against the grain" as far more complex and even ideologically radical than they at first appeared to be. Although the levels and nuances are present in other melodramas of the decade, it is the films of Douglas Sirk that have, by feminist film critics in particular, been identified as the most satisfyingly politicized.[16] It is this politicization of seemingly reactionary films that especially links the 1950s melodramas to the New Look, for both embody deeply contradictory attitudes to femininity and the woman's form. In films such as *Magnificent Obsession* and *All that Heaven Allows,* the female costumes in particular, like the New Look and also like the conventional Hollywood melodrama in general, were fuelled by the repressive instinct, pregnant with nuance and meaning that is only barely and superficially repressed.

The plot of *Magnificent Obsession* seems totally unlikely if recounted: Helen Phillips's (Wyman) husband dies at the start of the film, a death that is blamed on Bob Merrick (Rock Hudson), sportsman and playboy, who, after a speedboat accident, commandeers the area's only available defibrulator, which could have saved Helen's husband's life. Bob tries to make it up to Helen, but initially she will have none of his contrition and sympathy. In an early scene showing Bob trying to make amends, Helen, still very much in mourning but able to assure a friend with whom she has just had lunch that she does not intend to "hibernate," is wearing a striking black silk New Look ensemble of full skirt, tight jacket, hat with small net veil, long gloves set off by her two strings of pearls and matching pearl earrings. This is a striking and dynamic costume, not at all like the slightly dowdy and middle-aged New Look outfit worn by Laura in *Tea and Sympathy,* and it is little coincidence that it is in this scene that Bob Merrick articulates his growing attraction to Helen by inviting her to have dinner with him. She brushes aside this invitation (demonstrating the confidence that goes with her non-matronly New Look) and gets into a waiting cab. Bob pursues her into the cab and Helen, annoyed, asks him to get out and not "make a scene"; when he does not, Helen leaves by the other door and is promptly knocked down by another vehicle and, as a result, goes blind. Keeping his identity a secret, Bob then befriends Helen, and as they get closer her gowns get more adventurous and striking. As in the earlier melodrama *Dark Victory,* in which it is Bette Davis's turn to go blind elegantly, Helen's costumes in *Magnificent Obsession* are cruelly arresting; the blind or almost blind heroine cannot see them, but we are dazzled by them. The contradiction between the gowns' colorfulness and their subtly staid cut perfectly reflect both Wyman (who, though a sought-after star, was never a leading sex symbol) and the ambivalences of the New Look. The U.S. doctors having resigned themselves to failure, Helen goes for treatment in Europe and gets engaged to Bob Merrick, still in disguise. After this, however, she disappears. Bob, now a fully trained brain surgeon, is summoned by her stalwart friend (played by Agnes Moorhead) to the dying Helen's bedside to try and save her life. Bob performs a radical operation on Helen and restores her sight.

Throughout *Magnificent Obsession* but particularly when blinded, as I have suggested, Wyman is dressed in ostentatiously noticeable clothes, clothes that are stubbornly, cruelly colorful, considering she cannot see them herself. They are there only, therefore, for the gratification of others, especially Bob and us, the audience. On the sandy shores of a lake, for example, before departing for Europe, Helen wears two especially notable outfits in contrasting colors. The first of these is in dusty pink silk, wide at the shoulders with cupped sleeves, and the second is a vibrant green halter-necked summer dress. This latter gown is more revealing: a full skirt, a tight bodice that lies flat across the chest bodice with white lines extending from neckline waist, and a thick halter strap that leaves a considerable amount of Helen's flesh exposed. For much of this scene Helen, in conversation with Bob (in disguise) and a girl named Judy, whom she has befriended, is positioned centrally within the frame and so is the scene's focal figure; with her eyes shielded by dark glasses her gaze is in the direction of the camera, more assertive than passive. The vibrant New Look gowns here are extremely expressive, particularly of something that had been hinted at before when the sighted Helen, in her elegant widow's weeds, had subtly hinted at her attraction to "Robbie Robinson." The New Look becomes a perfect foil for Helen's desires, a mechanism for disavowal as she can show herself off to the man she is falling in love with whilst at the same time managing to seem demure, engagingly prim and innocent. The blindness is a comment and a punishment, perhaps: a comment on her inability to see, until late in the film, that people can change, or a comment on her own sexual attraction for an unsuitable man. The latter is definitely suggested by the use of tight-bodiced dresses and lowish necklines on the beach. The innocence of blindness only partially masks her desire.

Once Helen has got to Europe in search of a cure, she is told by one doctor that there is no hope of restoring her sight. The intricacy of the lacework on the otherwise slightly prissy gown she wears to this meeting is strikingly suggestive. Beneath a high neckline trimmed by a white bow, the beige gown is covered in an ornate laced and embroidered pattern. The intricacy of the lace work is not merely a sadistic touch (as it requires particularly good sight to be admired) but, I would posit, evokes Helen's repressed desire and certainty. Lace is intricate and involved but also fragile and hyper-feminine. Not unlike Lisa Freemont's black and white dress in *Rear Window*, it emphasizes both Helen's vulnerability, for she seems over-dependent on appearance, and her self-assurance,

7.1A. *Magnificent Obsession.* The now blind Helen arrives at the lakeside.

for how many blind women would dress up to go to the doctor? It is in this scene that Helen is told her situation is hopeless and her blindness incurable. That evening, she returns to her hotel with her daughter Joyce and, as Joyce leaves her alone, she feels her way round her dimly-lit room in the brightest dress of all, a full-skirted red and fuchsia house dress that reaffirms the non-matronliness of the New Look. This is *Magnificent Obsession*'s most perverse outfit for Helen: rich pink and deep red, both in-

7.1B. *Magnificent Obsession.* Helen at the beach with Robbie/Bob and Judy.

tense and intensely feminine colors, worn as she has been told there is no hope for her sight. The lushness of this dress is achingly sensuous during the moment of loss of one of her crucial senses. The screen is especially moody and dark at this moment—in one sense manifestly synchronized with and empathetic to Helen's blindness—which makes the design details on the dress at times hard to decipher. As Helen emerges from her room, the limited amount of light that there is picks out the pink silk scarf that shields her neck and cleavage and appears to be tucked into the darker maroon housedress or dressing gown. This shape seems important at this particular juncture as the potentially revealing plunge of the dark V-neckline is filled in by the scarf, perhaps connoting a temporary rejection of Helen's sexuality and the New Look's erotic potential. Alternatively, with the screen as dark as any in a Sirk melodrama, the vibrancy and opulence of the dress with its pinks and reds as well as its very shape (floating and feminine) are, despite being hard at times to see, arrestingly perverse: again, why would a blind widow in a dark house dress to make

7.2A. *Magnificent Obsession.* Helen visits doctors in Switzerland, hopeful they will be able to restore her sight.

herself as noticeable as possible? The complexities of femininity are here almost smothered by despair, but the perversity of the choice of dress is explained by "Robbie's" arrival in Switzerland, having been summoned by Joyce. "Robbie" tempts Helen out of her room and takes her to a dinner dance. In a scene reminiscent of so many Hollywood moments when a woman is compelled to put herself on show, Helen—for all the anxiety that accompanies the presumed passivity of this objectification—is at her happiest and most lusciously feminine, dressed in a stunning strapless ivory evening gown with a plunging back and full, floor-length skirt. This dress functions as the affirmation of her desire for "Robbie" and her need to be found desirable; it is quintessentially feminine in that it both sexualizes Helen and resonates with her acquiescence and romantic longing. The white dress contrasts with, rather than complements, the overwhelming vibrancy of Sirk's color scheme, accentuating Helen's innocence maybe, although her exposed back especially connotes a mature and confident femininity.

In the following year, the winning formula of Hudson and Wyman is used again in *All that Heaven Allows* (1956) in which the New Look is again prominently featured. At the start of the film Cary Scott is a widow. She is being courted gently by an older man, Harvey, but becomes more interested in her gardener, Ron Kirby (Rock Hudson). The younger Ron is not from the same affluent Connecticut middle class as Cary, so is perceived by her friends not to be a good match, despite his physical charms. Ron proposes and at first Cary accepts, but then calls off the engagement, succumbing to pressure from others, primarily her ghastly college-age children, Ned and Kay. The complex Oedipal dynamic between Cary and her children is, from the outset, focused on her appearance. As Harvey comes to take Cary to a party at the Country Club, she puts on a red dress that becomes the site of tremendous conflict and equivocal responses: a New Look gown, with hem falling just below the knee, and thin straps with a tight, relatively décolleté, top (although the squareness of the neckline, echoing the squareness of Wyman's haircut, is more dry than desirable). The dress's redness connotes aspects of her personality that have been systematically repressed: her sexuality, her desire to be aroused again and not condemned to the "tomb" of widowhood, as her Freud-spouting daughter terms it. Cary has, after all, already met Ron the lusty gardener, who has clipped for her a branch from a tree that grows in her garden—and which, he tells her, only thrives in a house where there's love. The ostentation of the red dress is repeatedly—and rather tryingly—alluded to in a reminder that, according to unspoken etiquette, Cary is breaking with her widowed state too soon. The dress, however, like Deborah Kerr's gowns in *Tea and Sympathy,* is in its shape and cut staid and markedly unsensuous, more reminiscent of Queen Elizabeth's New Look gowns, which observed the rules of rationing, than of Grace Kelly's. Ironically, it is the safe, domestic New Look femininity that Cary's awful children would like her to embody, not the sensuous and erotic alternative, as suggested by Ned's hyperbolic, hysterical Oedipal excitability as he drools and remonstrates with his mother at the same time (remarking that, in her low-cut evening gown, she might frighten Harvey off). The irony here, of course, is that Ned's comments are about a dress that in its styling seems middle of the road, not bursting with erotic potential. The attention the dress attracts from all parties carries the implication that it is inappropriate for a widow, a woman who should not have sexual thoughts. However, Cary (having kept a twig from the tree that only grows in a house where there's love) is already unconsciously aware that there is a life beyond not only her widow's weeds but also the Queen's version of the New Look style. As in *Magnificent Obsession*, Cary's clothes become longer, more flowing, exciting, and figure-accentuating. Again, the red dress is a site of conflict and Wyman, more than most other stars of the time, exemplifies the ambivalence of Hollywood's rendition of the New Look: its link to domesticity and the perfect 1950s woman as well as its link to sexuality. At the beginning of the film, Cary puts herself on show, even as she dismisses or fails to register reactions to her; she is always incomplete, never having to engage wholly with the feelings of lack suggested by the interaction between her costumes and character's situation. In *Magnificent Obsession* this internalized conflict was also expressed through color, as Wyman's gowns got increasingly extravagant and feminine as her attraction to Hudson grew.

I want to conclude by referencing some of the more contemporary and nostalgic uses of the New Look. Obviously, there is Todd Haynes's *Far From Heaven* (2002), a homage to Minnelli as well as Sirk in its use of, for example, color coordination. Sandy Powell's costumes are an essential component of this nostalgia; they accentuate and exaggerate the features of the New Look so that the skirts are wider and more extravagant than they ever were in the films of Minnelli and Sirk, their colors are more vibrant, and they are more self-consciously accessorized. Exaggerated nostalgia is, in fact, a recurrent feature of Powell's cinematic work, from earlier films such as Sally Potter's *Orlando* to more recent designs for Scorsese's *Gangs of New York* and *The Aviator*. Again, the Look exemplifies the contradictory nature of femininity: a nostalgia for an era when the woman was more traditional, less aspirational and independent, is marked out here, but also there is the linking of this look to the strains of femininity, its troubles and especially its sexual tensions: Kathy (Julianne Moore) is only superficially content; her marriage (to an actively gay man) is in tatters. The costumes are extreme versions of what we have become used to, but interestingly are more in line with the Dior originals—the yards of silk, the voluminous underskirts, the exaggeratedly curvy silhouette that makes Kathy look more like a doll than a woman. Kathy is a hyper, unreal version of the archetypal 1950s housewife, in only an outwardly perfect marriage. She is particularly and defiantly matronly in retaliation; she could not be more feminine. Julianne Moore was pregnant at the time of the filming and her figure much fuller than we are used to seeing it, which brings this heightened difference to the fore. However, Kathy is also rendered insignificant through her perfection; unlike Lisa in *Rear Window,* Kathy, more like Laura, the heroine in Minnelli's *Tea and Sympathy,* blends into the background, a technique that, however aesthetically appealing, emphasizes the fragility of Kathy's attachment to the "perfect" and "quintessential" New Look and her romanticized ideal of how a woman should be—or rather appear—even as her marriage is being exposed as a sham. The brittleness of her subservience to this hyper-symbolic rendition of the perfect wife/woman is articulated via her costumes. She never relaxes her style, is never seen in casual wear—this is her, even after she has started to fall for Raymond, her black gardener. As Julianne Moore says in an interview included on the DVD: Kathy "doesn't have an outlet for anything in her life" but "she finds it in her clothes."

In another, more recent context, the women in the television series *Mad Men,* which boasts high production values and a hip cult status, also offer contemporary retrospectives on the New Look, principally in the costuming of Betty Draper, one of the three pillars of *Mad Men* femininity: Betty is the wife, Joan the diva (conventional underneath, but sexually daring), whilst Peggy is the proto-feminist career woman. The costuming of Betty epitomizes the paradoxical nature of the New Look as it has been appropriated by mainstream American culture. She is caught in the trap (as Betty Friedan articulated it) of "the feminine mystique," but we are repeatedly being told that there is more to Betty than her outwardly domestic, conformist appearance. In the second season, horseback riding is a notable outlet for repressed desires and frustrations that are also suggested by her complex clothes—the riding outfits, the skimpy swimsuits, a candy-colored spotted New Look dress. It is impossibly apposite for the purposes of this article that Betty Draper's psychological collapse in the second season occurs when she is dressed in a comic-book version of the sanitized late-era New Look: a garishly spotted evening gown that is both preppish, "safe," and eye-catching underneath which nestle several springy petticoats that give it a dollish bounciness.

The dress in many of these instances is the outlet for women's repressed and thwarted emotions—desire that is often impossible or unrequited—or their unhappiness with their lot as conventional women. It is significant that the New Look becomes shorthand for the ultrafeminine within Hollywood, while at the same time retaining its "safe" and maternal connotations—it is illicit desire confused with outward decorum: the scarf flying off, the echo of Kerr's dress in Tom's ridiculous costume, the Oedipal shock Cary's red dress provokes. The New Look in these instances becomes a site for conflicting views about womanhood and conflicting patterns of desire; it has come some distance since the style's launch in 1947 as a riposte to wartime austerity and functionality and has in the process come to symbolize a far less glamorous form of femininity.

NOTES

1. See Colin McDowell, *Forties Fashion and the New Look.*

2. Stephen Gundle, *Glamour: A History,* 199.

3. Margaret Maynard, "'The Wishful Feeling About Curves'," 44.

4. Gundle, 202.

5. Ibid.

6. Maynard, 44.

7. McDowell, 197.

8. Ibid., 178.

9. Elizabeth Wilson, *Adorned in Dreams,* 46.

10. Ibid., 100.

11. McDowell, 175–78.

12. Pamela Church Gibson, "New Stars, New Fashions and the Female Audience," 92.

13. Edith Head, *Edith Head's Hollywood,* 69–70.

14. Geoffrey Nowell-Smith, "Minnelli and Melodrama," 73.

15. Stella Bruzzi, *Undressing Cinema,* 13.

16. For example, Laura Mulvey, "Notes on Sirk and Melodrama."

WORKS CITED

Bruzzi, Stella. *Undressing Cinema: Clothing and Identity in the Movies*. London: Routledge, 1997.

Church Gibson, Pamela. "New Stars, New Fashions and the Female Audience: Cinema, Consumption and Cities, 1953–1966." In *Fashion's World Cities*, ed. Christopher Breward and David Gilbert, 89–108. Oxford: Berg, 2006.

Cook, Pam. *Fashioning the Nation: Costume and Identity in British Cinema*. London: BFI, 1994.

Gaines, Jane. "Costume and Narrative: How Dress Tells the Woman's Story." In *Fabrications: Costume and the Female Body*, ed. Jane Gaines and Charlotte Herzog. London: Routledge, 1990.

Gundle, Stephen. *Glamour: A History*. Oxford: Oxford University Press, 2008.

Head, Edith (with Paddy Calistro). *Edith Head's Hollywood*. New York: E. P. Dutton, 1959.

Laver, James. *Taste and Fashion: From the French Revolution to the Present Day*. London: GG Harrap, 1945.

Maynard, Margaret. "'The Wishful Feeling About Curves': Fashion, Femininity and the 'New Look' in Australia." *The Journal of Design History* 8, no. 1 (1995): 43–59.

McDowell, Colin. *Forties Fashion and the New Look*. London: Bloomsbury, 1997.

Mulvey, Laura. "Notes on Sirk and Melodrama." In *Home Is Where the Heart Is: Studies in Melodrama and the Woman's Film*, ed. Christine Gledhill, 75–79. London: BFI, 1987.

Nowell-Smith, Geoffrey. "Minnelli and Melodrama." In *Home is Where the Heart is: Studies in Melodrama and the Woman's Film*, ed. Christine Gledhill, 70–74. London: BFI, 1987.

Wilson, Elizabeth. *Adorned in Dreams: Fashion and Modernity*. Berkeley: University of California Press, 1985.

FILMOGRAPHY

All that Heaven Allows. Dir. Douglas Sirk. Costumes (gowns), Bill Thomas. Universal Pictures, 1955.

The Aviator. Dir. Martin Scorsese. Costumes, Sandy Powell. Forward Pass. Miramax Films, 2004.

Belle de Jour. Dir. Luis Buñuel. Costumes, Yves Saint Laurent. Paris Film Productions, 1967.

Dark Victory. Dir. Edmund Goulding. Costumes, Orry-Kelly. First National Pictures, 1939.

Designing Woman. Dir. Vincente Minnelli. Costumes, Helen Rose. Metro-Goldwyn-Mayer, 1957.

Les Enfants terribles. Dir. Jean-Pierre Melville. Costumes (dresses), Christian Dior. Melville Productions, 1952.

Far From Heaven. Dir. Todd Haynes. Costumes, Sandy Powell. Focus Features, 2002.

Gangs of New York. Dir. Martin Scorsese. Costumes, Sandy Powell. Miramax Films, 2002.

Magnificent Obsession. Dir. Douglas Sirk. Costumes (gowns), Bill Thomas. Universal Pictures, 1954.

Orlando. Dir. Sally Potter. Costumes, Sandy Powell. Adventure Pictures, 1992.

Rear Window. Dir. Alfred Hitchcock. Costumes, Edith Head. Paramount, 1954.

Stage Fright. Dir. Alfred Hitchcock. Costumes, Milo Anderson and Christian Dior (both uncredited). Warner Bros, 1950.

Stazione Termini. Dir. Vittorio de Sica. Costumes (Jennifer Jones), Christian Dior, Columbia Pictures, 1954.

Tea and Sympathy. Dir. Vincente Minnelli. Costumes (Deborah Kerr), Helen Rose. Metro-Goldwyn-Mayer, 1956.

TELEVISION

Mad Men. Prod. Matthew Weiner. Costumes, Katherine Jane Bryant.

American Movie Classics, 2007– present.

EIGHT

Adornment in the Afterlife of Victorian Fashion

MAURA SPIEGEL

Among the variety of dress-reform movements that emerged in the second half of the nineteenth century, the female "aesthetic dress" movement, which originated with the Pre-Raphaelites and the Arts and Crafts Movement near mid-century, is distinctive for having a significant fashion influence. It caught on in the 1870s and had an impact on fashion design until the end of the century. Walter Crane, an artist and illustrator associated with the Pre-Raphaelite Movement, tells us that the aesthetic dress Look drew inspiration "from the purer and simpler lines, forms, and colours of early medieval art."[1] The archetypal "aesthetic dress," according to fashion historian Patricia Cunningham, had a "loose bodice, sleeves set in high on the shoulder so they would not restrict movement, and a full skirt worn without extending petticoats or crinolines."[2] Beyond design influence, these clothes seemed to open up a new or at least distinctive notion of feminine self-fashioning, a look for the artistic nineteenth-century woman, defining a kind of feminine subculture of intellectual, artistic, and cultivated women (Sarah Bernhardt and Isadora Duncan both developed their style out of this look). These loose-fitting and uncorseted, wide-wasted and distinctively simple, unornamented dresses offered the intelligent woman an anti-fashion fashion engagement.

Anti-fashion fashion, like the aesthetic dress movement, is, arguably, a creation of the nineteenth century. It isn't after all very surprising that while fashion was gaining momentum as a consumable middle-class marker of taste, a backlash was building, or a variety of backlashes.[3] One influential source of fairly consistent anti-fashion opinion was the high-minded Victorian novel, where fashion and fashionableness are almost consistently coded negatively. The conventional opposition between the fashionable or "ornate" woman and the "anti-fashionable" woman is often configured, especially in this period, as one between ornateness and plainness—and indeed the aesthetic dress movement favored simplicity and plainness over the more elaborate adornment and detailing of fashionable styling. In novels of the period we repeatedly encounter this opposition as a contest between the "ornate woman" and the "plain woman," and it almost always resolves in the triumph of the plain woman—who gets her man. The original of the plain heroine, whose antithesis, the ornate woman of fashion, is traditionally reviled, is a creation of the nineteenth century.[4] Female fashion, associated in novels of this period with ornament, with "frills and furbelows," conveyed the image, for many serious novelists, of a woman whose self-presentation was either imperfectly or too perfectly managed. (A host of characters from Dickens comes to mind, from the bedecked and bedraggled Miss La Creevy, "a mincing young lady of fifty"—doubtless a bit out of fashion—to the "over-dressed" Miss Knag, both found in *Nicholas Nickleby*.) The woman of fashion serves primarily, in these novels, to make the plain woman look good, to provide a contrast to her virtues, to morally enhance her final victory. To list some of the most obvious examples: Jane Eyre, our ur-"plain Jane" who even declines Mr. Rochester's gift of a wedding trousseau, has both Adèle and Blanche as anti-types; *David Copperfield*'s Agnes has Dora; *Middlemarch*'s Dorothea Brooke and Mary Garth, two variants on the plain woman, are contrasted with Rosamond as an ornate type; and *Wuthering Heights*' Cathy Earnshaw famously embodies both types in herself—to her peril. Plainness in the Victorian novel is associated with the good middle-class English virtues of earnestness, modesty, integrity, autonomy, and character; and, in some instances it is also linked to the perhaps compensatory traits of female intelligence, verbal agility—wit. Ornament is linked to any number of faults, including vanity, silliness, falseness, sentimentality, and Catholicism. In these novels, intelligence falls on the side of plainness, while sophistication (or too much worldliness) falls on the side of fashionableness or the ornate.

The man who chooses the ornate over the plain woman has, in many instances, exposed an unredeemable flaw of character, and he usually finds himself ruing his choice.

In the afterlife of Victorian narrative, in movie adaptations, historical fictions, and films, the moral and sexual contest between the plain and ornate woman lives on. A staple of the nineteenth-century female *Bildungsroman,* this opposition continues to occupy a place in coming-of-age stories of our own era. *Legally Blonde* (2001), for example, a popular, high-grossing film, gains comic traction by inverting the familiar Victorian paradigm, shuffling the terms so that the seemingly superficial, fashion-conscious, ultra-"fem" heroine, Elle Woods, turns out to be more clever than her New England–styled "plain" rival, and also to have more integrity, heart, and grit than her anti-type. Ms. Woods, who majored in fashion in college, can make it at Harvard Law School *and* maintain a perfect manicure. When we of the twentieth and twenty-first centuries return to tell stories set in the "Victorian era," these two types almost invariably make an appearance. Their opposition provides a scaffolding to explore ideas about sexuality and gender, ideas that have a special place in nineteenth-century ideology and scientific speculations. Theories of "Victorian sexuality" (itself a fetish, and of course something that could not be named in its own time but that remains a reference point for sexuality to this day) come into play in the costuming of post-nineteenth-century renderings of Victorian society. Adornment—and the very idea of fashion—is tied in a number of ways to issues of sexual expression, sexual selection, and gender. In the two films I will explore in this chapter, both adaptations of revisionist Victorian novels—that is, novels written about but not during the Victorian period—John Fowles's 1969 *The French Lieutenant's Woman* and A. S. Byatt's 1992 *Angels and Insects* (or *Morpho Eugenia*), ornament carries ideological freight in its relation to sexuality, gender, and to *nature,* a word Raymond Williams described as "perhaps the most complex in the language," and in relation to fashion, too.[5] In both of these films, the "plain" women win out against their ornate rivals, and the plain characters are the ones with whom the viewer identifies.[6] In the texts from which these films were adapted, however, the two terms, the *ornate* and the *plain,* take on new meanings, meanings that reflect their authors' revisionist agenda vis-à-vis Victorian sexuality, and also, unsurprisingly, meanings regarding the period of their own production.

Additionally, the nineteenth-century themes of sincerity, modesty, and female autonomy that played a significant role in narratives treating the types of the plain and the ornate woman in Victorian novels also play a role in these two films. Those positively valenced Victorian values of sincerity and modesty that were conventionally associated with plainness in the nineteenth century, are exposed in the films as mere ideology; plainness is rendered as no less a performance than fashionableness.

THE DECLINE OF ADORNMENT

In some quarters, the ornate and the plain are to this day quite reductively gendered. Ornateness is associated (at least in the human species) with the female, and so, by a familiar equation, its value is discounted; and plainness, correlated with the male, comes to signify dignity and power. Once women begin to aspire to some parity with men, at the end of the eighteenth century, the great era of ornateness (wigs, powder, brocade, cod-pieces, beauty spots) begins its decline, followed by what fashion historians call "the great male renunciation," that is, the rise of men in black.[7] Ornateness, however, receives its most enduring assault from the female side, in Mary Wollstonecraft's founding feminist document, *A Vindication of the Rights of Women* (1792), where she rails against the role of fashion in women's lives, observing that women of fashion "take pride in their weakness."[8] "Soft," "cunning," and far too attentive to their clothes, women confuse style with knowledge. Women are betrayed, Wollstonecraft remonstrates, by such "trivial employments" as fashion, which reduces the mind and trains the female to be vain and artificial.

Indeed, Wollstonecraft urges women to renounce their frills, to dampen their display, contending that to gain social power, women must forfeit sexual power; they must forfeit their frivolous attachment to fashion and accede to rationality, to behave more "like men." This argument remained persuasive for a very long time; one sees its influence, for example, in the second wave of feminism in the 1960s. In an earlier iteration, with a eugenics-inspired twist, Charlotte Perkins Gilman applies this premise to her female utopian novel *Herland,* published in 1915. The novel is attentive to female attire and self-fashioning throughout, including an enthusiastic description of the revolutionary introduction of pockets into the unadorned tunic-like dresses these highly evolved women have devised. Convinced that the display and enhancement of female secondary sexual characteristics both degraded the female *and* was responsible for the devolution of the entire species, Gilman contended that women must phase out these corruptions through determined acts of will. Comparing female adornment to the male peacock's celebrated fan—in her view significant only as a physical handicap to the animal—she makes the case that "exaggerated differences" between male and female secondary sexual characteristics are correctable mutations. Gilman's objective, a decrease in observable gender differences, relies upon a diminution or tamping down of both artificial and physiological ornamentation. As the women of Herland demonstrate, in plainness lies power.

In an altogether different theory for the fall of ornament from grace, Anne Hollander proposes that fashionable dress loses prestige in the nineteenth century because of the fashion plate, new mass-produced images found in *Godey's* and other early women's magazines. Fashion-plate artists developed an illustrative style that showed no impulse to keep pace with serious art, Hollander explains—which for centuries had represented the dynamic between the "beauty of the natural world and the beauty of rich clothes." The result was that fashion lost moral ground along with aesthetic prestige. The images in the fashion plates became more and more elaborate; the fashions appear increasingly insipid and, in Hollander's account, "spiritually burdensome" and "at odds with earnest pursuits."[9] Hollander goes on to observe that while photography was developing at great pace, it was long remiss in dealing with the image of female elegance, up until the 1920s when it first found a fashion language.

Plainness and ornateness in dress have taken on many meanings in film representations through the decades. Hollywood wardrobe designers of the 1930s understood themselves as the arbiters of the fashion language of feminine sophistication. In this era, the intelligent woman is *pro*-fashion.[10] Being fashionable suggests confidence, independence—

Modes de Paris 1855. N°24

sexual and financial—and knowingness. Hollander observes that in the 1920s and '30s "the female clothed body was given its own dignified visual unity for the first time since antiquity."[11] Indeed, as Hollywood virtually invents the language of glamour, elegance of line, casualness and motion are stressed; ornament is eschewed. Sophistication has switched sides; now on the side of plainness, streamlined fashion asserts itself as empowering to women. In 1930s films representing *contemporary* life, the ornate woman is the matron, the insignificant or naïve ingénue, the social aspirer, the woman without taste; she is garish, she is Stella Dallas. Her antithesis does not suggest *restraint;* she is Jean Harlow, Carole Lombard, Greta Garbo. Ornament belongs, among other places, to the past, and in the 1930s Victorian costume movies, women are decorated more than attired. For the 1930s, the Victorian woman *is* the ornate woman; her self-adornment is without sexual or social force. Frilly clothing becomes associated with little girls.

THE PLAIN AND ORNATE IN THE AGE OF AQUARIUS

The 1981 film adaptation by Harold Pinter of *The French Lieutenant's Woman,* which was nominated for six Academy Awards, including best costume design for Tom Rand (won that year by Milena Canonero for *Chariots of Fire*), presents a self-conscious gloss on the Victorian novel, and offers a revised, very 1960s representation of our two types. Ernestina (Lynsey Baxter) is the ornate figure here; she is the pretty, well brought-up daughter of a self-made industrialist; she is affianced to the upper-crusty Charles (Jeremy Irons). Here's how Fowles introduces this ornate woman in his novel:

> The Young lady was dressed in the height of fashion, for another wind was blowing in 1867: the beginning of a revolt against the crinoline and the bonnet. The eye in the telescope might have glimpsed a magenta skirt of an almost daring narrowness—and shortness, since two white ankles could be seen beneath the rich green coat and above the black boots . . . ; and perched over the netted chignon, one of the impertinent little flat "pork pie" hats with a delicate tuft of egret plumes at the side.[12]

8.1. Three-tiered skirts, beribboned bonnets, a double-breasted jacket, and a mantle place these 1855 fashion-plate figures in an inelegant confusion of the plain and the ornate. *Courtesy of University of Washington Libraries, Special Collections, UW28769z.*

8.2B. Looking distinctly Pre-Raphaelite in this publicity photograph for *The French Lieutenant's Woman*, Meryl Streep's plain outfit of stark wool is arranged dramatically in folds that suggest depths, secrets, and an erotic charge of equal parts shame and defiance. *Courtesy of United Artists/Photofest.*

absence of corseting, and the tailoring that allows her freedom of movement, reference the Look of aesthetic dress, as her attitudes and the
poses she strikes echo various Pre-Raphaelite paintings. What's more,
her fashioning would seem to confirm Anne Hollander's thesis in *Sex
and Suits* that women's clothes have gained elegance by aspiring to the
single-lined look of the man's suit; notably, in the period of the film's
production, circa 1980, tailored suits for women, "power suits," had their
apotheosis.[15]

Ornateness in this story is associated with Ernestina, whose Victorian earnestness is limited, proper, conventional, and obediently re-
strained. And now the plain woman, far from her Victorian prototype,
has become wild and sexually alive, flirting with madness, defying convention. Her defiance appears to serve her more successfully than Ernestina's conformity, as she comes out a well-adjusted artist at the end.
Unlike in later costume movies (*The Piano*, directed by Jane Campion
in 1993 with costume design by Janet Patterson, for example), Victorian
clothes do not here create erotic tension as a product of their restraining
features. Restraint is not eroticized in the 1960s or '70s; *transgression* is.
This repressed version of the ornate woman represents the anti-type of
the liberated woman of the 1960s or '70s, and a type that still resonated,
evidently, until the release of the film in 1981. Sarah's virtues, unlike her
Victorian forebears', are spontaneity and, implicitly, diffused erogenous
zones—another fashion of the mid- to late twentieth century. Indeed,
the film's original audience would have been contemptuous of Ernestina
for mislocating her sexual power in the details, willingly participating in
her own oppression.

What this Victorian plain woman of the 1960s and a fictive plain
woman of the 1860s have in common is that their plain dress functions
as a protest against their gender constraints, against fashion itself, in a
period when sophisticated fashion became anti-fashion. The Pre-Raphaelite aesthetic dress movement of the 1860s and '70s is comparable to the
anti-fashion mood of feminists in the 1960s and '70s—when a version of
androgyny was emerging as a feminist ideal.

The novel ends with Sarah working for and residing in the home of
the artist Dante Gabriel Rossetti. (Although Rossetti remains unnamed
in the novel, several identifying clues are provided, including the recent

death of the painter's young wife Elizabeth Siddal, the presence in the
house of an artistic brother, William Michael Rossetti, and of a "scan-
dalous poet," Rossetti's friend, A. C. Swinburne). Charles is beguiled
by her appearance; no longer dressed in black, Sarah strikes him as an
"electric and bohemian apparition." She has "flagrantly reject[ed] all
formal contemporary notions of female fashion."[16] The "simplicity and
attractiveness" of this "uniform of the New Woman" is contrasted to
the more conventional "wretched bustles, stays and crinolines."[17] Notably, Fowles's fashion statement is again revised by the film's costume
designer Tom Rand. In the novel, Fowles describes Sarah's colorful
outfit:

> Her skirt was of a rich dark blue and held at the waist by a crimson belt with
> a gilt star clasp; which also enclosed the pink-and-white striped silk blouse,
> long-sleeved, flowing, with a delicate small collar of white lace, to which a small
> cameo acted as tie. The hair was bound loosely back by a red ribbon.[18]

In the film, in contrast, Sarah's outfit is far less elaborate; she wears
a handsomely tailored white blouse with faint beige stripes, a light beige
skirt that falls simply to the ankle, a gray belt, and a pale pink ribbon
hanging loosely, almost like a man's tie, at her collar. Absent the bright
colors, stripes, lace collar and jewelry accents, her Look in the film conveys continuity with her anti-fashion, aesthetic dress statement of earlier on (although the skirt and blouse are conceivably a nod to the "New
Woman" Look Fowles anachronistically invokes). More pertinently, in
keeping with the plain versus ornate theme of the film's female costuming, Sarah's apparel remains solidly on the plain side of the divide.[19]

ORNAMENT AND THE POST-NATURAL

Angels and Insects, the 1994 adaptation (directed by Phillip Haas) of A. S.
Byatt's 1992 novella, *Morpho Eugenia,* presents a fabulously ornate "ornate woman" played by Patsy Kensit. The contest between the two figures, the ornate and the plain woman, is played out rather conventionally
in a contest for a man—but there are a number of clever twists to this
story. The man in question is William Adamson (Mark Rylance), a natu-
ralist specializing in insects and butterflies. Of modest origins—he is the
son a butcher—Adamson has returned from ten years in the Amazons,

penniless, having survived a shipwreck which cost him all but a few of his precious specimens. Adamson is introduced into the aristocratic family Alabaster by the patriarch, Reverend Alabaster, who shares his fascination with insects. Irresistibly attracted to the older daughter of the family, Eugenia, our ornate woman, Adamson is astonished when he is encouraged by her father, and then by Eugenia herself, to marry her. In due time Adamson discovers that Eugenia and her brother Edgar are lovers and that the children he thought were his are the offspring of incest. He eventually finds his way clear of them with the aid of, or more accurately, through the well-wrought design of the story's plain woman, the governess Matty Crompton (Kristin Scott Thomas).

The costumes of the wealthy, overbred, anemic Eugenia Alabaster are somewhat whimsically fashioned from a glittering palette of silvers, lavenders, bright reds, and deep velvet blues. They are wildly elaborate, but not fussy or bourgeois (like Ernestina's), and not without elegance. They are the best money can buy, and unlike in *The French Lieutenant's Woman,* money *can* buy taste in this 1990s version of Victorian society. In contrast, Matty, our plain woman, is dressed mostly in blacks and dark blues, her simplicity of dress matching her position in the household. Unlike in *The French Lieutenant's Woman,* the plain woman is not introduced to us with a romantic long shot or lingering close-up; in fact, our ornate Eugenia is much more the favorite of the camera in this film, as if her brilliant ornamentation irresistibly draws our eyes to her.

And unlike in *The French Lieutenant's Woman,* in the world of this film, nature and ornament are not opposed or clashing. Standing out of doors, Eugenia Alabaster's costume puts us in mind—through exaggerated visual analogy—of the fabulous ornamentation of a bumblebee. The fashioning of Eugenia's clothing so emphatically echoes the film's treatment of the exquisite ornamentation of certain insects, especially butterflies, that we are urged to ponder the significance of the comparison. If sometimes nature itself (in the universe of this film) is excessively ornate, even "over the top," what are we to make our ornate Eugenia? Is the reliable Victorian novelistic alignment of *plainness* with nature being overturned? More fundamentally, is the film endorsing the very nineteenth-century mental habit of drawing analogies between animal and human behavior as a way to test the human behavior's "natural-

sonal biological function of luring a mate? In this dinner sequence there are so many delicious ironies at work, as Adamson, while engaged in this discussion, sneaks peeks at Eugenia around the centerpiece, through which she appears framed in leaves and flowers.

The idea of ornamentation as sexual signal is set up at the very start of the film when, under the opening credits, painted and feathered "savages" dance orgiastically by firelight, and subtle emphasis is placed on their crude ornamentation. This scene dissolves into another scene of ornamented dancers, the formally attired attendees of an English ball, the men in black, the women arrayed in brilliant hues. Does the film want to suggest, we wonder, a relativism regarding the uses of adornment, whether in "savages" or English ladies? And if so, is this relativism pro- or anti-adornment? Does it validate the sexual power of adornment, or does it view it as a biological lure or snare that puts the male at a disadvantage—as Adamson appears to be in his helpless and irresistible attraction to Eugenia? At this point in the narrative, we are not sure what to make of the pile-up of sorties into questions of gender, sexuality, and nature. One further turn of the screw is given in the observation Adamson offers that in butterflies and birds, it is the *male* that is brilliantly colored, not, as Eugenia assumed in a prior scene, the female.

Ornamentation, sexual selection, and gender are complexly interwoven in this film, urging us to engage the question, what *is* nature? And even to question further, does "nature" have any explanatory power—as the Victorians seemed to have believed it did—with regard to human society? What's more, if we take the natural world (or our *reading* of the natural world) as a map of what is or of what is possible, if we anthropomorphize or draw analogies of our own choosing, do we misread the world as it is? Adamson, for example, cannot recognize or even *see* the incest that is taking place in his immediate proximity because it is not part of his idea of what is natural, of what can occur. And likewise, he cannot see Matty Crompton, our plain heroine, because she too is an apparent anomaly having no place in nature—a woman of intellect who is also a sexual being.

But the danger is not only in misreading the world, it is also in drawing moral precepts from a Victorian idea wherein what is deemed to belong to "nature" can be loosely equated with how things are meant to be. Perhaps this story is drawing us toward an even more dramatic post-Victorian and postmodern conclusion, that there are dangers in reifying "nature," in trying to draw lessons from nature, in trying to read our "oughts" analogically from what we observe in the natural world? *Angels and Insects* presents us with the spectacle of an army of red ants as they organize themselves and attack a black ant farm for the purposes of enslaving them; we learn that before long the black ants take on the behaviors of the red ants. Certainly the analogies between the insect world and that of nineteenth-century imperial England are plain enough, and the viewer is invited to imagine how in the nineteenth century this scenario could have represented a natural allegory for imperial dominance, Social Darwinism enacted in miniature and affirmed by the fact that nature "will have it so." But the film, I believe, urges us to consider that there is nothing in this ant story for us to emulate; indeed, the film deconstructs the logic of the "natural order." The natural world does not give us clues to how things are, or how they are supposed to be. Thus, ornamentation in the "natural world" offers no meaningful cues regarding the "nature of gender in human beings."[20]

Through the opposition of the plain and ornate women, the very premises of "nature" are upended in this film. Additionally, in perhaps a less consequential reorientation, plainness and its conventional association with sincerity and modesty are similarly undone. Dressed in blacks, dark blues, and grays, Matty's restraint is a uniform she wears; it is not internalized, except perhaps to sharpen her ambition. Her plainness is in fact not so very plain in this film, where her costume includes stylish detailing and accessories; in the novel, in contrast, she is described wearing musty black gowns and brown stuff dresses, "severe and unornamental."[21] In the film adaptation, her plainness is a costume, too; it is not the opposite of ornament (or of wealth), nor the authentic expression of a demure nature. It is a social accommodation rendered in a narrative gesture that serves, I think, to undermine the very logic of sincerity and authenticity, to demystify plainness as the pose of the "virtuous" girl.

While Adamson believes in a static paradigm of the natural, Matty knows better, because by these terms and the logic of her day, she herself is unnatural—a scientifically minded woman who writes books. Matty is

8.4a. The plain heroine of *Angels and Insects* is given some interesting detailing by costume designer Paul Brown. A woman of intellect, her dress is a study in symmetry, with the designs on her sleeves pointing to her fecund head.

an observer of mutations and transformations, like black ants adopting the behavior of red ants. Nature is not orderly, consistent, logical—nor is it romantic or associated with passion. In this film, we are post-natural, and thereby post-gender.

Or in perhaps a darker reading, the film could be offering a new take on the Darwinian narrative of sexual selection. To return to the dinner scene discussed above, Eugenia's decision to spill her wine can be interpreted as a wry intervention into the male-centered dispute about whether female beauty in all its radiant adornment is evidence of God's existence or support for Darwin's theory of natural selection; that is, her gesture might suggest that her self-adornment is neither God nor instinct at work, but her own deliberate move in a complicated social schematic where the only reliable premise seems to be the egotism and gullibility of the male.

Like Sarah Woodruff in *The French Lieutenant's Woman* and many of her "plain" Victorian predecessors, Matty is the author of a scheme

8.4B. The ornate woman of *Angels and Insects* appears in satin, lace, and jewels, awaiting Adamson's proposal of marriage. *Courtesy of Samuel Goldwyn Company/Photofest.*

to reposition herself in society, to find a way to have a life of her own. Unlike Sarah's, Matty's plan extricates the male, her chosen mate, Adamson, from the snare he's fallen into as a functionary, a worker ant in this great anthill of a house, an analogy the film plays with quite wittily. At the end we see the two lighting out together in the dark of night—presumably to make their way to the Amazons, to the Victorian salvation of meaningful work. Surely Matty will do without fashions where she is going, but this need not be interpreted as an anti-fashion statement *per se.*

Sarah of *The French Lieutenant's Woman* turns out in the end to have been deploying her madness and her tragic airs, expressed in part through her unconventional attire, in order to ensnare the clueless Charles, because she needs to escape her gender-locked circumstances and he is a likely mark. When we see Sarah at the end, when she has allowed the desperate, lovesick Charles to finally track her down, she is living comfortably, working as an assistant to a famous Pre-Raphaelite artist—and her wardrobe has changed along with her mental status. She is still not

FILMOGRAPHY

Angels and Insects. Dir. Philip Haas. Costumes, Paul Brown. Playhouse International Pictures and The Samuel Goldwyn Company, 1995.

The French Lieutenant's Woman. Dir. Karel Reisz. Costumes, Tom Rand. Juniper Films, 1981.

Legally Blonde. Dir. Robert Luketic. Costumes, Sophie de Rakoff Carbonell. MGM, 2001.

The Piano. Dir. Jane Campion. Costumes, Janet Patterson. Australian Film Commission, 1993.

NINE

Sofia Coppola's *Marie Antoinette:* Costumes, Girl Power, and Feminism

DIANA DIAMOND

Sofia Coppola's film *Marie Antoinette* (2006) portrays the French queen as a fashion icon. Indeed, the film was featured on the September 2006 *Vogue* cover with the headline, "Kirsten Dunst as the Teen Queen Who Rocked Versailles." The film has inspired a range of consumer products, including perfume for the teen fashion line Juicy Couture, whose ad shows a seemingly nude teenage model with a cotton-candy pink pouf hairstyle—the signature coiffure of Marie Antoinette—holding a bottle with a semblance of a royal seal. The film also inspired a range of fashion accessories and couture lines, notably a masquerade and bondage collection for Dior designed by John Galliano that features hoop-skirted Marie Antoinette gowns printed with tableaux of the queen's life, such as her frolicking as a shepherdess and her being executed by guillotine. "Guillotine chic" was the term given to one Galliano creation, a blood-red high-necked dress marked with crosses and guillotines[1] (see Figure 9.1b). "Judging from the faux blood-splattered hems and the wild, haunted look in all of the models' eyes, the revolution was in full swing, and the poor Queen had already lost her head," remarked one fashion commentator.[2] These images show that Marie Antoinette has been worshiped and ridiculed, guillotined and resurrected, parodied and paraded over and over again on the runway.

One fashion commentator summed up the recurring Marie Antoinette fashion craze by saying, "there is something inherently 'Let them Eat Cake' about haute couture,"[3] an obvious reference to the queen's

alleged comment about the poor—a comment which Fraser[4] and others now attribute to malicious gossip against the queen. In resuscitating
and reinterpreting the fashion trends of the ancien régime, designers
offer new and imaginative syntheses of past and present in fashions
that often serve the function of travesty or social commentary.[5] Cathy
Horyn makes this point in "From Paris, Revolution and Roses," where
she refers to the relevance of Galliano's blood-spattered creations:

> If you are gifted like Mr. Lagerfeld, or like John Galliano at Dior, you don't have
> to ask whether couture is dead. It's relevant if you can make the meaningful
> connections between the past and present. On Monday, Mr. Galliano sent
> out a provocative collection with allusions—in the rough work boots and red-
> splattered white organza—to the French Revolution and, not incidentally, to the
> recent riots in France.

A number of designer forays into the ancien régime were timed to
coincide with and capitalize on the release of Coppola's film,[6] and in
the years subsequent to the film's release, the Marie Antoinette theme
continues to haunt the fashion world. For example, in 2007, when the
sixtieth anniversary of Dior was celebrated at Versailles, the *New York
Times* headline read "At Versailles: Let Them Wear Cake,"[7] while the
Juicy Couture ad for fall 2008 features a bevy of teenage girls in athletic
gear with the banner "Let Them Eat Juicy Couture" floating over their
heads.[8] That the ghost of Marie Antoinette still hovers over us was evident in one of the 2007 Christmas windows at Bergdorf's where a Park
Avenue princess preens with the shadowy figure of Marie Antoinette
suspended eerily above her.

The current fascination with Marie Antoinette in the fashion world,
while clearly linked to the pre-2007 economic boom, has not died with
its demise. With our economy in a deep recession, and fashion in "a
deep retail rut," Karl Lagerfeld for Chanel located his most recent show
(2009), which featured "light wearable luxury,"[9] in a farmhouse that
was reminiscent of one that belonged to Marie Antoinette at le Petit
Trianon—the country retreat given to her by the King—a place where
she favored simplicity, if not economy. The embroidered linen dresses
worn with clogs, the natural linen jackets, "the blues, reds and creams in
the embroideries and crochet could have come from her [Marie Antoinette's] hair ribbons."[10] The show culminated with models described as

"coquettish country courtesans...wearing dirndls and naughty aprons"[11] frolicking with male models in a haystack in the middle of the setup. A newer fashion incarnation of Marie Antoinette from the spring 2009 collection perhaps owes more to costume designer Milena Canonero's filmic version of the teen queen than to the original costumes in portraits of the queen. It seems clear the film will have an impact on fashion for years to come, and that as one fashion commentator put it, "M.A., it seems, is officially a brand."[12] The newest post-recession incarnation of Marie Antoinette–inspired couture affirms this prophecy.

In France the release of Coppola's film revived a centuries' old fascination, if not obsession, with the ancien régime's last queen, as evidenced by five-course Marie Antoinette meals, the restoration and opening to the public of her beloved retreat,[13] and a play in which citizens are asked to vote on the queen's fate. Although long awaited, the film was booed when it opened in Cannes mostly because of its sanitized portrait of France's revolutionary history and its portrayal of the teen queen as an American "valley girl," although Frodon, editor of *Le Cahier de Cinema* praised Coppola's "genius" at portraying adolescent alienation.[14]

In response to her critics, Coppola has stated that she was interested in showing "the real human being behind the myths and just the sort of icon that we've heard about as the frivolous, evil French queen."[15] Coppola was not interested in being a "fetishist" about historical accuracy. "I'm just, like, making it my thing," she declared.[16] Her goal was to immerse herself in the subjectivity rather than the historical circumstances of her subject, to "capture in the design the way in which I imagined the essence of Marie Antoinette[']s spirit. . . . so the film[']s candy colors, its atmosphere and teenaged music all reflect and are meant to evoke how I saw that world from Marie Antoinette[']s perspective."[17] Her film presents an impressionistic portrait of Marie Antoinette and the court of Versailles refracted through the prism of contemporary culture to highlight the passion for consumption and cult of celebrity—which the teen queen's obsession with fashion and fame helped to spawn.

Coppola has called *Marie Antoinette* the last chapter of a trilogy that began with *The Virgin Suicides* (1999) and *Lost in Translation* (2003) about young women marooned in that treacherous and elusive developmental history, politics, and creative expression. Feminist scholars have discovered, in short that "clothes are ideas,"[33] and that there is much to be gained by analyzing and understanding rather than deriding this enduring realm of female spectatorship.

If fashion bears the imprint of history, in the era of Marie Antoinette it became a historical force influencing the fate of its heroine and of the nation. In her groundbreaking book, *Queen of Fashion: What Marie Antoinette Wore to the Revolution,* Caroline Weber demonstrates how Marie Antoinette sought to carve out her own power base through her various masquerades, which included towering, preposterous pouf hairstyles, silk gowns studded with gems, free-flowing uncorseted muslin peasant dresses, and masculine riding costumes (the redingote). Indeed, Weber makes the point that the contemporary fashion industry was born in the era of Marie Antoinette. My own analysis owes much to her formulations as well as to the painstaking documentation of Marie Antoinette's life found in Antonia Fraser's biography—both of which set the foundation for the spate of books and articles that have rehabilitated the teen queen and expanded our view of her historical significance.

The history of the era in which Marie Antoinette lived was encoded in her costumes and hairstyles, and emblazoned on her physical being. In Coppola's *Marie Antoinette,* fashion and particularly the fluctuations in fashion, hair, and dress do indeed become the vehicle for analyzing not only the historical milieu in which the teen queen flourished and perished, but also the social milieu and functions of fashion for today's teens. Indeed, the ways in which the fashion industry both reflects and at times exploits the anxieties around identity and the quest for outlets for adolescents' budding and burgeoning sexuality through fashion represents the primary linkage between Coppola's film about the teen queen of Versailles and the fashion obsession of many contemporary teens. Despite the movie's faithful depiction of the pageantry and opulence of Versailles, where it was actually filmed, Kirsten Dunst as Marie Antoinette remains "a modern counterfeit posed within the semi authentic trappings of Versailles."[34]

The ironic tension maintained in the film between eighteenth-century France and our era is highlighted by the opening shot showing Marie Antoinette reclining on a satin chaise scooping the frosting from

9.2. Kirsten Dunst as Marie Antoinette, opening shot.

a luscious cake while assisted by her chambermaid in trying on a new pair of shoes. Canonero states, "This opening shot catapults us into a contemporary version of Marie Antoinette."[35] She turns her head to the camera in a gaze which is playful, seductive, and ironic, while the rock group Gang of Four blares the following words from their 2006 song, "Natural's Not in It":

> The problem of leisure
> What to do for pleasure.
> I do love a new purchase
> A market of the senses
> The problem of leisure
> What to do for pleasure
> Coercion of the senses
> We're not so gullible
> Our great expectation is a future for the good.
> Fornications make you happy
> No escape from society.
> Natural is not in it.

9.3. Sneaker amidst shoes by Manolo Blahnik.

The pop rock soundtrack that merges themes of eroticism and consumption, the contemporary and at times colloquial dialogue ("uh, like I love your hair," "This is ridiculous"), and the dizzying montages featuring a cornucopia of fashion consumer items (fabrics, dresses, shoes, hats) establish the film as much as an ironic comment on celebrity youth culture, with its submersion of rebellion into fashion and the pleasures of consumption, as a historical chronicle. Milena Canonero comments: "listen to the music of the movie. There is modern music at times. The dialogue is often very contemporary so one has to be in harmony with the movie. This is the kind of movie that Sofia was making and I wanted to be in tune with it. I like my work, from the head down, to be part of the whole of the director's vision."[36] Coppola, who as the daughter of Francis Ford Coppola is herself Hollywood royalty,[37] conveys her identification with the teen queen both acoustically and imagistically through inserting contemporary images, like a pair of lavender high top sneakers into a spectacular visual cascade of period-appropriate satin and fur-trimmed slippers (designed by Manolo Blahnik)—a touch that Coppola acknowledges was an attempt to make the film relevant to today's fashion-obsessed teens.

That fashion is equated with girl power is evident in a recent ABC News program on teen fashion where a sixteen-year-old is quoted as follows: "I have over 20 pair[s] of sneakers, . . . And boots, I probably have like 20. . . . If I could have a shoe for every day, I wouldn't repeat a pair of shoes once."[38]

Given the centrality of couture for Marie Antoinette's political fate in Coppola's film, it is not surprising that in this film the costumes become a major vehicle of narration in that transformations in the internal lives and external circumstances of the characters are conveyed through changes in costume. Canonero conveys Marie Antoinette's journey from sheltered, awkward, pubescent Austrian princess to fashion-icon queen to despised symbol of the excesses of the ancien régime, all through modifications of couture. The shifts in style, color, cut, coiffure, accessories, jewelry, headgear, and even necklines narrate the complexities of Marie Antoinette's position at court, her relation to her courtiers and subjects, and even the state of her erotic and internal life. Commenting on her work on this film, Canonero states:

> The costumes were correctly cut. The reinterpretation of the period was more in the colors, the coordination with the make up and hair—that is where I took liberties. Obviously I looked at the original portraits of Marie Antoinette. When one does period movies one always does a lot of historical research, but then of course one throws everything away. I followed more the inspiration that came in light touches by Sofia Coppola. She had an approach that crystallized and inspired me as we went along. The main object was to keep it graphic and fresh—less laces and trimmings, some jewelry but not too much. Whenever I would propose ideas for the looks or colors she always went for the timeless touches. She inspired me about the colors of the young queen Marie Antoinette, when she is in full swing as a fashion victim, by sending me a big box of Ladurée macaroons. As you can see from the movie it is certainly not a docudrama of that sad queen, but I like the cut and the quality of the materials to be absolutely of the period in question.[39]

Thus, throughout the film Canonero retains the spirit of historical authenticity, replicating the elaborate patterns, fabrics, and styles of the original clothes, crafted of silks and satins, brocaded and embroidered, ruffled and flounced, some being faithful copies of the originals, while at the same time introducing contemporary touches that offer an ironic commentary on the queen's life and fate. Marie Antoinette's interior journey from innocence to experience, from obscurity to empowerment, from frivolity to gravitas, from ignorance to knowledge, from sexual inexperience and frustration to sexual pleasure and maturity—all are conveyed primarily through Canonero's costumes. Although a perusal of portraits and documentaries on Marie Antoinette indicates the meticulous historical research that went into the costumes, Canonero cunningly incorporates aspects of contemporary fashion so they tell a saga of past and present.

We are introduced to Marie Antoinette as a barely pubescent girl in a girlish, unstructured white dress, her blond hair flowing loosely down her back, as her stout and stalwart mother, the formidable Queen Maria Teresa, informs her that she is to marry Louis Auguste, the dauphin or future king (Louis XVI) of France in order to cement alliances and diffuse ancient tensions between the two countries. When she arrives in France, Marie is told, "all eyes will be on you." The film documents how, as the ultimate object of exchange, the young queen dealt with the scrutiny of the court by constructing herself as a spectacle. At first we view the actual physical exchange of the princess from the Austrians to the French. Transported out of Austria in a gilded coach she was denuded of everything—her clothes, her companions, even her beloved lap dog, so that her body might be inscribed with the mores and customs of France, symbolized by the change of clothes. Before meeting her fiancé, the dauphin, and his father, King Louis XV, she is stripped of her simple travel suit of pale cream and plain undergarments and completely re-outfitted in a much more elaborate, fitted, and adorned suit of a light French blue, her silhouette instantly transformed into that of a *poupée* or doll.[40] She is presented to the dauphin with a large blue bow tied around her neck—an exaggerated replica of a neck bow in a portrait of the young Marie Antoinette—chosen, perhaps, to highlight her status as an object of exchange. She also wears a matching blue tricorner hat, a miniature version of the one worn by Louis XVI; when they meet, a shot of them face to face shows their hats mirroring each other, pointing toward each

9.4A. *The Dauphine Marie Antoinette, Archduchess of Austria, future Queen of France, Chateaux de Versailles,* oil on canvas, Jean Baptiste Charpentier (1728–1806). *Reunion des Musées Nationaux/Art Resource, NY.*

other but not touching—a harbinger of the ambivalent and frustrating sexual dance that they will engage in for the next eight years, as well as a signifier of the queen's latent striving for power which will eventually emerge. As she enters the palace of Versailles for the first time, she is followed by two little girls artfully outfitted in peach, their hair as elabo-

9.4B. Coppola's Marie Antoinette enters the court of Versailles for the first time.

rately powdered and coiffed as Marie Antoinette's, and these children dressed as courtesans provide another visual clue that her marriage has brought an abrupt end to her childhood.

In the wedding scene she is dressed in cream silk, her hair simply coiffed with tiny diamonds, highlighting her extreme youth. Indeed, in the first part of the film she appears only in pastel colors or fresh prints, showing her vulnerability as a princess who has not yet produced an heir. Her major adornment is a simple bow around her neck; this accessory becomes progressively smaller, perhaps indicating that the exchange, in which Marie Antoinette functioned as a "seal" on the treaty between Austria and France,[41] has been accomplished. Commenting on the changes in color Canonero states: "In the beginning I used innocent colors, but as we went on I used stronger colors until in the end we finished with grays, sad mauves, and dark blues. Black on the other hand is a special issue which was used to make specific points in the film."[42]

Marie Antoinette's increasing political acumen and sophistication in a court where she is surrounded by enemies who opposed the recent Franco-Austrian alliance that her marriage symbolized is indicated through subtle shifts in color and couture. As she begins to make the rounds of court dinners and events with the dauphin, the color and cut of her clothes and the nature of her accessories subtly change. Candy pinks deepen to salmon and fuchsia, light blues to deeper, more sophisticated shades of ice and French blue, plain satins to more elaborately patterned and embroidered fabrics; chaste necklines become more revealing; and she begins to don increasingly elaborate jewelry.[43] At the same time as Marie Antoinette drifts through the halls and gardens of Versailles, her increasingly elaborate and constricting gowns supported by rigid corsets reflect her ensnarement in the stultifying social rituals and invisible web of gossip and intrigue that comprised daily life at court. In one shot, we see her in a pale patterned yellow silk dress collapsing against a pale patterned yellow silk wall that mirrors her dress so perfectly she seems to merge with it—perhaps reflecting her despair and her desire to disappear after she reads another of her mother's critical letters about her failure to consummate her marriage.

The inexperience and sexual inhibition of the dauphin and dauphine is contrasted with the relationship between Louis XV and Madame du Barry, a former courtesan and now the King's mistress. Du Barry boldly strides through the halls of Versailles dressed in garish shades of coral, purple, red, or emerald green, adorned with animal furs, and encrusted with jewels. In her signature colors that signify free, uninhibited sexuality, du Barry contrasts with Marie Antoinette's increasing enslavement to the mores of the court that suppress spontaneity in eating, dressing, toileting, and sex—all of which are performed according to strictly observed rituals. At first she is shamed and humiliated as she stands shivering in the early morning waiting for the princesses of the blood to decide whose right it is to put on her underwear, but she gradually begins to greet the array of relations waiting to dress her with a seductive pose and ironic smile. When she finally acquiesces to her father-in-law by receiving the notorious du Barry, whom she initially spurned out of a sense of moral purity, she dons black for the first time—this shift in color a harbinger of her own incipient rebellion. At times, the queen, whose husband still pre-

9.5A. Marie Antoinette with her hairdresser Leonard, who designed the first pouf.

fers hunting and turning locks in a private forge to dancing or gambling, becomes a victim to fashion and decadence. Dressed in black tulle with a black tulle mask she attends a masked ball where she whirls with abandon through the maze of dancers until she spins into the arms of her future lover—the Swedish Count Ferson. As Canonero comments, "In the real world of 18th century, black for women was considered a serious color, more reserved for elderly people or people in mourning. In the movie I use black to give a sense of sophistication and sensuality."[44]

When the queen learns that her sister-in-law has given birth to a son, she runs through the palace to escape jeering courtiers and subsequently embarks on a shopping spree set to Bow Wow Wow's 1980s hit, "I Want Candy." "Got everything that I desire," crows the group's adolescent singer as a cornucopia of luxury goods, including sumptuous silk and brocade gowns, embroidered fans, mountains of artfully decorated pastries, rivers of champagne cascading from a pyramid of glasses, and a dazzling array of Manolo Blahnik's bejeweled and fur-trimmed pumps are

9.5B. Marie Antoinette's pouf features a miniature replica of the French Frigate to celebrate a key victory over the British.

paraded in front of the queen and her companions. Canonero reports, "I wanted to have the input of Manolo Blahnik so that the whole look from the head to the feet would have a contemporary cast. With the approval of Sofia, I asked Manolo Blahnik to collaborate and design special shoes for Marie Antoinette."[45] The film erupts in a manic montage of colors, patterns, and styles in a synethesia of music, couture, shoes, pastries, fabrics, jewels, and coiffures. The spectacular collection of Manolo Blahnik shoes takes its inspiration from the multicolored satin slippers trimmed with bows and jewels that are featured in portraits of Marie Antoinette, but these are clearly hybrids, with anachronistic stiletto heels. This visual extravaganza ends with Marie Antoinette emerging with her hair coiffed in a towering pouf and standing face to face with an effete male courtier (her hairdresser Leonard, reportedly the first celebrity hairdresser) also elaborately poufed—an ironic reminder of the earlier shot of her and her husband face to face. That this scene begins with her humiliation

and ends with the unveiling of the first pouf hairstyle reveals Coppola's use of fashion—the tower of powdered hair representing a compromise between the queen's desire to be both the phallic subject and the desired object. A fleeting shot of her with a battleship in her pouf—a miniature replica of the French Frigate designed to celebrate a key victory over the British—makes the point that, although still childless, she is emerging as a major political and social force at court and in the country at large. Indeed, when Marie Antoinette finally takes her place as queen, her pouf hairstyle (mirroring the king's crown), her gold encrusted gown, and her elaborate jewels foreshadow the legitimacy their finally consummated sexual union will give her and her future empowerment over the king and the court in general.

The full scope of her sexuality, femininity, and creativity, however, is only realized after Marie Antoinette sets up an alternative court at le Petit Trianon to escape the stifling rituals of Versailles and to return to her bucolic Austrian roots. In this miniature Arcadia, Coppola depicts Marie Antoinette reading Rousseau, frolicking with her daughter in the grass along with lambs and goats and chickens, acting in theatrical productions of her own making, playing the parts of shepherdesses and milkmaids. Here she also composes and plays music. Again this expansion of spirit and body and release of inhibitions is reflected in changes of costume; she adopts free-flowing, uncorseted muslin, silk, or linen chemises worn with lightly powdered, uncoiffed hair.

Just as the homespun white chemises and simple straw hats embraced by Marie Antoinette (pictured in Figure 9.6a) at le Petit Trianon during her lifetime came to signify resistance to the constricting fashions and behavioral rules of Versailles and even flagrant promiscuity,[46] so Coppola's rendition of the queen's life at le Petit Trianon portrays her and her companions as rebellious teenagers engaging in sexual antics and frolicking out of sight of, but in close proximity to, the watchful parental eye of the court.

After Marie Antoinette finally consummates her relationship with Count Ferson,[47] Coppola collapses past into present, and we see a se-

9.6A. *Marie Antoinette* (1783). Louise Elizabeth Vigee-LeBrun, oil on canvas. *Courtesy of Bildarchiv Preussischer Kulturbesitz/Art Resource, NY.*

9.6B. Marie Antoinette at the Petit Trianon, in Milena Canonero's take on her more relaxed style.

ries of shots of the teen queen as contemporary it girl—nude except for white silk half stockings with garters with blue bows, feathers in her hair and a fan half hiding her nudity, wearing a seductive, mischievous expression—an image reminiscent of the first clips of the queen luxuriating on her chaise.

Rather than presenting the interior life of the doomed queen or contextualizing it in terms of the cataclysms of her time, Coppola and Canonero powerfully capture the way in which fashion may become the nexus for expressing female desire and empowerment, a route to female bonding, and a signifier of the unconscious wishes, conflicts, and fantasies of the wearer. In a court and an era where the queen was expected to begin breeding immediately and then retire to obscurity, to "be as peahens to the gaudy peacock husband; elegant, but drab and unshowy,"[48] Marie Antoinette's foray into fashion might be seen as the ultimate "femininity as masquerade"; that is, her use of costumes, clothes, and towering poufed hair was a means not only to shore up her sense of femaleness, but also to appropriate masculine power in a feminine guise.[49] As interpreted in Coppola's film, Marie Antoinette at first used fashion to provide a route to sensual pleasure. Once her marriage was consummated, which is celebrated in the film by a shot of her lying ecstatically in the grass in a multicolored dress, fashion became a means to political power, a signifier of economic power, and a shield against the envy and ridicule of a hostile court.

By focusing on the fetishistic aspects of Marie Antoinette's relationship to fashion, Coppola in turn reinforced the fetishistic aspects of how both fashion and film use Marie Antoinette. For both, she epitomized Freud's statement that "all women . . . are clothes fetishists" in that her frenetic consumption of shoes, gowns, and pouf hairstyles functioned simultaneously to disguise and display an erotic body that Arlene Richards calls "the essence of female allure and function."[50] In Freud's view:

> It is a question of the repression of the same drive, this time however in the
> passive form of allowing oneself to be seen, which is repressed by clothes and on
> account of which clothes are raised to a fetish. . . . Only now can we understand
> why even the most intelligent women behave defensively against the demands of
> fashion. For them clothes take the place of parts of the body.[51]

But while Freud certainly suggests that fashion may function as a fetishistic mechanism or perversion for women,[52] that is, a behavior that is preferred to or substituted for affectionate sexual activity, he also implies that the pursuit of fashion may involve its own pleasures and psychological purposes.[53] Both the pleasurable and perverse aspects of fashion are evident in Coppola's camera work, where id-charged images such as shots of fountains spurting, fireworks exploding, champagne cascading, and elephant trunks flailing are intercut with artful, often dizzying, montages of gowns, jewels, and shoes; and both are juxtaposed with scenes of the stultifying rituals surrounding dressing, eating, and sex at Versailles. As the camera plays impressionistically and intimately over the dresses, shoes, bonbons, and bodies of Marie Antoinette and her female companions, Coppola clearly suggests that fashion functions as a route to sensual female interaction and bonding, and an arena in which female desire can be legitimately expressed.

Here I am making the distinction between sensuality as body-centered, fantasy-elaborated diffuse pleasure, and sexuality as genitally focused, fantasy-elaborated erotic arousal. Sensuality in the view of Lichtenberg[54] and others encompasses a range of pleasurable bodily sensations and accompanying fantasies experienced through a spectrum of relationships from parent–child and romantic attachments to same and opposite sex friendships and even to fleeting pleasurable moments with self, others, and pets. The myriad scenes of Marie Antoinette cavorting and consuming with her companions both at Versailles and especially at le Petit Trianon are redolent with such sensual currents.

However, while *Marie Antoinette* may be seen in part as the legacy of these recent intellectual forays into the ways that fashion may function as a mode of sensual bonding and an arena of self-definition for women, it also highlights the ways in which fashion may serve the needs of a cultural milieu that fetishizes and exploits female sexuality, particularly that of teenage girls. The sexual suggestiveness of teen and preteen fashions and the sexually provocative images of teenage girls in advertisements and music videos are a testament to the ways that popular culture may exploit and even pervert as well as express the developmental needs and proclivities of adolescent girls and women. Laura Mulvey and others have remarked that the trend over the past fifty years is to focus the erotic male gaze with ever greater intensity on prenubile rather than adult women, a trend that has contributed to the objectification and fetishization of the female body.[55] Indeed the ideal images of beauty and particularly the ideal body and facial type are increasingly those of pubescent and prepubescent girls, as evident in the plethora of erotically coded images of adolescent girls that pervades popular culture.[56] One study by anthropologist Douglas Jones showed that when images of various models were fed into a computer that matched the size and proportions of people's faces to their age, the models' ages were estimated to be about six or seven.[57] Furthermore, even those in the medical profession have contributed to equating female attractiveness with characteristics of the pubescent female body and visage. For example, at a recent meeting of the American Academy of Dermatology, a prominent leader in academic medicine asserted that women's lips reach their fullest at age fourteen, and that after that, "it's an uphill battle"; hence the rush toward such procedures as plastic surgery and botox, among women in their early twenties.[58] Daphne Merkin recently deplored the developmental arrest in our conception of female beauty, saying, "you might wonder given the feminist legacy of self-determination and the long ago . . . vision of power dressing, why women have suddenly been pushed back to, if not quite the cradle, then certainly to a state of prepubescence."[59] In a consumer society the pubescent adolescent female's body has become the site of a spectacle where "pleasure, desire and commodification intersect."[60] Let us not forget that Marie Antoinette was a child by contemporary standards when she was given away in the interest of the state.[61]

Thus, although *Marie Antoinette* was not a great critical success in the United States, it captured the current zeitgeist of the American consciousness in its idealization of female adolescents and in its portrayal of adolescent alienation, and the ways it finds its expression in conspicuous consumption that provides the illusion of access to wealth and privilege. It is ironic that interest in Marie Antoinette, the royal whose spectacular consumption and sumptuous lifestyle was paraded in front of an impoverished and starving populace who wreaked their revenge by sending her and her family to the guillotine, has skyrocketed in a climate of near unprecedented economic inequality.[62] Despite these inequalities, Eric Konigsberg, quoting economist Robert H. Frank, reminds us that even in the midst of an economic crisis, Americans are not known for their class consciousness, nor for any striking capacity to perceive self, world, or events through a prism characterized by their objective economic circumstances. He comments, "There are many Americans who see themselves—accurately or not—in Marie Antoinette."[63] Thus it may be that the life and death of Marie Antoinette are signifiers for fantasies about access (or lack of it) to financial power and to the massive wealth that has been amassed in recent years by a few and that is completely out of reach for the average consumer. These economic and social strivings may be especially true for teens of all social classes who are among the major consumers of our time, spending over $170 billion in 2007—double the amount just ten years earlier, and more than the budget of the state of Texas. Total U.S. teen spending exceeds the gross national product of countries such as Finland, Norway, or Greece,[64] with the bulk of the money (33%) spent on clothes. In general, clothes top the list of items purchased by female adolescents with twice as many female as male teens purchasing or planning to purchase fashion items (43% for females, 21% for males).[65]

The film reminds us of Arlene Richards's comment that, given certain cultural conditions, fashion and consumption of clothes cross over from the realm of normative pleasure to the realm of paraphilia and sexual fetishism. Coppola's *Marie Antoinette* represents an ironic commentary on the tenuousness of the boundaries between pleasure and paraphilia in fashion. The film, like most Hollywood films, is characterized by the interplay of contradictory and diverse codes, which together convey the ideologies of gender, privilege, and cultural location that are not all necessarily part of the conscious intention of the filmmaker.[66]

Ultimately, Marie Antoinette's obsession with fashion trends constituted a "program of singular sartorial defiance,"[67] connecting her to the wider community of women who frantically sought to emulate her, but it ultimately narrowed her vision in ways that contributed to her demise. In the final images of the doomed queen, Coppola perhaps unwittingly conveys that constriction and distortion of focus that can be the legacy of fashion obsession. Coppola does not show Marie Antoinette's imprisonment and execution, to which she apparently submitted with extraordinary dignity (even while continuing to order modest gowns from her dressmaker Rose Bertin).[68] Tellingly, Coppola's Marie Antoinette does not age noticeably as the country plunges into revolution and the monarchy collapses. Instead, what Coppola has called the queen's essential "dignity and character,"[69] as well as her sadness and sense of impending doom are conveyed in the muted grays, mournful mauves, black lace trim, and simple cuts of Canonero's costumes toward the film's end. Coppola gives us a glimpse of what one eyewitness called the queen's "air of grandeur and heroic courage in the face of danger"[70] in a scene where Marie Antoinette appears before the enraged revolutionary mob in a white dressing gown with blue bows, the latter a reminder of her original presentation at Versailles, and bows her head to them in a gesture that anticipates her ultimate beheading by guillotine. Finally, however, Coppola conveys the queen's demise through images of the defilement of her clothes, furniture, and objects. In the final scene, after showing us her bedding and clothing slashed, her furniture and chandeliers smashed, rock music begins to play—reminding us of the ways that past and present are conjoined in the film.

Perhaps, more than any other film, Coppola's *Marie Antoinette* captures the dialectic of our contemporary view of fashion. *Haute couture,* now recognized to have been invented by Marie Antoinette,[71] in particular continues to represent an arena of female spectatorship that is exclusive and elite; yet fashion in a broader sense represents an arena of innovation and experimentation that provides an outlet for creative expression. In its ties to innovation and performance, fashion in *Marie Antoinette* also captures the spirit of the contemporary moment and its relation to the past. In conflating the past and the present, the film celebrates the timeless power and creativity of fashion; but it also represents an example of how fashion and the popular culture that it reflects may create a froth of fantasy as an escape from the revolutionary power of the past and from the trauma of the present.[72] Indeed, Coppola succinctly sums up her film, which portrays the teen queen and her companions partying at the edge of the abyss, in the following statement: "This is a more playful version of history that reflects teenagers in a decadent time. At the same time there is always a sense that while they're partying into oblivion the revolution is right around the corner.... She [Marie Antoinette] was in a total silk and cake world.... it was a complete bubble right up until the very end."[73]

NOTES

I thank Milena Canonero, whose generous responses to my questions about her artistry in the costumes in *Marie Antoinette* helped me to do justice to the originality of her vision. I am also grateful to Allison Groffman for giving me the perspective of a young adult fashionista. This paper is dedicated to my grandfather, Zanville Diamond, who represented French *haute couture* through his work in the advertising agency Diamond and Barnett, and who instilled in me a love of fashion as an enduring art form.

1. Jess Cartner-Morley, "Guillotine Chic a Slice of Excess."

2. Alix Browne, "Let Them Wear Couture."

3. Ibid.

4. Antonia Fraser, *Marie Antoinette: The Journey.*

5. Pam Cook, "Sofia Coppola: Portrait of a Lady," 36–40.

6. See Browne.

7. Cathy Horyn, "At Versailles," G1–G2.

8. The ad appeared in *Vogue,* September 2008.

9. Horyn, "Just a Bunch of Hayseeds."

10. Ibid.

11. Armand Limnander, "Group Hug."

12. Browne.

13. Elaine Sciolino, "Marie Antoinette's Devotees, Including Bakers, Celebrate."

14. Alexander Zevin, "Marie Antoinette and the Ghosts of the French Revolution," 32–35.

15. Todd Gilchrist, "Interview: Sophia Coppola."

16. Emanuel Levy, "Sofia Coppola's Marie Antoinette."

17. Quoted in Levy.

18. See Gilchrist.

19. A. Lane, "Lost in the Revolution"; Daniel Mendelsohn, "Lost In Versailles."

20. See Gilchrist.

21. Sofia Coppola, *Marie Antoinette,* 2.

22. Quoted in "The Making of Marie Antoinette," DVD featurette.

23. See Gilchrist.

24. Canonero, phone interview with author, January 26, 2010. This is a modification of a statement originally quoted in Patricia Zohn's "Culture Zohn off the C(H)uff."

25. Kennedy Fraser, "Teen Queen," 640.

26. Debra S. Rosenblum et al., "Adolescents and Popular Culture," 319–38.

27. See Harriet Kimble Wrye, "Introductory Remarks"; Diana Diamond, "Fourth Wave of Feminism"; and Jennifer Baumgardner and Amy Richards, "Manifesta."

28. Baumgardner and Richards, 130.

29. Ingrid Sischy, "Body Politic," 225.

30. According to Martha N. Lauzen's 2008 report, "The Celluloid Ceiling."

31. See Cook.

32. Written by Guy Trebay.

33. Ibid., 10.

34. Stuart Klawans, "The Queen is Dead," 34.

35. Canonero, phone interview with author, January 26, 2010.

36. Canonero, e-mail message to author, January 3, 2010.

37. Kristin Hohenadel, "French Royalty as Seen by Hollywood Royalty."

38. John Stossel, "Teen Spending on the Rise."

39. Canonero, e-mail message to author, January 3, 2010.

40. Canonero, phone interview with author, January 26, 2010.

41. See Kennedy Fraser.

42. Personal communication, February 3, 2010.

43. Allison Groffman, personal communication, September 15, 2009.

44. Canonero, e-mail message to author, January 3, 2010.

45. Canonero, phone interview with author, January 26, 2010.

46. Caroline Weber, "Queen Please, Remembering Marie Antoinette."

47. On the affair with Ferson, see Antonia Fraser.

48. Liesl Schillinger, "The Queen's Wardrobe," 15.

49. Joan Riviere, "Womanliness as a Masquerade."

50. Arlene Richards, "Ladies of Fashion," 338.

51. Louis Rose, "Freud and Fetishism," 156.

52. See Louise Kaplan, *Female Perversions.*

53. See Richards.

54. Joseph Lichtenberg, *Sexuality and Sensuality across the Divide of Shame.*

55. Laura Mulvey, "Visual Pleasure and the Narrative Cinema."

56. Valerie Walkerdine, *Daddy's Girl.*

57. Daphne Merkin, "2007: A Face Odyssey."

58. Natasha Singer, "Defy Another Day," 40.

59. Merkin, 91.

60. Henry A. Giroux, "What Comes between Kids and Their Calvins," 16.

61. See Antonia Fraser.

62. David Leonhardt, "Obamanomics."

63. Konigsberg, "A Looking Glass."

64. Ann Holdsworth, "Teens Cash in."

65. "Teen Buying Behavior."

66. Glen O. Gabbard, ed., *Psychoanalysis and Film.*

67. Caroline Weber, *Queen of Fashion,* 291.

68. Weber.

69. Gilchrist.

70. Weber, 216.

71. Weber.

72. See Herbert Marcuse, *Eros and Civilization;* and, Konigsberg.

73. Quoted in Levy.

WORKS CITED

Baumgardner, Jennifer, and Amy Richards. "Manifesta: Young Women, Feminism and the Future." New York: Farrar, Strauss, and Giroux, 2000.

Browne, Alix. "Style: Let Them Wear Couture." *New York Times,* February 26, 2006. http://query.nytimes.com/gst/fullpage.html?res=9C03EFDA113EF935A15751C0A9609C8B63.

Cartner-Morley, Jess. "Guillotine chic a slice of excess." *The Age,* January 29, 2006, Fashion section. http://www.theage.com.au/news/fashion/guillotine-chic-a-slice-of-excess/2006/01/28/1138319489792.html.

Cook, Pam. "Sofia Coppola: Portrait of a Lady." *Sight and Sound* 16 (November 2006) 11: 36–40.

Coppola, Sofia. *Marie Antoinette: Written and Directed by Sofia Coppola.* New York: Rizzoli, 2006.

Diamond, Diana. "The Fourth Wave of Feminism: Psychoanalytic Perspectives." *Studies in Gender and Sexuality* 10, no. 4 (October 2009): 213–23.

Fraser, Antonia. *Marie Antoinette: The Journey.* New York: Random House, 2001.

Fraser, Kennedy. "Teen Queen: The Style of Marie Antoinette." *Vogue* 196 (September 2006): 640–47.

Gabbard, Glen O., ed. *Psychoanalysis and Film.* London and New York: Karnac, 2000.

Gilchrist, Todd. "Interview: Sofia Coppola." IGN (U.K. edition), October 17, 2006. http://uk.movies.ign.com/articles/739/739308p1.html.

Giroux, Henry A. "What Comes Between Kids and Their Calvins." *New Art Examiner* 23 (1996): 16–21.

Hohenadel, Kristin. "French Royalty as Seen by Hollywood Royalty." *New York Times,* September 10, 2006.

Holdsworths, Ann. "Teens Cash In." Susan Combs: Window on State Government, Fiscal Notes, 2005. http://www.window.state.tx.us/comptrol/fnotes/fn0508/teens.html.

Horyn, Cathy. "At Versailles: Let Them Wear Cake." *New York Times,* July 5, 2007 (Style section): G1–G2.

———. "From Paris, Revolution and Roses." *New York Times,* January 26, 2006.
http://query.nytimes.com/gst/fullpage.html?res=9A0CE7DA103FF935A15752

CoA9609C8B63&sec=&spon=&page
wanted=1.

———. "Just a Bunch of Hayseeds,
Dressed by Lagerfeld." *New York Times,*
October 7, 2009. http://www.nytimes
.com/2009/10/07/fashion/07REVIEW
.html.

Kaplan, Louise. *Female Perversions.* New
York: Jason Aronson, 1997.

Klawans, Stuart. "The Queen is Dead."
The Nation, November 6, 2006: 32–34.

Konigsberg, Eric. "A Looking Glass:
Marie Antoinette, Citoyenne." *New
York Times,* October 22, 2006. http://
www.nytimes.com/2006/10/22/
weekinreview/22marie.html.

Lane, A. "Lost in the Revolution: Marie
Antoinette." *New Yorker,* October 23,
2006: 93–95.

Lauzen, Martha N. "The Celluloid Ceiling: Behind-the-Scenes Employment
of Women in the Top 250 Films of
2008." San Diego State University,
2009. http://womenintvfilm.sdsu
.edu/files/2008_celluloid_ceiling
.pdf

Lee, Nathan. "Pretty Vacant: The Radical
Frivolity of Sofia Coppola's Marie An-
toinette." *Film Comment,* September–
October 2006: 24–26.

Leonhardt, David. "Obamanomics." *New
York Times,* August 24, 2008.

Levy, Emanuel. "Sofia Coppola's Marie
Baumgardner, Jennifer, and Amy
Richards. "Manifesta: Young Women,
Feminism and the Future." New York:
Farrar, Strauss, and Giroux, 2000.

Lichtenberg, Joseph. *Sexuality and Sensuality Across the Divide of Shame.* New
York: Analytic Press, Taylor and Francis Group, 2007.

Limnader, Armand. "Group Hug: Chanel,
Valentino et al." *T: New York Times
Style Magazine,* October 7, 2009.
http://tmagazine.blogs.nytimes.
com/2009/10/07/group-hug-chanel-
valentino-et-al.

"The Making of *Marie Antoinette." Marie
Antoinette,* DVD. Directed by Sophia
Coppola. Sony Pictures, 2007.

Marcuse, Herbert. *Eros and Civilization:
A Philosophical Inquiry Into Freud.* Boston, Mass.: Beacon Press, 1955, 1966.

Mendelsohn, Daniel. "Lost In Versailles." Review of *Marie Antoinette,*
directed by Sofia Coppola. *New York
Review of Books* 53 (November 30,
2006): 19–22.

Merkin, Daphne. "2007 A Face Odyssey."
T: New York Times Style Magazine,
April 15, 2007: 90–91.

Merskin, Debra. "Reviving Lolita: A
Media Literacy Examination of Sexual
Portrayals of Girls in Fashion Advertising." *American Behavioral Scientist* 48
(2004): 119–29.

Mulvey, Laura. "Visual Pleasure and the
Narrative Cinema." In *The Sexual Subject: A Screen Reader in Sexuality,* ed.
M. Merck, 22–33. New York: Routledge, 1992.

Rich, Frank. "Let Me Entertain You."
New York Times, January 18, 1997:
(section 1) 23.

Richards, Arlene Kramer. "Ladies of
Fashion: Pleasure, Perversion or
Paraphilia." *International Journal of Psy-
choanalysis* 77 (1996): 337–51.

Riviere, Joan. "Womanliness as a Masquerade." *International Journal of Psychoanalysis* 10 (1929): 303–13.

Rose, Louis. "Freud and Fetishism:
Previously Unpublished Minutes of
the Vienna Psychoanalytic Society."
Psychoanalytic Quarterly LVII (1988):
147–66.

Rosenblum, Debra S., Peter Daniolos,
Neal Kass, and Andres Martin. "Adolescents and Popular Culture: A Psy-
chodynamic Overview." *Psychoanalytic
Study of the Child* 54 (1999): 319–38.

Schillinger, Liesl. "The Queen's Wardrobe." Review of *Queen of Fashion:
What Marie Antoinette Wore to the*

Revolution, by Caroline Weber. *New York Times Book Review,* October 15, 2006: 15.

Sciolino, Elaine. "Marie Antoinette's Devotees, Including Bakers, Celebrate." *New York Times,* June 1, 2006. http://www.nytimes.com/2006/06 /01/world/europe/01marie.html?scp =1&sq=Sciolino,%20Marie%20Antoi nette%E2%80%99s%20Devotees,%20 Including%20Bakers,%20Celebrate &st=cse.

Scott, A. O. "A Lonely Petit Four of a Queen." Review of *Mary Antoinette,* directed by Sofia Coppola. *New York Times,* January 21, 2008. http://movies .nytimes.com/2006/10/13/movies/13 mari.html?scp=1&sq=A+Lonely+Petit +Four+of+a+Queen&st=nyt.

Singer, Natasha. "Defy Another Day: Natasha Singer on the Anti-Aging Glut." *T: New York Times Style Magazine,* April 15, 2007. 40.

Sischey, Ingrid. "Body Politic: Will Feminism's Fourth Wave Begin on the Runway? A Rumination." *T: New York Times Style Magazine,* February 25, 2007.

Stossel, John. "Teen Spending on the Rise: Teens Charging Up Chic Wardrobes." *ABC News 20/20,* December 12, 2008. http://abcnews.go.com/2020/ story?id=124346&page=1.

"Teen Buying Behavior." In *Teen Market Profile,* published by Magazine Publishers of America, 8. May 3, 2003. http:// www.magazine.org/ASSETS/905DE

1D985A04046ABAC7754572F1163 /teenprofile04.pdf

Trebay, Guy. "Admit It. You Love It. It Matters." *New York Times,* September 2, 2007: 1, 10–11.

Walkerdine, Valerie. *Daddy's Girl: Young Girls and Popular Culture.* Cambridge, Mass.: Harvard University Press, 1997.

Weber, Caroline. *Queen of Fashion: What Marie Antoinette Wore to the Revolution.* New York: Henry Holt & Co., 2006.

———. "Queen of the Zeitgeist." *New York Times,* October 21, 2006.

———. "Queen Please, Remembering Marie Antoinette." *T: New York Times Style Magazine.* November 2, 2009. http: //tmagazine.blogs.nytimes.com/2009 /11/02/queen-please-remembering -marieantoinette/?scp=1&sq=Queen %20Please,%20Remembering%20 Marie%20Antoinette&st=Search. Marie%20Antoinette&st=Search.

Wrye, Harriet Kimble. "The Fourth Wave of Feminism: Psychoanalytic Perspectives Introductory Remarks." *Studies in Gender and Sexuality* 10, no. 4 (October 2009): 185–89.

Zevin, Alexander. "Marie Antoinette and the Ghosts of the French Revolution." *Cineaste,* March 22, 2007: 32–35.

Zohn, Patricia. "Culture Zohn Off the C(H)uff: Milena Canonero, Oscar-Winning Costume Designer Collaborates at the Metropolitan Opera." *Huffington Post,* September 21, 2009. http:// www.huffingtonpost.com/patricia-zohn-off-the-chuf_b_291306.html.

FILMOGRAPHY

Lost in Translation. Dir. Sofia Coppola. Costumes, Nancy Steiner. Focus Features, 2003.

Marie Antoinette. Dir. Sofia Coppola. Costumes, Milena Canonero. Columbia

Pictures, 2006.

The Virgin Suicides. Dir. Sophia Coppola. Costumes, Nancy Steiner. American Zoetrope, 1999.

PART THREE

Fashioning National Identities

A theme woven through the two earlier sections of *Fashion in Film* concerns the many ways fashion shapes nation through its Look. That theme begins in Drake Stutesman's chapter and surfaces implicitly in Guiliana Bruno's exploration of the ethnically tailored films of Wong Kar-wai. In her focus on French silent films, Caroline Evans reveals how filming fashion shows helped to define France as the West's fashion capital. Maura Spiegel and Diana Diamond, in their discussions of films set in Victorian England and pre-Revolutionary France, indicate how national values shape both the fashion of a given moment and later evaluations of it. In this section of the volume, the topic of fashion and nation takes center stage.

Jacqueline Reich, in "Slave to Fashion: Masculinity, Suits, and the *Maciste* Films of Italian Silent Cinema," argues for the centrality of cinematic representations to the consolidation of Italian masculinity. Drawing on ethnographic, racial discourses from before unification, nascent Italian masculine identities "converged onto the cinematic representation of the muscled, male body, both naked and clothed, in the first decades of the twentieth century." Her chapter follows the meteoric career of Italian silent film star Bartolomeo Pagano, who became widely known by the name of Maciste, the character he played in an increasingly influential series of silent films that were part of a popular genre known as Strong Man films. Maciste evolves his masculine image from a toga-wearing black slave to a suit-wearing white Strong Man that eventually became the model for fascist masculinity.

No volume about fashion in film should ignore films explicitly about fashion. Narrative fashion films contain much of what one would expect: mannequins, beautiful clothes, glamorous settings, and an inside view of aspects of the fashion industry. Adrienne Munich, in "The Stars and Stripes in Fashion Films," finds another, less predictable element in three Hollywood fashion films, and that is their various uses of a patriotic subtext. The national message uses fashion to promote national pride, sometimes in alliance with fashion and sometimes as its enemy. Each of the three films draw in spectators with fashion's allure, with spectacle, and with the promise of personal transformations. Then they subtly or not so subtly sing the nation's praises—two are musicals with a score from the Great American songbook, and one features an American icon of rock and roll, Diana Ross. However, given fashion's reputation for superficiality, frivolity, and the intimate pleasures of fabric caressing skin, traditional American values cannot entirely fall for fashionability. The three films in the chapter have their fashion only when its drape and dimensions can be altered to fit the Stars and Stripes.

Kristin Hole in "Does Dress Tell the Nation's Story? Fashion, History, and Nation in the Films of Fassbinder" situates Werner Fassbinder's influence on high fashion as part of his cohort's program of recreating and reimagining a post-fascist nation in film. Hole explains that Fassbinder adapted his fashion Looks from Hollywood films, particularly film noir, gangster, and melodrama, to give his films a postmodern edge. That particular fashion combination is central to what Hole considers the reimagining of a national identity. Her analysis elevates the importance of fashion in a national project to reformulate a country through restyling it: "The ability of fashion to project desired identities, identities that signify a break with or reworking of the past, is key to understanding one of the central meanings of fashion in Fassbinder's films." Fashion plays a major role in what Fassbinder considers history lessons.

Offering an introduction to those unfamiliar with Indian cinema, Sarah Berry in "Subversive Habits: Minority Women in Mani Ratnam's *Roja* and *Dil Se*" first contextualizes the importance of costume in representing political, gendered identities. Pointing out that women have been traditionally used in Indian cinema to represent nation, Berry's analysis reveals that the director genders the costumes and uses women's attire to signify a conflict between traditional values and modernity, whereas men's costumes signify desire that moves toward cosmopolitan attitudes. But the costumes perform much more complex cultural work. The tailoring of particular costumes and scenes reflects conflicts of ethnicities; conflicts concerning the role of women within and among different Indian subcultures; conflicts about nationalism, religion, and regionalism. Berry's chapter captures some of the immense complexity of conceiving an Indian nation through the prism of Indian cinema.

TEN

Slave to Fashion: Masculinity, Suits, and the *Maciste* Films of Italian Silent Cinema

JACQUELINE REICH

In the late nineteenth century, the newly formed Italian nation faced questions of national identity, specifically: what did it mean to be an Italian, when the country itself consisted of stark regional differences (most evident in language and customs), and economic as well as social discontinuities? Italian national identity itself did not come ready-made in cultural or geographic terms, but instead had to grow out of the active dynamics of both national and racial self-positioning. These historical developments affected the formation of a modern masculinity associated, as George Mosse observes, with the emergence of racially defined nationalist ideals.[1] During this period of Italian history, in the years between unification and World War I, the concept of nation is inseparable from the concept of race: in the eugenic and anthropological discourses of Cesare Lombroso and Sergio Niceforo, for instance, race was an essential component to the construction of a national Italian identity, one that advocated the superiority of the North over the South and found pseudo-scientific justifications for these assumptions. Simultaneously, the "stereotype" of modern masculinity in Western Europe had begun to take shape, and greater attention was being placed on the athletic male body. After 1861, both Italian schools and the Italian army institutionalized gymnastics as a means of creating "manly men." Within early-twentieth-century nationalism, the male stereotype was a symbol of a new national consciousness. The sculpted body and the brave soldier contrasted with the degenerate enemies of the gendered status quo: the effeminate man or manly woman, the androgyne, the homosexual, and the Jew.[2]

It is my central thesis that these very discourses of nation, race, and masculinity in Italy converged in the cinematic representation of the muscled male body, both naked and clothed, in the first decades of the twentieth century. If, as Nicholas Mirzoeff has observed,[3] the twentieth century has witnessed a growing tendency to visualize things that are not usually visible, then early-twentieth-century media culture in Europe and the United States—photography, silent cinema, and early sound films in particular—visualized the male body as a multifaceted vessel of discriminating nationalism. The male nude photography of Eakins and others, Muybridge's movement studies, Edison's films of Eugen Sandow's muscles, the first filmed sporting events (boxing in particular), and Italian futurism's paintings (and print manifestos) copiously featured the male body in stasis and in motion. Moreover, their reproducibility augmented their reach.

This ideal of the sculpted male body and brave soldier found its expression in Italian silent cinema in the character of the "Strong Man" Maciste, played by Bartolomeo Pagano, the most popular and highly paid male actor of his day, and a recognizable figure in Italy, Europe, and the United States. Who exactly was Maciste? In silent cinema of the 1910s and '20s, the Strong Man films, commonly referred to in Italian as the *forzuti* or *uomini forti*, were an extremely popular genre that revolved around a specific character placed in various situations and featured the powerful, sculpted male body performing feats of bravery that showed off his strength and virility. Maciste, though arguably the most famous, was not the only Strong Man. Others included Sansone (Luciano Albertini), Saetta (Domenico Gambino), Ausonia (Mario Guaita Ausonia), Aiax (Carlo Aldini), and in one case a woman, Astrea. The Strong Man genre evolved from various cultural practices: 1) the circus, specifically the clown and the strongman's acts of strength; 2) a new interest in physical culture, exemplified in the birth of gymnasiums in cities such as Torino, Bologna, and Milano, where the nascent film industry flourished; and 3) variety theater (*il teatro di varietà*) and the comic tradition. These were all precursors to the focus on novelty and the act of display in the early "cinema of attractions."[4] Cinematically, it had its origins in the

historical epics that populated early silent cinema: Giovanni Pastrone's
La caduta di Troia (The Fall of Troy, 1910), the character of Ursus (Bruto
Castellani) in *Quo Vadis?* (1913), *Spartaco* (Spartacus, 1913, starring Albertini and Ausonia), and ultimately Pastrone's masterpiece, *Cabiria*
(1914), in which the character of Maciste was born as an African slave.[5]
Maciste subsequently appeared as protagonist in approximately twenty
silent films after *Cabiria,* some full-length and others serialized, including *Maciste* (1915), *Maciste alpino* (Maciste the Alpine Soldier, 1916), *Ma-
ciste innamorato* (Maciste in Love, 1919), *Maciste in vacanza* (Maciste on
Vacation, 1920), *Maciste imperatore* (Maciste the Emperor, 1924), *Maciste
contro lo sceicco* (Maciste Against the Sheik, 1926), and *Maciste all'inferno*
(Maciste in Hell, 1926).

In this essay, I argue that the character of Maciste comes to serve
as the paradigm for the Strong Man's metamorphosis from an icon of
ancient glories in the classical film epics so popular in the early years
of Italian cinema, to an exemplary symbol of modern Italian masculinity. The initial two *Maciste* films accomplish this transformation in
three distinct ways: they change his race from African to Italian and his
skin color from black to white, they set his films in contemporary Italy,
and they align him with pressing national and political imperatives.
His films enact and inscribe this transformation through Maciste's
whitened, muscular body and his clothing.[6] He becomes the model
Italian to lead the relatively young Italian nation by example through
important historical developments, such as intervention into World
War I, modernization, and later Fascism, with both his bare muscles
and fashionable suits playing equally important roles. Why is the suit
so important for Maciste? Clothing is an integral sign of the ways in
which cinema makes meaning and constructs and/or subverts gender identities,[7] and in the *Maciste* films the clothes Maciste wears, like
the red shirts of General Giuseppe Garibaldi's brigade during Italian
unification before him and Fascist black shirts after, have discursive,
political, and symbolic implications:[8] they are essential elements in the
construction of Maciste's character as national hero, as I will show, both
diegetically and extradiegetically. Moreover, the twentieth-century suit
functions, particularly in the Maciste films, as an iconic marker of modern bourgeois identity, a signifier of Italy's increasing urbanization,

industrialization, and modernity epitomized in its emerging middle class.

Modern men's fashion, however, is a story that has an earlier beginning. In the nineteenth century, the principal centers of European influence in menswear were France and England. In England in particular, the Industrial Revolution brought about changes in both the manufacturing of clothing and how and where it was purchased, increasing its accessibility. At the same time, what Flügel has termed the "great masculine renunciation" and the emergence of the suit as the epitome of a capitalist style gradually purged unnecessary, feminizing accessories.[9] The modern suit, according to Anne Hollander, was born out of shift in perception of the body. In the late eighteenth and early nineteenth centuries, the heroic male nude of classical antiquity, with his broad shoulders, muscular chest, flat stomach, small waist, and long legs became the "new anatomical foundation."[10] Even though clothing persisted as a marker of class difference throughout the nineteenth century, it gradually became less colorful and more practical, with the conservative black, grey, and brown emerging as the dominant colors symbolizing modern, bourgeois, capitalist identity.[11] Since Italy was on the slow end of social and industrial transformation with respect to the rest of Europe, these changes began to manifest themselves in the early twentieth century, with England being the dominant industrial and sartorial model for men.

That is not to say that fashion was not important on the Italian peninsula before World War I, the major historical reference point for this paper. Beginning in the 1700s, various regions in the Italian peninsula (Milan and Parma in particular) cemented their status as centers of textile production, in particular of cotton, linen, and wool, while Italian silk has a much longer history dating back to the Middle Ages.[12] Eugenia Paulicelli underscores that "fashion has been one of the privileged vehicles with which Italy has sought to create, promote, and define a national identity for itself," a process which reaches its height in the autarchic policies of the Fascist period.[13]

As it would continue to do in later years, early film culture established fashion trends in Italy and influenced modes of dress and behavior, appealing to the middle-class spectator and dresser as well as playing on mythologies of the upper middle class, aristocracy, and nobility.[14]

Angela Dalle Vacche argues that clothes are critical to the construction of the Italian silent film actress or *diva*'s persona both on and off the screen, and that their costumes and fashion choices influenced the female film-going public. For example, in 1913, when the popular film diva Lyda Borelli sported loose-fitting pants and a pilot's beret in *La memoria dell'altro* (The Memory of that Man, 1913) and then was photographed a few days later wearing the outfit in Florence, hoards of women wanted to copy her Look.[15]

Yet just as the connection between women and fashion has an earlier beginning than 1951, generally regarded as the birth date of the Italian fashion industry,[16] so does the connection between clothing, national character, and cinema. In a 1918 article in the film magazine *In Penombra*, the writer Teresita Guazzaroni discusses the role of clothing in film in these revealing terms:

> Since we are dealing with artists of the silent art, one must know how to do without their words, and to understand what they are saying from their faces, their gestures, and their clothes.
>
> Above all from their clothing, which is one of the greatest means given to the film artist to assert her taste, personality, we would say, even her race: that which every day improves, since good blood flows to the white screen from the theater and from the most respectable of social strata.[17]

Thus fashion in film in Italy's second decade, like the film products themselves, carries both racial and national overtones. Note the use of racial language in the above quotation: not just the employment of the word "race" itself but also the way that its "good" blood infuses the "white" screen. Italian fashion and Italian film articulate notions of the Italian national and racial identity, and one of the means through which they accomplish this task is through costume. But in order to better understand how the national and the racial interacted with fashion, cinema, and the muscular male body, it is important to examine two contemporary cultural intertexts, to use Gaylyn Studlar's term: (1) futurism and the avant-garde, and (2) modernism and modernity, and to see how each interacted with questions of nationalism, race, and masculinity.[18]

Emilio Gentile, in his analysis of early-twentieth-century political movements, sees this period in Italian history as one in which Italy questioned its role as a national entity due to changes produced precisely by modernization. He interprets that period's radical nationalism in light of what he terms *political modernism:* "those ideologies and political movements that arose in connection with modernization and tried to make human beings capable of mastering the processes of modernization in order not to be overwhelmed by the vortex of modernity."[19] Radical nationalism involved new cultural movements, such as the futurists and the Florentine avant-garde.

These cultural movements all integrated both a nationalistic, racial, and gender discourse into their rhetoric. Barbara Spackman notes how throughout F. T. Marinetti's futurist *manifesti,* virility consistently invoked nationalism.[20] A paradigmatic text to which Spackman briefly alludes, but which I believe requires further examination, is *Maschilità.* Written in 1915 by the Italian poet, editor, and sometime futurist author Giovanni Papini (1881–1956), *Maschilità* was a collection of essays previously published in important literary journals of the day.[21] Concerned with Italy's cultural heritage, Papini also engaged in the nationalistic debates that flourished in Italy at the time. He writes that Italy "lacked courage"[22] because it lacked genius (*genio*—his principal concern and ultimate symbol of masculinity), greatness, and originality. In two essays in particular, "Le due tradizioni letterarie" ("Two Literary Traditions") and "Miele e pietra" ("Honey and Rock"), he discusses two "dynasties" (he even uses the term "razze" or "races") of literature: the "masculine," representing everything "unyielding, sturdy, hard, atrocious, solid, concrete and plebian" in Italian literature and best epitomized by Dante, Machiavelli, Cellini, Foscolo, Alfieri, and Carducci, among others. On the other side, there is the "feminine," Petrarchian tradition, or everything "gentle, elegant, musical, harmonious, decorative, conventional, literary, and empty" represented by the *Petrarchisti* of the fifteenth, sixteenth, and seventeenth centuries, the Romantics, and the *decadenti* of the late nineteenth century, including the renowned interventionist poet Gabriele D'Annunzio.[23] He goes on to further clarify how he signifies these gender constructs:

> There are not only biological but also spiritual sexes. When I say male I intend, now, strength, energy, toughness, and pride; when I speak of female I intend feebleness, sweetness, bland voluptuousness, modesty, easy tears, silly gossip and a faint and wearisome musicality.[24]

The words Papini uses to elucidate the more masculine Italian literature that he clearly favors could easily describe Maciste himself: force,
strength, hardness, energy (clearly a reference to Futurism as well), and
pride; in a subsequent essay, he criticizes the decadent style as lacking
"muscles and bones,"[25] a quality the Strong Men clearly embody. The
metaphor of the rock (concreteness, solidity) aligns itself with classical
notions of strength and virility, as does his description of the "good,
masculine" D'Annunzio, in which he extols the virtues of this "superman" (*superuomo*). It is perhaps no coincidence that Maciste arose from
D'Annunzio's primary cinematic contribution, the above-mentioned
Cabiria, and his appearance in this film clearly draws on classical references, as does his name, which D'Annunzio believed to be an ancient
nickname for Hercules.[26]

D'Annunzio, aside from being Maciste's nominal benefactor, is an
important figure in Italy at the turn of the nineteenth into the twentieth century, not solely as an accomplished poet and author but also as
model of masculinity. A man of many incarnations, he played many roles
in contemporary Italian culture: literary dandy, nationalist superman,
war hero (he enlisted in World War I and received a total of eight medals), and political leader. In whatever he did, however, he was always
impeccably dressed: he would have thirty shirts made at one time, and
his war uniforms were personally tailored. Although much shorter in
stature than his creation, Gabriele D'Annunzio, like Maciste, was and
came to be a man of war, a national symbol, and a fashion icon.[27] One of
the reasons he took on the project of writing intertitles for *Cabiria* was
to cover the debts he incurred while living in France, including the vast
sums he owed to his tailor.[28]

Set during the Punic Wars of the third century BC and scripted by its
director, Giovanni Pastrone, *Cabiria,* whose full title includes the phrase
"Historical Vision of the Third Century BC" ("Visione storica del terzo
secolo A.C."), recounts the kidnapping of a young Roman girl after the
eruption of Mount Etna and her subsequent liberation from Carthage
during the Second Punic War, and features strategic appearances by the
Roman military leader Scipio and his Carthaginian antagonist Han-
nibal. The heroes of this rescue, after ten years of trials and tribulations,
are Fulvius Axilla, a Roman patrician living secretly in Carthage as a

spy, and his faithful African slave Maciste. It was, as I stated above, one
of the many historical epics that constituted Italian cinema's golden era,
capitalizing on the genre already popularized in the literary culture of
the late nineteenth century (the novels *Quo vadis?* and *The Last Days of
Pompeii (Gli ultimi giorni di Pompeii)* were bestsellers at the time).[29] More
than just spectacular displays of production design, however, these films
had important political resonances, evoking the nation's Roman glories,
national unification (which had occurred a mere fifty-three years before
the release of *Cabiria*), and past and future colonial ambitions.[30] It was
a resounding success both in Italy and abroad, a fact well documented
in newspaper reviews all across the world.[31] The film's instantaneous
impact sprang from its cinematic innovations: its highbrow literary references, its moving camera, and the historical accuracy of its elaborate sets
and costumes, which betray more of an Egyptian than a Carthaginian
influence.[32]

Neither the film credits, nor the historical record, attribute a specific
name to the costume designer of *Cabiria* or any of the *Maciste* films.
In early cinema, costume design was a collaborative process, involving
the creative force behind the film (usually the director), the film studio, and the production designer, in this case the well-regarded Camillo
Innocenti, also known for his costume designs.[33] The correspondence
between D'Annunzio and Pastrone indicates that Pastrone oversaw the
production of the film's intricately detailed pieces, sewn by a team of
fifteen tailors. During preproduction the director had traveled to Paris
to see the Carthaginian exhibit at the Louvre, studied catalogs from the
British Museum, used the sources of the Egyptian Museum in Torino,
and read the *Répertoire de la statuaire grecque et romaine (Catalog of Greek
and Roman Statuary)* by Saloman Reinach, sent to him by D'Annunzio.[34]
There is speculation that Romano Luigi Borgnetto, an Itala Film Studio
collaborator, played a role in the costume design. Since Borgnetto would
then go on to direct or co-direct several other Maciste films, this collaboration begs further exploration, for it suggests that Borgnetto had a
hand in dressing Maciste from the very beginning.[35]

In order to play the African slave, Pagano's skin had to be darkened
(nor is he the only actor to appear that way in the film), and the toga he
wears in the opening scenes, as well as his subsequently scant outfits,

10.1. Maciste's first appearance in *Cabiria*.

highlight both the size and the color of his muscles (Figure 10.1). He always appears bare-chested, often only wearing a leopard-print loincloth, with the most coverage at any time being the white cloth casually draped over his shoulders or his head. Maciste's body dominates Fulvio Axilla, and almost everyone else, in the film's various mise-en-scène. His size, however, is only threatening to those who challenge his goodness.[36]

The extraordinary popularity of the Maciste character explains much of the film's appeal. While D'Annunzio thought of the name Maciste, it was Pastrone who made him black. As he writes to D'Annunzio in an undated letter (most likely from 1913, during the film's preproduction), "Most ingenious the name of Maciste, for whom we must find another country of origin: I made him a mulatto."[37] Audiences clearly responded to Maciste despite his blackness, as evident in newspaper articles from 1914 that cite ecstatic reactions to "il buono e gigantesco Maciste" ("the good and gigantic Maciste").[38] Moreover, this appeal jumped out from the screen, as Pagano routinely made appearances, often in black makeup but wearing modern dress, during screenings of *Cabiria*.[39] Thus began both the soon-to-be-essential fusion between character and star and Pagano/Maciste's incarnation as a national symbol. As a notice in the 9 May 1914 *Corriere della sera* newspaper recounts:

> Whether young or old, the audience befriends Maciste; they admire the superb beauty of his Herculean form which makes him a rare champion of *our race* (he was discovered in Genova, where he practiced the humble and noble profession of dock worker), they applaud him, feel the agony of his imprisonment, rejoice in his liberation, smile with him, detach his black figure from the screen and turn that into a friendly companion, always accessible in their imagination, in order to tell stories about his deeds and glorify the natural beauty of his actions.[40] (italics mine)

The use of the word *race*, particularly when Pagano would make these regular public appearances with darkened skin, is telling: although it was not unusual for race to be equivocated with the idea of the nation, color is, as personified by the figure of Maciste, superceded by the national. The fact that the character Maciste is conflated with the actor, that the divide between screen and public life is ruptured, and that he is appropriated as a symbol of the national ("our race") lays the pattern for future on-screen and off-screen representations of Maciste/Pagano. Also telling in this description is the positioning of Maciste as both ordinary (the humble dockworker) and extraordinary (Herculean), as well as the audience's instantaneous appropriation of both his greatness and his humility. The audience both befriends and exalts him, a classic dialectic at work in star–spectator positionings.[41]

Following the phenomenal international success of *Cabiria*, the Itala Film Company decided to produce a film with Maciste as protagonist. Titled simply *Maciste* (1915), it shows our hero once again saving an unnamed damsel in distress, this time from a cohort of bandits who have also imprisoned her mother. The title character undergoes several radical alterations as if to reinforce the elements stressed in the *Corriere* article (his immediacy, his greatness, and his ordinariness): he moves from Ancient Rome to modern-day Italy (it was shot in Torino); he changes from an African to a white Northern Italian; and from slave to a well-dressed member of the *borghesia*.

The film's opening scenes neatly explain this transition to the audience. His first appearance onscreen is in his guise as the fictional char-

10.2A. Maciste's first on-screen appearance in *Maciste*.

acter from *Cabiria*. The unnamed woman takes refuge from her pursuers in a crowded beaux-art theater where *Cabiria* is being shown, complete with full orchestra and posters featuring Pagano as Maciste in an exterior shot (they are in fact some of the original publicity materials for the film). The title card on the theater's screen reads "CABIRIA—GABRIELE D'ANNUNZIO/ITALA-FILM FORINO," followed by a singular intertitle reading "MACISTE." The image presented of Maciste here is not one from the actual film (it is most likely an outtake), although it features him in the same recognizable toga. When she enters the theater, she sees Maciste on screen, and, as if mimicking the reaction described in the newspaper article cited above, collapses the distance between spectator and screen as she realizes that he is the only one who can save her. The film self-consciously reinforces this collapse as the screen within the screen disappears, and the audience of *Maciste*, like our heroine, is left watching in full screen the scene in which Maciste contorts the metal bars of his

10.2B. Maciste's whitened chest in *Maciste*.

prison window in order to rescue the imprisoned Cabiria. She herself minimizes this distance as, while viewing the scene, she physically approaches the screen. She then writes to Maciste at the Itala film studio (also featured in the film) seeking his help.

Maciste receives her letter at the film studio, and it is there that the spectator is introduced to the character in "real life" as he works out in what appears to be the studio's gymnasium (Figure 10.2A). This positioning is significant for several reasons. First, and perhaps foremost, it reinforces the character's whiteness, in contrast to the darkness of his on-screen *Cabiria* counterpart. The contrast between the lightness of his muscular yet hairy chest and the darkness of his pants (as opposed to the slave Maciste's dark chest and white toga) highlights his light skin. The shot that immediately follows, as Maciste towels off to read the unnamed woman's plea for help (Figure 10.2B), has spotlighting directed toward his torso, creating a slight halo effect later perfected in silent cinema to signify purity and holiness. Second, it positions Maciste in a gymnasium

10.3. Maciste and his double-breasted suit in *Maciste*.

performing feats of strength; he is an extraordinary strongman who lifts not only the barbell but also several men attached to the barbell. The gymnasium and gymnastics, and the physically fit body which emerges from it, was at the time in Italy a symbol of both national and masculine pride.[42] Lastly, the gymnasium and the city of Torino, in its nascent stages as the Italian center of industrialization with the founding of Fiat (1899) and the new film industry, are symbols of Italian modernity. Torino had been an established center of film production since 1907,[43] and the Itala film studio is explicitly featured in *Maciste*. The muscled body in action epitomizes the well-oiled industrial machine.

In his first fully-clothed appearance onscreen, Maciste wears a classic double-breasted suit (Figure 10.3).[44] His suits are impeccable and representational of fashion at the time. According to Farid Chenoune, there were two kinds of suits popular in Europe in the 1910s: the double-breasted model, with a long jacket featuring wide lapels, tapered waist, and slight flaring, as perfectly shown off by Maciste; and the single breasted, with a nipped-in waist and sloping shoulders. Both came to epitomize the classic bourgeois suit that the Futurists railed against in fashion manifestos of the time.[45] In proposing his "anti-neutral" suit in 1914, the futurist painter and theorist Giacomo Balla lambasted the traditional suit's "neutral shades and colors, degraded by black, stifled by belts, and imprisoned by folds of fabric" as well as its "symmetrical cut and static lines that tire, depress, sadden and bind the muscles; the uniformity of ill-fitting lapels and all wrinkles; useless buttons and starched collars and cuffs."[46] Although Maciste's suit almost exactly matches both Chenoune's and Balla's description, the sheer size of it (and Maciste himself) cannot hide, mask, or restrict his muscles. In fact, during the film, Maciste performs most of his feats of bravery and strength fully and impeccably clothed, never restricted by his size or his suit.

Maciste's transformation from African slave to white Northern Italian necessitated an iconographic, corporeal metamorphosis, and fashion was one of the tools through which the film accomplished this task: the new film re-presented Maciste's body as it refashioned it along different racial, national, and class lines. No scene better illustrates the self-reflexive positioning of well-dressed character, race, and a national, modern identity than one near the end of *Maciste*, when Maciste attempts to rescue the unnamed heroine's mother. Maciste, throughout the film, presents himself as a master of disguise. As he goes to encounter the unnamed woman for the first time, he unpacks a suitcase, which contains several changes of clothes, wigs, and disguises. This spectacle of vested transformation has a precursor both on stage and on screen in Italy in the vaudeville performer Leopoldo Fregoli. Known as the "wizard of disguise," he was famous for his ability to change costumes in a matter of seconds on the stage (the quick-change artist). He quickly saw the potential of film to increase his creative capacity by allowing greater velocity in the costume changes, and to widen his audience beyond that of the stage. He created his own "Fregoligraph," a projection system that toured the country primarily between 1897 and 1899. Maciste's costume changes and multiple disguises clearly draw on this tradition.[47]

Maciste here dons black facial makeup and masquerades undercover as a servant while he attempts to discover the whereabouts of her mother. His cane, long checkered jacket, and top hat evoke the image of the black

10.4. Maciste in blackface from *Maciste*.

dandy, popularized by American minstrel shows and their cinematic incarnations (Figure 10.4). Most evocative, however, is the figure of the dandy itself, and the importance that dress plays in his incarnation in and out of both American black minstrel and various European traditions.[48] Whether the minstrel show was a popular form of entertainment in Italy at the beginning of the twentieth century begs further examination, but the fact that American films did circulate widely in Italy at this time, and that in most of those films, ninety-five percent according to Gerald Butters, the blackfaced white man, not the African American, appeared on-screen, speaks to the presence of the blackface tradition in Italian theaters.[49]

The desired effect in this scene is clearly comic, given its exaggerated physicality (for instance, Maciste's physical dominance over the other actors and the recurring motif of his insatiable appetite). But there is also self-conscious play with racial overtones. Clearly, the spectator knows (and the film itself takes pains to stress) that Maciste/Pagano's blackness is performative: there are shots showing him putting on and removing his blackface makeup. This artificial blackness self-consciously reinforces his whiteness by revealing blackness, both in this film and, by association, in *Cabiria,* to be a disguise, like the many others he wears in the film. His whiteness in terms of race is thus fully constituted. Darkness or otherness becomes a masquerade, something he can take on and off, like the dandified suit that he wears. Blackface and dandyism are the prerogative of the white male star.

The relationship between clothing, masculinity, and nationalism reaches further heights, both literally and figuratively, in *Maciste alpino* (1916), in which the emphasis on clothing shifts from the civilian to the military uniform. During World War I, military uniforms became much more functional, simple, and less ornate: they lost their national colors in favor of providing better cover. Simultaneously, the military jacket, with its "military belt, the blazer with lapels and civilian style neck/collar with large, folding pockets" became a fashion piece in and of itself.[50] The war was a boon to the fashion industry: the production of military uniforms as well as the civilian clothes that sported their influence contributed to its economic growth.[51] Although World War I military uniforms became more practical with the use of khaki, camouflage fabric, and cargo-style pockets and trousers, they still, through their emphasis on the broad shoulders and chest, connoted "discipline, self-control, reliability, competence, loyalty, political allegiance, ideology, aggression, and heroism."[52] It seems fittingly natural that Maciste, as national symbol par excellence, should don the most masculine and most national of Italian military wear, the alpine soldier's uniform.

Maciste alpino, like *Maciste* before it and most of the Maciste films after it, begins with the title character filming a movie, this time at the Austrian border when Italy enters World War I. Subsequently imprisoned for his patriotic outbursts, Maciste escapes and later enlists in the army to fight for his homeland. In order to do so, however, he must first be fitted for his alpinist uniform. In one of the film's many comical scenes, Maciste tries on jacket after jacket and rips the seams on each "glorious uniform" with his bulging chest and shoulders, much to the frustration of the tailor trying to fit him (Figure 10.5). When ultimately able to suit up, he wears the uniform that everyone else dons, but not

10.5. Maciste at the tailor's in *Maciste alpino.*

quite: what sets him apart is not only his physical size but the oversized feather which adorns the characteristic alpinist hat, which, as one intertitle says, does not restrict him in conquering the Alps and bringing glory to the Italian nation. Whether the feather is metonymic reinforcement of his greatness, a comic or a phallic symbol, in *Maciste alpino* "Maciste embodies the virtues of patriotism in the name of the Italian nation," and by enlisting he becomes the "common man with exceptional qualities."[53] The uniform, like the star himself, serves as a leveling device: like many Italians who did not ask for the war, he is nonetheless ready to sacrifice himself.[54]

A compelling aspect to the early Maciste films is not only the fact that Maciste wears new and finely tailored clothes but that, like the blackface, we see him both putting them on and taking them off. As I have argued elsewhere, fashion is integral in the representation of Italian masculinity on screen, often masking an unstable masculinity.[55] With Maciste, however, the fact that we see him first (and often) bare-chested carries two connotations essential to the construction of his character and the role of fashion in that character formation. First, the strategic revelation of his muscled, sculpted chest performing feats of strength aligns him not only with the emerging physical culture movement (which would later become an integral part of Fascist masculine subject formation) but also with the ideals of classical antiquity that Hollander cites as fundamental to the suit's early signifying practices: "Dressed form was now an abstraction of nude form, a new ideal naked man expressed not in bronze or marble but in natural wool, linen, and leather."[56] Second, while male fashion may hide gender instability, it never fully masks the male body. The show of muscle through clothing was an important feature of men's dress up through the nineteenth century, and muscular, lean legs showcased by tights epitomized athleticism in costume.[57] Men's dress reinforced rather than hid the body, highlighting broad shoulders, narrowed waist, and fit arms and legs; the dominant historical styles imply physical fitness rather than fat.[58] Though trousers and modern suit jackets often have a looser fit than older styles, Maciste's muscles remain visible whether he is bare-chested or fully clothed, with the contours of the modern suit reinforcing the masculine physical elements that Maciste's body and character come to personify: strength, courage, and moral and civic fortitude, all in an extra-large size.[59]

In conclusion, the rise of nationalism and racial discourses affected the positioning of the male body in the emerging mass media of early-twentieth-century Italy. The Italian Strong Man's body, and particularly that of Maciste, functioned as the visual personification of modern Italian masculinity through its association, in part, with the most modern of media, the cinema, and what was soon to become the most Italian of industries, fashion. Moreover, classical ideals of masculine beauty inform these contemporary nationalist ideas of the male body. Attached to new ideals of male physicality was an increased attention to male fashion, a phenomenon enhanced by new patterns of production and consumption, and dramatically influenced by World War I and its exhibitions of male heroism and moral nationalism.

Rather than a glance backwards, however, Maciste and his clothes embody the future—modernity feeds on the past in order to become more modern than the present. Echoing but then ultimately abandoning the glories of Ancient Rome, the Maciste films reincorporated and rewrote the virile feats of the valiant Roman soldier for the twentieth century through a characterizing process that erased Maciste's original blackness and reinscribed ideals of Italian masculine virility on the muscled, whitened body of the Italian male star, dressed in the bourgeois uniform *per eccellenza* but still allowing enough of the hyper-masculinized, classically infused body to bulge through. As the rise of Fascism and its anti-bourgeois orientation coalesced in the October 1922 March on Rome, it is not surprising that Maciste, as both political and national symbol, would shed his middle-class uniform in favor of even more symbolically oriented costume dramas such as *Maciste the Emperor* (1924), *Maciste against the Sheik* (1926), and *Maciste in Hell* (1926). While the sign of the muscled torso remains visible, what is signified shifts, to evoke instead the soon-to-be ubiquitous masculine presence, Benito Mussolini.

NOTES

I would like to thank Claudia Gianetto, Stella Dagna, Marco Grifo, and Silvio Alovisio of the National Film Museum in Turin, Italy, for granting me privileged access to both film prints and archival materials, and scholarly solidarity; Livio Musso and Andrea Devalle for their detailed answers to my inquiries on film costume in Torino in the 1910s and 1920s; my two anonymous readers for challenging me to better articulate my argument; Adrienne Munich for her editorial and professional guidance throughout my years at Stony Brook; Giorgio Bertellini and Ellen Nerenberg for their invaluable feedback, inspiration, and collegiality; and E. Ann Kaplan, a true feminist inspiration. All translations from Italian are mine unless otherwise noted.

1. George Mosse, *The Image of Man*, 1998.

2. Ibid.

3. Nicholas Mirzoeff, *An Introduction to Visual Culture*, 5.

4. Tom Gunning, "Now You See It, Now You Don't," 41–51.

5. For more on the Strong Man films, see Gian Piero Brunetta, *Storia del cinema italiano*, 87–89, 317–19; Vittorio Martinelli, "Lasciate fare a noi, siamo forti," 9–28; Alberto Farassino, "Anatomia del cinema muscolare," 29–50; Monica Dall'Asta, "La diffusione del film a episodi in Europa," 277–323; Marcia Landy, *Stardom, Italian Style*, 7–15; Steven Ricci, *Cinema & Fascism*, 81–87.

6. For fashion terminology, I rely on the definitions cogently relayed by Andrew Reilly and Sarah Cosbey in their excellent introduction to *The Men's Fashion Reader*. They define fashion as the "social process involving collective consumer acceptance of a newly introduced style" or the reference to a popular style at a particular time; clothing as a general term which refers to "any tangible or material object connected to the human body"; apparel as garments made of fabric; and costume as clothing specific to a historical period or culture, and "dress associated with rites of passage, rituals and performances" (xv).

7. This is the main argument put forth by Stella Bruzzi in her groundbreaking *Undressing Cinema.*

8. Susan North, "Men's Fashion and Politics," 192; Simonetta Falasca-Zamponi, "Peeking Under the Black Shirt," 148.

9. Christopher Breward, *The Hidden Consumer,* 24–25; Colin McDowell, *The Man of Fashion,* 113.

10. Anne Hollander, *Sex and Suits,* 84.

11. Cristina Giorgetti, *Moda maschile dal 1600 al 1990,* 42–47.

12. Elisabetta Merlo, *Moda italiana,* 23–49.

13. Eugenia Paulicelli, *Fashion Under Fascism,* 2. Although the sixteenth-century sources she cites mostly deal with men's clothing, Paulicelli's focus on fashion and fascism largely neglects the masculine sphere, something not uncommon in previous studies on Italian fashion, yet still somewhat surprising given its prominence over the past thirty years. Recently, scholars have devoted much more attention to men's fashion, as evidenced by the publication of two books of the title *The Men's Fashion Reader* in 2008 and 2009, by Fairchild and Berg, respectively.

14. Arturo Carlo Quintavalle, "Fashion: The Three Cultures," 21–25.

15. Angela Dalle Vacche, *Diva: Defiance and Passion in Early Italian Cinema,* 111.

16. Valerie Steele, *Fashion, Italian Style,* 19–20.

17. Cited in Melita Mandalà, "Scenografia, trucco, costumistica," 96.

18. Gaylyn Studlar, *This Mad Masquerade,* 6–7.

19. Emilio Gentile, *The Struggle for Modernity,* 2.

20. Barbara Spackman, *Fascist Virilities,* in particular 1–33.

21. Giovanni Papini, *Maschilità.*

22. Ibid., 38.

23. Ibid., 84–85.

24. Ibid., 95.

25. Ibid., 99.

26. Brunetta, *Cent'anni di cinema italiano,* 117.

27. Martinelli, *La guerra di D'Annunzio,* 6–9. In a lovely convergence for this author, *T: The New York Times Style Magazine,* in its Fall 2009 fashion issue, showcased D'Annunzio's dandy style and his legacy as male fashion icon on an international level. Grazia D'Annunzio, "The Randy Dandy."

28. Alfredo Bonadeo, *D'Annunzio and the Great War,* 14.

29. Jon Solomon, *The Ancient World in Cinema,* 3; Maria Wyke, *Projecting the Past,* 25–26.

30. Brunetta, *Storia del cinema italiano,* 173; Wyke, 45.

31. Many of these reviews are anthologized in the collection Alovisio and Barbera, *Cabiria & Cabiria.*

32. Paolo Fiorina, "Cartagine, teatro dell'immaginario," 81–101.

33. Riccardo Redi, "Gli scenografi e gli operatori nel cinema italiano degli anni Dieci," 119. Another name which is often mentioned in relation to costume, early cinema, and Torino is Luigi Sapelli, also known as Caramba, who also worked with lyric opera at La Scala in Milano (116), but there is no evidence that I have found that links him to *Cabiria* or the *Maciste* films.

34. Paolo Cherchi Usai, *Giovanni Pastrone,* 61, 74; Fiorina, 100–101.

35. Marco Grifo, "Alla ricerca del cast perduto," 125.

36. Cristina Jandelli 2006, "'Per quanto immagini, sono riusciti a farsi amare come persone vere,'" 127–37; Fabio Pezzetti Tonion, "Corpo della visione, corpo della narrazione," 138–45.

37. Cherchi Usai, 74. The term *mulatto* meant a person of mixed race, with one parent white and the other of black skin.

38. Jandelli, *Breve storia del divismo cinematografico*, 47–53.

39. According to an anonymous 1931 biography of Giovanni Pastrone, Pagano wore a checkered jacket to these appearances, typical of the costumes American (and African American) blackfaced actors would wear on and off screen. In addition, he was told to remain silent, smile broadly at the audience, and shake hands when requested (Cherchi Usai, 66). This use of African American minstrel culture re-emerges in *Maciste* (see below).

40. I would like to thank Cristina Jandelli and Giorgio Bertellini for providing me with this particular reference.

41. Edgar Morin, *The Stars*; Richard Dyer, *Stars*.

42. Suzanne Stewart-Steinberg, *The Pinocchio Effect*, 139–83.

43. Gianni Rondolino, "'Affatica meno e rende di piu,'" 22.

44. There is no film credit, nor does there exist any information at the National Film Museum in Turin, Italy, where the *Maciste* films are housed, about the film's costume designer.

45. Farid Chenoune, *A History of Men's Fashion*, 135–42.

46. Emily Braun, "Futurist Fashion," 39.

47. Aldo Bernardini, "Leopoldo Fregoli, 'Cinematografista,'" 181–85; Wanda Strauven, "From 'Primitive Cinema' to 'Marvelous,'" 105–20.

48. Eric Lott has written brilliantly on the racial ambiguities of the figure of the black dandy in American minstrel culture (Lott, *Love and Theft*, 131–35). More recently, Barbara L. Webb has examined the transatlantic crosspollination of the black dandy in American culture, noting that "the Blackface dandy claims a genealogy traceable to the everyday performances of dandies in Europe and their imitators in the United States" (Webb, "The Black Dandyism of George Walker," 9). There is little reason to doubt that the reverse was not the case, as *Maciste* eloquently illustrates.

49. Gerald Butters, *Black Manhood on the Silent Screen*, 7.

50. Blignaut and Popova, *Maschile, femminile e altro*, 83–84.

51. Merlo, 52.

52. Craik, "Uniforms and Men's Fashion," 435.

53. Landy, 13–14.

54. Alonge, *Cineme e guerra*, 72.

55. Reich, *Beyond the Latin Lover*, 24–48.

56. Hollander, 92.

57. Banner, "The Fashionable Sex," 9.

58. Harvey, "Showing and Hiding," 74.

59. The notion of Maciste's size is of key importance and sets him apart from other fashionable male stars, such as John Barrymore and Rudolfo Valentino (see Studlar, 90–149 and 150–98).

WORKS CITED

Alonge, Giaime. *Cineme e guerra. Il film, la grande guerra e l'immaginario bellico del novecento.* Torino, Italy: UTET, 2001.

Alovisio, Silvio, and Alberto Barbera, eds. *Cabiria & Cabiria.* Torino, Italy: Il Castoro, 2006.

Banner, Lois. "The Fashionable Sex." In *The Men's Fashion Reader*, ed. Andrew Reilly and Sarah Cosbey, 6–17. New York: Fairchild Books, 2008.

Bernardini, Aldo. "Leopoldo Fregoli, 'Cinematografista.'" In *A nuova luce. Cinema muto italiano I. Atti del convegno internazionale, Bologna, 12–13 novembre 1999*, ed. Michele Canosa, 181–85. Bologna, Italy: Clueb, 2000.

Blignaut, Helène, and Liuba Popova. *Maschile, femminile e altro. Le mutazioni dell'identità nella moda dal 1900 ad oggi.* Milano, Italy: Franco Angeli, 2005.

Bonadeo, Alfredo. *D'Annunzio and the Great War.* Madison, N.J.: Fairleigh Dickinson University Press, 1995.

Braun, Emily. "Futurist Fashion: Three Manifestoes." *Art Journal* 54, no. 1 (Spring 1995): 34–41.

Breward, Christopher. *The Hidden Consumer: Masculinities, Fashion and City Life, 1860–1914.* Manchester, U.K.: Manchester University Press, 1999.

Brunetta, Gian Piero. *Cent'anni di cinema italiano.* Roma-Bari, Italy: Laterza, 2000.

———. *Storia del cinema italiano, v. I. Il cinema muto 1895–1929.* Roma, Italy: Riuniti, 1993.

Bruzzi, Stella. *Undressing Cinema: Clothing and Identity in the Movies.* London: Routledge, 1997.

Butters, Gerald R., Jr. *Black Manhood on the Silent Screen.* Lawrence: University of Kansas Press, 2002.

Chenoune, Farid. *A History of Men's Fashion.* Trans. Duke Dusinberre. Paris: Flammarion, 1983.

Cherchi Usai, Paolo, ed. *Giovanni Pastrone. Gli anni d'oro del cinema a Torino.* Torino, Italy: UTET, 1985.

Craik, Jennifer. "Uniforms and Men's Fashion: Tailoring Masculinity to Fit." In *The Men's Fashion Reader,* ed. Andrew Reilly and Sarah Cosbey, 429–44. New York: Fairchild Books, 2008.

Dall'Asta, Monica. "La diffusione del film a episodi in Europa." In *Storia del cinema mondiale, Volume I: L'europa. Miti, luoghi, divi,* ed. Gian Piero Brunetta, 277–323. Torino, Italy: Einaudi, 1999.

Dalle Vacche, Angela. *Diva: Defiance and Passion in Early Italian Cinema.* Austin: University of Texas Press, 2008.

D'Annunzio, Grazia. "The Randy Dandy." *T: The New York Times Style Magazine,* September 13, 2009: 120–25.

De Marly, Diana. *Fashion for Men: An Illustrated History.* New York: Holmes and Meier, 1985.

Dyer, Richard. *Stars.* New edition. London: BFI, 2008.

Falasca-Zamponi, Simonetta. "Peeking Under the Black Shirt: Italian Fascism's Disembodied Bodies." In *Fashioning the Body Politic: Dress, Gender, Citizenship,* ed. Wendy Parkins, 145–65. Oxford: Berg, 2002.

Farassino, Alberto. "Anatomia del cinema muscolare." In *Gli uomini forti,* ed. Alberto Farassino and Tatti Sanguineti. Milano, Italy: Mazzotta, 1983.

Fiorina, Paolo. "Cartagine, teatro dell'immaginario. Su alcune trace archeologiche nei film muti italiani di ambientazione punica." In *Cabiria & Cabiria,* ed. Silvio Alovisio and Alberto Barbera, 87–101. Torino, Italy: Il Castoro, 2006.

Gentile, Emilio. *The Struggle for Modernity: Nationalism, Futurism, and Fascism.* Westport, Conn.: Praeger, 2003.

Giorgetti, Cristina. *Moda maschile dal 1600 al 1990.* Firenze, Italy: Octavo, 1994.

Grifo, Marco. "Alla ricerca del cast perduto: la troupe di *Cabiria.*" In *Cabiria & Cabiria,* ed. Silvio Alovisio and Alberto Barbera, 110–26. Torino, Italy: Il Castoro, 2006.

Gunning, Tom. "'Now You See It, Now You Don't': The Temporality of the Cinema of Attractions." In *The Silent Cinema Reader,* ed. Lee Grieveson and Peter Krämer, 41–51. London: Routledge, 2004.

Harvey, John. "Showing and Hiding: Equivocation in the Relations of Body and Dress." *Fashion Theory* 11, no.1 (2007): 65–94.

Hollander, Anne. *Sex and Suits.* New York: Knopf, 1995.

Jandelli, Cristina. "'Per quanto immagini, sono riusciti a farsi amare come persone vere.' Attori, recitazioni, personaggi in *Cabiria*." In *Cabiria & Cabiria*, ed. Silvio Alovisio and Alberto Barbera, 127–37. Torino, Italy: Il Castoro, 2006.

———. *Breve storia del divismo cinematografico*. Venezia, Italy: Marsilio, 2007.

Landy, Marcia. *Stardom, Italian Style: Screen Performance and Personality in Italian Cinema*. Bloomington: Indiana University Press, 2008.

Lott, Eric. *Love and Theft: Blackface Minstrelsy and the American Working Class*. New York: Oxford University Press, 1993.

Mandalà, Melita. "Scenografia, trucco, costumistica." In *Cinema muto italiano: tecnica e tecnologia. Volume I: Discorsi, precetti, documenti*, ed. Michele Canosa, Giulia Carluccio, and Federica Villa, 82–107. Roma, Italy: Carocci, 2006.

Martinelli, Vittorio. "Lasciate fare a noi, siamo forti." In *Gli uomini forti*, ed. Alberto Farassino and Tatti Sanguineti, 9–28. Milano, Italy: Mazzotta, 1983.

———. *La guerra di D'Annunzio. Da poeta e dandy a eroe di guerra e commandante*. Udine, Italy: Paolo Gasperi Editore, 2001.

McDowell, Colin. *The Man of Fashion: Peacock Males and Perfect Gentlemen*. London: Thames and Hudson, 1997.

McNeil, Peter, and Vicki Karaminas, eds. *The Men's Fashion Reader*. Oxford: Berg, 2009.

Merlo, Elisabetta. *Moda italiana. Storia di un'industria dall'Ottocento a oggi*. Venezia, Italy: Marsilio, 2003.

Mirzoeff, Nicholas. *An Introduction to Visual Culture*. London: Routledge, 2000.

Mora, Emanuela. "La moda italiana e l'uomo integrato." In *Mascolinità all'italiana. Costruzioni, narrazioni, mutamenti*, ed. Elisabetta dell'Agnese and Elena Ruspini, 103–126. Torino, Italy: Utet, 2007.

Morin, Edgar. *The Stars*. Trans. Richard Howard. Minneapolis: University of Minnesota Press, 2005.

Mosse, George L. *The Image of Man: The Creation of Modern Masculinity*. New York: Oxford University Press, 1998.

North, Susan. "Men's Fashion and Politics: '. . . A Son of Liberty Will Not Feel the Coarseness of a Homespun Shirt.'" In *The Men's Fashion Reader*, ed. Andrew Reilly and Sarah Cosbey, 180–98. New York: Fairchild Books, 2008.

Papini, Giovanni. *Maschilità*. Firenze, Italy: Libreria della Voce, 1919.

Paulicelli, Eugenia. *Fashion Under Fascism: Beyond the Black Shirt*. London: Berg, 2004.

Pezzetti Tonion, Fabio. "Corpo della visione, corpo della narrazione: Maciste in *Cabiria*." In *Cabiria & Cabiria*, ed. Silvio Alovisio and Alberto Barbera, 138–45. Torino, Italy: Il Castoro, 2006.

Quintavalle, Arturo Carlo. "Fashion: The Three Cultures." In *Italian Fashion: The Origins of High Fashion and Knitwear*, ed. Gloria Bianchino, Grazietta Butazzi, Alessandra Mottola Molfino, Arturo Carlo Quintavalle, 21–25. Milano, Italy: Electa, 1985.

Redi, Riccardo. "Gli scenografi e gli operatori nel cinema italiano degli anni Dieci." In *Cinema muto italiano: tecnica e tecnologia. Volume II. Brevetti, macchine, mestieri*, ed. Michele Canosa, Giulia Carluccio, and Federica Villa, 115–35. Roma, Italy: Carocci, 2006.

Reich, Jacqueline. *Beyond the Latin Lover: Marcello Mastroianni, Masculinity, and Italian Cinema*. Bloomington: Indiana University Press, 2004.

———. "Undressing the Latin Lover: Marcello Mastroianni, Fashion, and *La dolce vita*." In *Fashion Cultures*, ed. Stella Bruzzi and Pamela Church

Gibson, 209–220. London: Routledge, 2000.

Reilly, Andrew, and Sarah Cosbey, eds. *The Men's Fashion Reader.* New York: Fairchild Books, 2008.

Ricci, Steven. *Cinema & Fascism: Italian Film and Society, 1922–1943.* Berkeley: University of California Press, 2008.

Rondolino, Gianni. "'Affatica meno e rende di piu.' Il cinema muto a Torino." In *Cabiria e il suo tempo,* ed. Paolo Bertetto and Gianni Rodolino, 19–30. Torino, Italy: Il Castoro, 1998.

Solomon, Jon. *The Ancient World in Cinema.* Revised and expanded edition. New Haven, Conn.: Yale University Press, 2001.

Spackman, Barbara. *Fascist Virilities: Rhetoric, Ideology, and Social Fantasy in Italy.* Minneapolis: University of Minnesota Press, 1996.

Steele, Valerie. *Fashion, Italian Style.* New Haven, Conn.: Yale University Press, 2003.

Stewart-Steinberg, Suzanne. *The Pinocchio Effect: On Making Italians, 1860–1920.* Chicago: University of Chicago Press, 2007.

Strauven, Wanda. "From 'Primitive Cinema' to 'Marvelous'." In *The Cinema of Attractions Reloaded,* ed. Wanda Strauven, 105–20. Amsterdam: Amsterdam University Press, 2006.

Studlar, Gaylyn. *This Mad Masquerade: Stardom and Masculinity in the Jazz Age.* New York: Columbia University Press, 1996.

Webb, Barbara L. "The Black Dandyism of George Walker: A Case Study in Genealogical Method." *TDR* 45, no. 4 (Winter 2001): 7–24.

Wyke, Maria. *Projecting the Past: Ancient Rome, Cinema and History.* London: Routledge, 1997.

FILMOGRAPHY

Cabiria. Dir. Giovanni Pastrone. Itala Film, 1914.

La caduta di Troia (The Fall of Troy). Dir. Giovanni Pastrone. Itala Film, 1911.

Maciste. Dir. Vincenzo Dénizot, Romano Luigi Borgnetto. Itala Film, 1915.

Maciste all'inferno (Maciste in Hell). Dir. Brignone. Cines-Pittaluga, 1926.

Maciste alpino (Maciste the alpine soldier). Dir. Giovanni Pastrone. Itala Film, 1916.

Maciste contro lo sceicco (Maciste Against the Sheik). Dir. Mario Camerini. Fert Film, 1926.

Maciste imperatore (Maciste the Emperor). Dir. Guido Brignone. Fert Film, 1924.

Maciste in vacanza (Maciste on Vacation). Dir. Romano Luigi Borgnetto. Itala Film, 1921.

Maciste innamorato (Maciste in Love). Dir. Romano Luigi Borgnetto. Itala Film, 1919.

La memoria dell'altro (The Memory of that Man). Dir. Alberto degli Abbati. Film Artistica "Gloria," 1913.

Quo Vadis? Dir. Enrico Guazzoni. Società Italiana Cines, 1913.

Spartaco (Spartacus). Dir. Giovanni Enrico Vidali. Pasquali, 1913.

ELEVEN

The Stars and Stripes in Fashion Films

ADRIENNE MUNICH

A moment arrives in a "fashion film" when the story pauses to feature a fashion show. Expecting it, the audience switches optical gears to a kind of spectatorship that transforms them momentarily into fashionistas. Viewers of whatever gender join the fashion cognoscenti to view the show, with ritual parade and twirling models robed in outfits that dreams and stories are made of.[1] For the female spectator, the fashion show coddles her, transports her into a fantasy land where she might don an alluring style. For his part, the male spectator takes his role as evaluator of fashionable femininity, escorting a woman to fashion. Once American fashion films captivate viewers into fashionability, they often deliver another message that has apparently little to do with fashion: Hollywood fashion films often arrive on the silver screen draped in an American flag.

It is true that even the Stars and Stripes bow to historical fashion adjustments, looking the same but coming in different sizes and bearing altered meanings. This chapter focuses on three Hollywood fashion films about twenty years apart—*Roberta* (1935), *Funny Face* (1956), and *Mahogany* (1975)—which, in three different ways and each reflecting its time's political and economic issues, use fashion to shape affiliations with America. As in other cases of political coalition, the alliance of fashion with nation involves a good measure of wariness on the part of each side toward its ally. In most fashion films, satire or irony figures in portrayals of fashion, its aesthetics, and its industry. A cosmopolitan perspective—wherein most concepts of fashion thrive—incorporates admiration mixed with condescension for traditional American traits, particularly those associated with authenticity, openness, and distrust of cosmopolitan urbanity. Fashion films with a nationalistic subtext cannot wholeheartedly champion a cultural institution that is associated with surface, with cosmetic appearance, with super-refinement. While providing a perfect medium for showcasing fashion, fashion films often lightly deride it. Yet without seeming to, some fashion films demonstrate that fashion can be imported and rebranded: Made in the U.S.A.

Hollywood fashion films make a preemptive move to enter America into competition as a global fashion center, while trading on European allure.[2] Tons of films reveal that the U.S., particularly New York and Hollywood, sought to appropriate or claim a dominant fashion position over Europe. To repudiate the sheer gorgeous magnetism of Paris or Rome as fashion capitals poses a formidable challenge; thus films take the viewer to Europe, but with eyes of an outsider, sometimes of a tourist. The three exemplary films I examine all take the viewer to Europe on a business trip and reflect a conflict about fashion, at once conceived as a fierce economic engine and a frivolous pastime for binding up female energies. That portrayal reveals a discomfort at recognizing fashion's central cultural position within a generally puritanical ethos, as the films affirm an American work ethic, but then question its expenditure on producing nothing more substantial than a quickly passing fashionable ensemble.

To focus on fashion in order to raise questions of nation and national definition reveals the centrality of fashion in identity formation. This applies not only, as is obvious, to personal and ethnic identities but also to an American identity that conceives itself as superior to Europe in knowing how to get things done. The fashion shows featured in the three films examined here appear at a culmination of the action, at a point where national identity is either affirmed positively or negatively in relation to fashion. America is at once too mighty to take fashion seriously yet too respectful of profitability to reject it. The films offer differing perspectives on fashion—and differing judgments of fashionability—to encourage loyalty to an American identity.

In the Depression-era film *Roberta*, fashion transports viewers to swanky settings, with luxurious, generally unaffordable clothing that provides rich furnishing for imaginary closets. Set in a never-never land called "Paris," the film deploys its plots, subplots, and characters in service of a romance with middle-American, small-town, plain forthrightness that might appear discordant with its *soi-disant* French setting. The American characters, all from Indiana, find themselves in a Paris dress shop. They include Roberta (Helen Westley), who is actually the Aunt Minnie of John Kent (Randolph Scott), a former football player and friend of bandleader Huck Haines (Fred Astaire), along with his high school girl friend, Lizzie Gatz (Ginger Rogers), who is passing herself off as the temperamental Comtesse Scharwenka with a quasi-Polish accent. Bearing names from American pop culture (Minnie Mouse, Huck Finn, and Lizzie Borden) the Indiana natives flaunt a midwestern openness and naïveté that extends even to Aunt Minnie, who unaccountably has made a huge fashion success in Paris, despite her matronly appearance, recalling the types of roles associated with Margaret Dumont. As if to confirm her unfashionability, the plot eventually reveals that sweet, rich old Minnie doesn't actually design clothes. That responsibility goes to her able Russian émigré assistant, Stephanie (Irene Dunne). Fashion, portrayed as almost decadent, is done by Europeans, but America exports its good business head in the person of Aunt Minnie.

The Americans also export popular music. Nothing could be more American than the Jerome Kern score and Huck's midwestern band, "The Wabash Indianians." The plot launches on an American pun. Huck's band sails to Paris for a nightclub gig under a Russian-born impresario's misapprehension that he was getting a band of Native Americans. It is a joke that so unselfconsciously alludes to non-European residents of America that it seems to suggest a fundamental difference in the way that Americans and Europeans perceive their national authenticity, the Europeans bogged down in class-consciousness, and the Americans blithely entitled one and all. (Unfortunately for the plot, the French Revolution necessitates a substitution of Russian for French aristocracy. The character of Stephanie, the Paris fashion designer, might make more sense were she French.)

Huck calls his band members "fellas," and Kent's repeated genial exclamation, "Gee that's swell," epitomizes wholesome American enthusiasm. To moderate their hick image, Huck and Kent French-polish their homey style, learning the language of speech and fashion without sacrificing their prairie openness, which shows itself as insouciance about details of fashion design, fabric, and fabrication.[3] Of course, they appreciate pretty dresses (plus the money made from them and the girls who wear them), but they are shown knowing what they like without knowing about fashion. Clearly, a real man's left hand doesn't know what his right hand is doing, and that's good for Indiana.

The word "Paris" serves more as a synonym for "fashion" than as a location. Stripped of its signature shots of famous landmarks, devoid of Parisians, made up of rooms with no views, Paris is a brand. The sets create an interiority that might just as well read as Indianapolis, where the shop name seems more at home. Thus, American business appropriates "Paris" and welcomes consumers. In the film these consumers are largely Eastern European titled émigrés, for whom fashionability and nightlife require their adornment in remnants of their authority—furs, tiaras, uniforms bedecked with flashy medals. The Russian/American contrast extends to musical performances. Irene Dunne, as Russian Stephanie, trills "Smoke Gets in Your Eyes" in an operatic register that comes across as cultured European highbrow. Middle-American business acumen absorbs European fashion sense in order to market it, a filmic mirror of the actual selling of *Roberta* fashions. Bernard Waldman's Modern Merchandising Bureau copied fifteen of the elegant *American* designer Bernard Newman's costumes for sale in the United States.[4]

The film's two romances, the Astaire and Rogers musical and the fairy tale of the fullback who loves a secret princess thinking she is a shopgirl, unite under the sign of fashion. Imperious aristocrat Comtesse Scharwenka behaves rudely and snottily as she demands obsequious service from the shop staff. Once unmasked as Indiana Lizzie, she freshens up, loses her caricatured accent, and turns into a dancing sweetie pie. John Kent's fiancée (Claire Dodd) sails over to meet him and orders Stephanie to sell her a dress that John has judged vulgar and unworthy of Roberta's style. Her bad taste, visualized as a black dress with a bathing suit back, betrays her bad character, a measure of fashion's moral valence. Stephanie's good taste, though Russian, qualifies her for John.

The denouement features the long-awaited fashion show. A fanfare prepares the viewer for a full-screen, engraved invitation to enjoy Roberta's "entertainment" (on one line) and "gowns" (on another). The invitation constructs viewers of both genders as part of the fashion show audience within and outside the film. The long fashion sequence follows the clock, featuring afternoon attire, then cocktail dresses, and finally evening gowns. Models circulate among the male and female viewers near round tables, stopping while ever-agile Huck stands next to them to deliver rhymed descriptions of the outfits. The first outfits exaggerate costumes specific to women's upper-class daytime activities, such as polo, skiing, sun bathing, meeting for tea, shooting, and flying planes. The ensembles burlesque real activities whilst Huck's verses embroider on the notion of activity as an outfit accessory: the polo outfit can be accessorized with a horse, the hunting outfit with a gun and two dead ducks, the aviatrix getup with a plane. Following daytime wear, cocktail fashion underscores the cocktail hour, an American custom. For the fashion show finale, the camera pans upwards toward a door atop a circular staircase. Mannequins in evening gowns appear in the doorway and then move slowly down to the viewer's level. Architectural space rotates the models in their finery as they descend.

Stephanie materializes, wearing a white gown with white fox trim and a relatively plain diamond necklace (though with huge stones) as her only jewelry. Her dress could have inspired Disney princess attire, with its fur collar framing the Russian princess's face and neck(lace) as she sings an operatic version of "Lovely to Look At."

After Stephanie introduces the opulent theme, other models follow, many with evening hats and full fur coats, muffs, or fur-trimmed dresses.[5] Emphasizing fur's opulence and its associations with sex, one spectacular example features two liveried footmen standing at attention at floor level. They move forward slightly as the stone-faced model reaches the bottom of the staircase and stands impassively facing the film viewer (as distinct from the guests seated at round tables) allowing the footmen slowly and deliberately to remove her floor-length sable wrap to reveal a metallic silver gown. Subsequent models repeat the ritual.

11.1. *Roberta.* Stephanie in fashion show white gown, white fox trim, and diamond necklace.

Roberta's solemn parade receives a comic gloss in the musical comedy, *Guys and Dolls* (musical 1950, film 1955), which includes a spirited strip-tease featuring extravagantly expensive clothes to the lyrics "Take back your mink" (Frank Loesser). Furs thus deliberately taken off suggest both opulence and the high-class burlesque sensibility represented by showgirls at such Parisian night spots as the Folies Bergère.[6]

Whatever its multiple purposes in the plot, *Roberta*'s fashion show offers sartorial information. The fashions initiate film viewers into an imaginary upper-crust life that takes place in well-dressed vignettes from noon to midnight. Selling fashion to ordinary Americans constitutes part of the movie industry's commercial history; here, fashion assumes a Parisian façade and claims cosmopolitan taste in order to sell its wares to American natives on the Great Plains. The fashion show patter inscribes

11.2A. *Roberta*. Lizzie as Comtesse Scharwenka in black satin ensemble; Huck slips off her fur-trimmed coat before the final dance number.

the actual American commercial connection to Waldman's dresses into the script. Huck announces a "gown ran up for Marie, Queen of Romania; we also ran up three for Mrs. Smudge in Pennsylvania." The choice of "Smudge" rather than a more tony Pennsylvanian name definitely suggests middle class. Mrs. Smudge brings high-falutin' fashion down to the level of the common woman, democratizing it while also allowing for gentle denigration of the fashion world. Is American Smudge trumping the Queen of Romania by ordering three to her one? Or do the multiples suggest a parvenu and hence a snobbish attitude toward democratization in mass-market fashion? The film has it both ways.

    Roberta's fashion show also links the fashion Look to love with the song "Lovely to Look At," and symbolically appropriates fashion for American purposes when Fred and Ginger take over. The fashion show

11.2b. *Roberta.* Lizzie dancing with Huck in tuxedo to "Smoke Gets in Your Eyes."

segues into the legendary couple ballroom dancing, first to a reprise (but with changed tempo) of "Smoke Gets in Your Eyes," thus appropriating the song from the Russian princess to associate it with the famous American dancing couple, and finally ending with them doing a fabulous, quintessentially American tap dance to the Kern tune, "I Won't Dance." The irony of the "won't dance" dance mirrors the film's double attitude toward fashion. Don't we do it even while we say we won't? Indeed, wouldn't women in the present moment still feel great in Ginger's slinky black satin gown, with a diamond brooch gently defining the bosom? Gee, *that's* swell.

Twenty years later, Fred changes partners from Ginger Rogers to the younger Audrey Hepburn in *Funny Face,* altering the romantic chemistry. American jingoism persists but has taken a different tonality, one that portrays the American fashion industry as depending upon French *savoir faire* while rejecting an intellectual life associated with French pretension. In the years of postwar recovery, America is jockeying for a top billing in the Western world's fashion show. The film's generally satiric tone undermines the claims of fashion but can't really efface the latter's glamour. The initial setting at *Quality,* a New York fashion magazine, portrays fashion not only influencing but dominating "the American woman;" fashion editor Maggie Prescott (Kay Thompson) characterizes her as a slave to the dictates of fashion.[7] *Quality* magazine represents the American woman's fashion bible, its religion founded on its evident dependence on Europe, confirmed by the magazine's requisite trip to Paris to shoot the *Quality* (American) woman.

Fashion films often feature a male enabler who transforms the fashion-challenged girl to a fashion insider. For a recent rendition of the type, think of Stanley Tucci's Nigel in *The Devil Wears Prada* (2006), who is shown pawing through racks of clothes to ramp up the un-chic college-girl taste of Anne Hathaway's Andy Sachs. Since many fashion movies promise transformation through the Look, this male figure plays the transformer. The Astaire character, Dick Avery (modeled on Richard Avedon, who served as an advisor to the film), plays the transformer role to the point of happily ever after.[8]

A signal moment opens the darkroom to viewers, revealing fashion photographers' secret technique. We watch Avery as he resorts to a precursor of photoshopping to transform the image of dowdy Jo Stockton (Audrey Hepburn), a fervent Greenwich Village intellectual and acolyte of a French philosophical movement satirically labeled "empathicalism" (a play on French intellectual "isms," notably existentialism). "Dick" desires to have a model who also thinks and sees the potential in Jo. To turn her from a brown study in jumper and sensible shoes into a fashion icon, he whites out the details of her features. We watch the transformative process as he draws out of the developing solution a deliberately overexposed image with the dove eyes, classical nose, and perfect lips of the girl who will become the *Quality* Woman, the

11.3. *Funny Face.* Photomontage of Americans in American-style clothes in Paris. Jo wears signature black pencil pants.

model for a new appearance of inner depth that will exemplify the Look for American fashion readers.[9] Again, as in *Roberta,* the film portrays both sides of an ambivalent attitude about fashion in Dick's quest for a beauty who's also smart. His developing technique visually indicates the autocracy of his desire, which is articulated toward the end of the film when he comments of the empathicalist Professor Flostra, "He's about as interested in your mind as I am." Talking out of both sides of his mouth, Avery speaks an ambivalence about women that the film connects to their seduction by fashion. Whiting out cancels individualism, rendering a "funny face" into a classical ideal, under control of the male photographer.

Duality of attitude also characterizes this fashion film in other ways. The film imports American envy of Parisian cultural authority and fashion status into its diegesis by portraying the three main characters, Prescott, Avery, and Stockton, loudly scorning those naïve American tourists besotted with Paris sights but then tracking them as they independently visit them all, singing their American hearts out.[10] Their chance encounter at the Eiffel Tower confirms Paris's irresistible attraction. The rest of the movie exploits that attraction for American competitive, consumer purposes.[11]

11.4. *Funny Face.* Jo floats down the Louvre staircase in red Givenchy gown and nike pose, with the Nike of Samothrace in the background.

As in *Roberta,* the score includes luminaries of the great American Songbook, this time Ira and George Gershwin, and calls attention to the film's allegiance to Stars and Stripes under the direction of an American photographer. We see Avery setting the mise-en-scène for Jo Stockton by telling her a story to induce an attitude; the model acts a part, and fashion here shows how an intellectual acolyte could imagine herself into a new identity by the clothes she wears, thus converting her to a fashion acolyte. David Campany describes the method whereby the photo shoot reveals fashion's constructed nature:

> the centerpiece of *Funny Face* is the long sequence of location shoots featuring Hepburn. Each has a different theme ... and each culminates in an ecstatic freeze-frame that mimics the snap of Astaire's shutter as it catches Hepburn's movements. . . . Each freeze is held for several seconds and put through heavy color filtrations of cyan, magenta, yellow, red, green, and blue, emphasizing the image as a malleable entity to be perfected for the screen or magazine page.[12]

A dialogue between moving pictures and stills in relation to fashion, along with the Gershwin music, produces entrancing filmic elements.[13] These moments beguilingly present aesthetic faces of fashion. Not simply as evanescent but as timeless, fashion receives a striking embodiment when the gauzy chiffon layers of a red evening dress appear around the corner of the Louvre staircase presided over by the Nike of Samothrace, which soaringly personifies the glory that was Greece. Jo, in an identification with the statue, calls out to Dick: "take the picture" as she floats down the staircase in the Victory (the meaning of "nike") pose.

As is true with most Hollywood fashion films, the conflicting messages about fashion indicate deep ambivalence about its allure. An apparent conflict between mind and body depends upon resolving the nationalist agenda in favor of what Maggie calls "pizzazz." In a way, however, the film ends up trashing intellectual behavior (mind), as it did at the beginning of the film when Maggie leads a fashion brigade in trashing the Greenwich Village bookshop where mousy Jo Stockton works and reads in order to rearrange it for a fashion shoot.

Such contradictions and ironies are also reflected in the French/ American costume designers, with Hubert de Givenchy designing Audrey Hepburn's Paris fashions and Edith Head named in the film credits as designer, winning and accepting an Academy Award despite Givenchy's gorgeous contributions.[14] In a further irony, Head's American casual garb in the film has had the greater impact on fashion.[15] Hepburn's skinny black pants, black turtleneck, flats, and pony tail endure as wearable fashion into the twenty-first century, with the casual clothes chain Gap featuring Hepburn on ads for its skinny pants Look. (See Hepburn's original costume in Figure 11.3.) To complicate matters more, the bohemian Look could be seen as an appropriation of Left Bank Paris by smoky Village cafés and similar hangouts throughout the States in the 1950s and early '60s.

Funny Face ends with a Gershwin tune, "S'Wonderful" that wittily rhymes fashion with love: "you make my life so glamorous, can't blame me for feeling amorous." Despite other ironies, such as Audrey Hepburn's less-than-American accent and a skepticism about fashion's dictates as a ploy for susceptible magazine readers—Maggie Prescott remarks of a major magazine campaign to "think pink" that she wouldn't be caught dead in the color—fashion emerges victorious.[16] And the real American gets the girl—as in fact he does in all three films.

Twenty years later, in the midst of racial upheavals in the United States and movements to involve African Americans in political races, the use of fashion and its national inflections take a more negative turn;

FASHIONING NATIONAL IDENTITIES

it is used not only to smooth or white out funny faces, but for the whitening of African American racial identity. *Mahogany* (1975), starring a non-singing Diana Ross, portrays the fashion capital in Rome, mainly in order to condemn that European setting as decadent and materialistic and to elevate American values that reject fashion. Race, so imperative for 1970s social consciousness, radically constructs the film's portrayal of fashion, showing a fashion industry controlled by white men and by white women who serve as acolytes (or worse) to male dominance.[17] Fashion, European and decadent, fundamentally corrupts through its worship of false gods, Mammon, and sexual perversity. The film's message resembles those of the preachers in the revivalist tent meetings of the time, except with a Black Power slant rather than a biblical one. Whilst *Funny Face* takes the form of a Cinderella tale, *Mahogany* tells a conversion narrative in which Cinderella finds a false prince and is unconverted from fashion worship to discover the true meaning of devotion in her man.

For the film's initial setting in Chicago during political agitation for black power, the white world of the department store where Tracy (Diana Ross) serves as an assistant to the haughty, prim, and probably racist buyer, Miss Evans (Nina Foch), contrasts starkly with the South Side black neighborhood where Tracy lives. Further illustrating the racial divide, Tracy visits her aunt (Beah Richards) sitting in a row of women behind sewing machines in the garment factory where she works. Most satirically, the viewer is asked to contemplate a block of ghetto walk-ups where the seriously disturbed celebrity fashion photographer Sean (Anthony Perkins) stages his fashion shoot. In this setting, ghetto blacks slouch off his camera but range themselves in the foreground of the film camera, looking miserable. They form a color-coded contrast to the stately elegance of the white models, who strike poses on the crumbling porches of the blacks' tenements. This graphic juxtaposition visually stages the binary terms of the film. Stunning fashion aesthetics disdain gritty reality to figure fashion as offensively frivolous, callous, and materialistic. Fashion here does not practice a Protestant ethic.

Sean, an American expatriate living in Rome, fulfills the male transformer role. Like Dick Avery, he recognizes Tracy's potential as a fashion model, chooses her to assist in his ghetto shoot, and then transports her from Chicago to Rome. Believing that the eternal city will provide a

more welcoming opportunity for her couturier ambitions, Tracy undergoes a transformation similar to that of Jo Stockton in Paris. She, too,
turns into a supermodel whose face seems to rival Roman attractions,
much as the flaming red gown of Jo in the Louvre seems to overshadow
the magnificence of the Nike of Samothrace. A fashion shoot in the Coli-
seum makes a similar point, this one showing Tracy in one of her own
outlandish fashions and a hairdo resembling a double helix.

To escape the exploitative conditions of American racism and to
fulfill her ambition, Tracy transforms into someone who sells her image
to the highest bidder, in one scene appearing on a billboard with a Revlon
ad (American cosmetics in Rome?) in front of a Roman ruin. Yet Tracy
carries to Italy the baggage of her race, which Sean relabels. By calling her
"Mahogany," he performs a similar erasure as Dick Avery, simultaneously
exoticizing her (mahogany does not grow in Illinois), reclassifying her
into the vegetable kingdom, and rendering her skin merely a vibrant, even
fashionable, color on a visual spectrum. Her hue, apparently an asset,
contrasts beautifully with the stone grey ruins Sean features in his photo
shoots. Thus, fashion negates race without producing true liberation.

The 1970s also experienced a feminist movement that built its vo-
cabulary on the foundation of civil rights language; the two social movements come together in Tracy's character. She longs for a career of her
own as a fashion designer, takes courses, designs a shimmering rainbow
top that her aunt runs up. Yet when she meets and enters into a romance
with Brian (Billy Dee Williams) a political activist running for office on
a platform of lifting his constituents' race consciousness and racial pride,
the idealism of his goals seems to stack the deck against her feminist
ambition, as embodied in a flashy blouse. It is clear that fashion serves as
an ideal vehicle to diagnose feminist desire for an independent career as
female narcissism. In the turmoil of the '70s social movements, fashion
served as an ideal target for feminists (it is more than interesting in this
regard that Sean collects guns to counterbalance his sexual impotence).
Feminists were discrediting fashion because it deflected female energies from self-liberation and it cemented women's role as sex objects.[18]
Consider the difference had Tracy wanted to go to Harvard Law School
as college fashion major Elle Woods does in the third-wave feminist film
Legally Blonde (2001).

11.5A,B. *Mahogany.* Tracy models her kimono for a charity fashion show, then, back to camera, receives applause for her Asian-inflected couturier collection.

Mahogany's Roman setting both allows the film to differentiate itself from fashion films set in Paris and to draw upon associations with a particular kind of Roman decadence that viewers might recall from films of Fellini, Antonioni, and Pasolini. Visiting Rome, Brian dismisses the glory of its antique ruins by remarking: "In Chicago, we call them slums." Tracy achieves her goals, both reigning as the Look and enjoying a smashing success as a fashion designer. Both successes, however, depend on white men. To satisfy the politics of the film, Sean, the fashion transformer, must be utterly discredited. Beyond his impotence (evidently not only with Tracy), his hostility to women (which he expresses by using a blown-up image of a former protégé for dart practice), and his self-destructiveness, which culminates in his suicide, he is a control freak. The other, older and married white man, Christian Rosetti,

underwrites her couture house only as a prelude to setting her up as his mistress. Once she is established as a couturier, Tracy emulates the overbearing tempestuous behavior associated with (clichéd) representations of temperamental fashion designers. It is "under whitey," as it were, that Tracy morphs from oppressed to oppressor. To overload the valences even more, both white men are feminized, or at least emasculated: neither manages to have sex with Tracy. Christian's name also echoes the Victorian woman poet, Christina Rossetti. When Brian appears in Rome, the other white men appear pallid in many senses compared to his '70s American masculinity—reflected in his casually suave American sportswear. At a fashion party in Rome that reeks of *la dolce vita,* Brian remarks on the gender-indeterminacy of fashionistas after a flagrantly swishy man tries to chat with him.

Diana Ross, given prominent billing in the opening credits as the costume designer, actually designed the costumes for the requisite fashion show, though there was possibly an uncredited wardrobe manager who created the non-Tracy-designed garb. Ross, with what must have been unconscious irony, designed blatantly orientalist fashions. She exuberantly displays herself in what resembles a barely modified kimono for her contribution to a charity auction. Then, in her own fashion show at the denouement, mannequins parade in exaggerated Asian-inflected garb, many with stylized, intensely madeup features resembling masks from Noh drama. Some carry parasols copied from fancy cocktail drinks. The faces erase identifying marks of human individual-

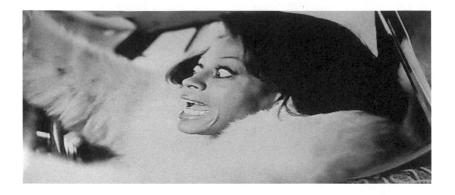

11.6. *Mahogany.* Tracy, in white fur, facing death in a car crash.

ity, conveying a message closely related to Hepburn's whited-out photo
in *Funny Face*. In this way, despite her fashion triumph, Tracy's talent
and career aspirations come across as completely lacking any allegiance
to the Stars and Stripes, so that when she renounces her fashion ambitions, she seems to have undergone a patriotic awakening rather than a
vocational sacrifice.

Sited among those Roman ruins, Tracy's fashion shows are associated with death. (And retrospectively, we might consider Dick Avery's overexposed funny face image to signify the timelessness linked
to death.) To reinforce the connection of fashion with death, Sean takes
over Tracy's sleek red custom convertible and embarks on a death drive.
Sitting in the driver's seat, foot on the accelerator, he snaps shots of a terrified Tracy. After the car crash that kills Sean, the film shows a bandaged
Tracy in bed in Christian's villa, being shown the blown-up black and
white photos of her terrified face; she is a person facing herself facing
Death. Walter Benjamin's words provide an apt gloss for this juxtaposition of fashion with death:

> Here fashion has opened the business of dialectical exchange between woman
> and ware—between carnal pleasure and the corpse.... For fashion was never
> anything other than the parody of the motley cadaver, provocation of death
> through the woman, and bitter colloquy with decay whispered between shrill
> bursts of mechanical laughter. That is fashion. And that is why she changes so
> quickly; she titillates death and is already something different, something new,
> as he casts about to crush her.[19]

The film joins death with fashion after Tracy's fashion show when she appears drained of emotion and energy, her body resembling a soft doll emptied of its stuffing. At the moment when Christian expects his sexual payback, she becomes corpselike, and he sends the body home. Fashion has attempted to sacrifice her, but Chicago, with all it represents in American lore, plus subservience to her Man and his Cause, resurrects her.

The theme song of *Mahogany*, "Do You Know Where You're Going To?" (Michael Masser and Gerald Goffin), signals the identity crisis that the film explores. Tracy, the "you" of the song, must turn westward, to Chicago, to spurn fame for love, to embrace a firm racial and gender identity. Political rallies replace fashion shows. Nevertheless, Tracy's final scene at a political rally showcases her in a fluffy white fun fur, fashionably setting off her rich dark skin and contrasting with the dark street clothes of her boyfriend's South Side constituents. The film—and its star costume designer—cannot quite relinquish fashion's allure.

Whereas Tracy's own designs reinforce prejudice against fashion, the beautiful dresses she wears, including the sequined gown she wears at her own fashion show, work against that negative message. The gown shows no orientalist proclivities, and, as with Rogers's black satin and Hepburn's red chiffon, ordinary women might imagine slipping into it. Exquisite fashions such as those associated with "Made in Italy" thrive in the lived world of the film. While inevitably favoring Brian's political goal of "making the world a better place" over filling the eye and clothing the body, the film flaunts a visually arresting counter-message. Elizabeth Wilson eloquently expressed this conflict between doing good and looking good: "Fashion in our culture is elaborate, fetishized, neurotic, because it goes against these [spiritual] values, against the grain of the cultural norm, representing the return of the repressed and the profound importance of the superficial."[20] *Mahogany* hints of the 1980s return of that repressed in third-wave feminism, a feminism that recognizes fashion's pleasures and the right to celebrate appearances.

Fashion shows from Hollywood set in motion a kind of double vision for viewers. They invite us to step into a looking-glass universe where fashion *matters* and you can have it all—love for great clothes and for the stars and stripes forever.

NOTES

I thank Herbert Sussman, Anya Taylor, Miriam Brody, and Richard Munich.

1. Maureen Turim's "Designing Women" discusses American silent film and its redefining femininity as glamour, "the pursuit of quiet splendor," 148. For a lively discussion of fashion and glamour in later "women's films," see section two in Jeanine Basinger, *A Woman's View.*

2. Joan DeJean, in *The Essence of Style,* portrays Louis XIV as the consummate fashion king, not only fashion-conscious in his person but also consciously supporting fashion industries in France to form its identity as the place where taste and fashion was defined. Caroline Weber, in *Queen of Fashion,* shows how Marie Antoinette adroitly built on the French fashion image. While the results were cataclysmic for her, Paris lived on as a fashion capital.

3. Rumors about Scott's sexual orientation do not figure ironically in his characterization as quintessentially manly, for the character of a football player here draws on Scott's cowboy roles as that kind of guy's guy.

4. Charlotte Herzog, "'Powder Puff' Promotion," 135; Sarah Berry, *Screen Style,* 67.

5. Jeanine Basinger wittily discusses uses of fur in 1930s films as making up for what ordinary women in the depression could not possibly afford, but could dream of when they went to the movies. Opulence and glamour are epitomized by fur: "displaying the star not only in a variety of fur coats, but also in fur hats, fur gloves, fur muffs, fur skirts, and fur-trimmed pajamas," 115. Basinger also points out how films presented dozens of outfits designed for only one activity, 116, which matches the organizing device of *Roberta*'s fashion show.

6. See, especially, Herzog's "Powder Puff Promotion" for a description of the fashion show shots, 139ff., and Berry also for discussion of fashion and musicals.

7. Susan Sellers explores interchanges between *Harper's Bazaar* and American ambition in the film as it

> serves as a departure for rethinking the incorporation of modern European design in the context of postwar American consumer culture.
>
> *Funny Face* sheds an alternate light on a familiar story; the incorporation of Eurocentric modern design in *Harper's Bazaar* and the meaning of that incorporation in the context of a publication produced for women. (Sellers, "'How Long Has This Been Going On?,'"13–14)

8. Peter Krämer, in "'A Cutie With More Than Beauty,'" points out that Astaire had taken a similar role of what he calls an "initiator" of younger women in other films and calls the character a "Svengali," 62. As we shall see, the fashion film uses this sort of transforming male for relationships with little or no age disparity. Krämer explores the biographical elements that create a narrative hodge-podge without acknowledging that fashion films generally show little respect for logic in plots.

9. Douglas Smith, "Funny Face Humanism in Post-War French Photography and Philosophy," extends discussion of the influence of philosophy on the film by situating photographers and Avery's photographic method in a humanist tradition. Such a promising direction exceeds my purposes here, though it is important to note.

10. For an exploration of what she calls the "European hinterland" imported into Hollywood musicals, see Fiona Handyside, "Beyond Hollywood, Into Europe."

11. Gaylyn Studlar, "'Chi-Chi Cinderella,'" explores the intersection between Parisian chic, Hepburn's roles, and French dependence upon American consumers: "American manufacturers and retailers longed to exploit once again the status of superiority enjoyed by Parisian designers. . . . French fashion houses were keenly aware of their postwar dependence upon U.S. business practice and American consumers who could afford French luxury goods. By the mid-1950s it was estimated that 70 percent of haute couture clients were Americans" (160). See also Elizabeth Wilson, "Gamine Against the Grain."

12. David Campany, "From Ecstasy to Agony," 42.

13. The Gershwin tunes are from their 1927 musical by the same name.

14. Rachel Moseley, *Growing Up With Audrey Hepburn,* provides documenta-

tion for Hepburn's influence in interviews with women who sew their clothes and who identify with her as an "image/text."

15. Hilary Radner makes a similar point ("Embodying the Single Girl in the 1960s," 185). See also Elizabeth Wilson, "Gamine Against the Grain," 30–32.

16. See Handyside, 87, for contextualization of Hepburn's European origins.

17. The film was not a critical success, and there is much to find fault with, particularly its heavy-handed use of racial stereotypes and its gratuitous hostility to fashion—which goes beyond satire, especially in terms of the homophobic stereotypes used to characterize Sean as what later decades would see as a homosexual dwelling in a fashion closet filled with gays.

18. For theoretical positions brought to bear on this film, see Jane Gaines, "White Privilege and Looking Relations."

19. Walter Benjamin, *The Arcades Project,* 63.

20. Elizabeth Wilson, "All the Rage," 38.

WORKS CITED

Basinger, Jeanine. *A Woman's View: How Hollywood Spoke to Women, 1930–1960.* Middletown, Conn.: Wesleyan University Press, 1995.

Benjamin, Walter. *The Arcades Project.* 1972. Trans. Howard Eiland and Kevin McLaughlin, ed. Rolf Tiedemann. Cambridge, Mass.: Harvard University Press, 1999.

Berry, Sarah. *Screen Style: Fashion and Femininity in 1930s Hollywood.* Minneapolis: University of Minnesota Press, 2000.

Campany, David. "From Ecstasy to Agony: The Fashion Shoot in Cinema." *Aperture,* no. 190 (Spring 2008): 40–47.

Cook, Pam. *Fashioning the Nation: Costume and Identity in British Cinema.* London: British Film Institute, 1996.

DeJean, Joan. *The Essence of Style: How the French Invented High Fashion, Fine Food, Chic Cafes, Style, Sophistication, and Glamour.* New York: Free Press, 2005.

Gaines, Jane. "White Privilege and Looking Relations: Race and Gender in Feminist Film Theory." *Cultural Critique* 4 (Autumn 1986): 59–79.

Handyside, Fiona. "Beyond Hollywood, Into Europe: The Tourist Gaze in *Gentlemen Prefer Blonds* (Hawks, 1953) and *Funny Face* (Donon, 1957)." *Studies in European Cinema* 1, no. 2, (2004): 77–89.

Herzog, Charlotte. "'Powder Puff' Promotion: The Fashion Show-in-the-Film." In *Fabrications: Costume and the Female Body,* ed. Jane Gaines and Charlotte Herzog, 134–59. New York: Routledge, 1990.

Krämer, Peter. "'A Cutie With More Than Beauty: Audrey Hepburn, the Hollywood Musical and *Funny Face.*" In *Musicals: Hollywood and Beyond,* ed. Robynn Jeananne Stilwell and Bill Marshall, 62–69. Exeter, U.K.: Intellect Books, 2000.

Moseley, Rachel. *Growing Up With Audrey Hepburn.* Manchester, U.K.: Manchester University Press, 2002.

Radner, Hilary. "Embodying the Single Girl in the 1960s." In *Body Dressing,* ed. Elizabeth Wilson and Joanne Entwistle, 183–198. Oxford: Berg, 2001.

Sellers, Susan. "'How Long Has This Been Going On'? Harper's Bazaar, *Funny Face,* and the Construction of the Modernist Woman." *Visible Language* 29 (Winter 1995): 13–34.

Smith, Douglas. "Funny Face Humanism in Post-War French Photography and Philosophy." *French Cultural Studies* 16, no. 1 (2005): 41–53.

Studlar, Gaylyn. "'Chi-Chi Cinderella': Audrey Hepburn as Couture Countermodel." In *Hollywood Goes Shopping,* ed. Garth Jowell David Dresser, 159–178. Minneapolis: Minnesota University Press, 2000.

Turim, Maureen. "Designing Women: The Emergence of the New Sweetheart Line." In *Fabrications: Costume and the Fashioned Body,* ed. Jane Gaines and Charlotte Herzog, 212–228. New York: Routledge, 1990.

Weber, Caroline. *Queen of Fashion: What Marie Antoinette Wore to the Revolution.* New York: Henry Holt, 2006.

Wilson, Elizabeth. *Adorned in Dreams: Fashion and Modernity.* New Brunswick, N.J.: Rutgers University Press, 1985, rev. 2003.

———. "All the Rage." In *Fabrications: Costume and the Female Body,* ed. Jane Gaines and Charlotte Herzog, 28–38. New York: Routledge, 1990,.

———. "Gamine Against the Grain." *Sight and Sound* (March 1993): 30–32.

FILMOGRAPHY

The Devil Wears Prada. Dir. David Frankel. Costumes, Patricia Field. Fox 2000 Pictures, 2006.

Funny Face. Dir. Stanley Donen. Costumes, Edith Head, Hubert de Givenchy, 1957.

Guys and Dolls. Dir. Joseph L. Mankiewicz. Costumes, Irene Sharaff. The Samuel Goldwyn Company, 1955.

Legally Blonde. Dir. Robert Luketic. Costumes, Sophie de Rakoff Carbonell. Metro-Goldwyn-Mayer, 2001.

Mahogany. Dir. Berry Gordy. Costumes, Diana Ross. Motown Productions, Paramount Pictures, 1975.

Roberta. Dir. William A. Seiter. Costumes (gowns), Bernard Newman. RKO Radio Pictures, 1935.

TWELVE

Does Dress Tell the Nation's Story? Fashion, History, and Nation in the Films of Fassbinder

KRISTIN HOLE

The September 2007 issue of American *Vogue* devoted an article to the "überglamorous leading ladies" of the films of Rainer Werner Fassbinder. The story examined how the director's forty-three film and television productions have influenced the world of high fashion, citing as examples recent collections that were inspired by films such as *The Bitter Tears of Petra von Kant* (1972), *Chinese Roulette* (1976), and *The Marriage of Maria Braun* (1979). Fassbinder belonged to a generation of West German filmmakers born during the period of World War II. His cohort inherited the legacy of fascism and struggled to create a new and viable German culture. The historical and cultural moment that was Germany from the late 1960s to early 1980s, the time when Fassbinder was active, is not necessarily the first that comes to mind when one thinks of fashionable films. Yet Fassbinder's oeuvre appropriates the thematic and visual language of Hollywood genres from film noir and gangster to melodrama, while evincing a decidedly self-reflexive and avant-garde character. The women in his films are nothing if not glamorous. From their garter-belts to their fringe-trimmed suits to their furs, the stars of Fassbinder films exude nostalgia for old Hollywood glamour. In an attempt to look closely at the meanings of fashion in Fassbinder's work, I will focus specifically on two films, *The Bitter Tears of Petra von Kant* and *The Marriage of Maria Braun*, taking these films off of the runway and returning them to their specific historical and national context. Inherently paradoxical, fashion maintains the tensions between truth and artifice; in Fassbinder's work,

the formal language of the film to distance the viewer from the action, at the same time, the artifice of fashion contains a seductive power that the film celebrates visually.

Fassbinder troubles any attempt to equate the artificial with the bad or to allow a simplistic conflation between dress and body. The opening scene of the film establishes a distinction between fashion and the body, as Petra's deceitfulness is rendered separate from her actual appearance. When we first witness Petra lying to her mother over the phone, she has not yet dressed or put on her wig and makeup. Fassbinder makes it clear that Petra does not need to be in costume to play a role. Petra proceeds to dress slowly and deliberately for the camera. She carefully spins around and buttons up her peignoir (a white floor-length number with fringe trim, a rhinestone belt, and a fur collar), and stands posed as if for a photo.[4] Petra turns to put on a wig in front of the mirror, and then slowly applies her makeup, from foundation to false eyelashes to lipstick. At key points in the dialogue that follows, her face is visible only as a reflection in her handheld mirror. The film's very self-conscious concern with Petra's first moment of getting dressed and "putting on her face" establishes its interest in fashion and beauty as role-playing, although as evinced in this scene, neither are necessary preconditions for the ability to play a deceptive role.

As Jane Gaines has argued in relation to classic Hollywood melo-drama, costume can work both to index character psychology, support-ing the film's narrative development, *and* to absorb the emotional surplus of the plot, even to the point of competing with the narrative trajectory itself.[5] Always shuffling between classical Hollywood and the avant-garde, Fassbinder utilizes costume as a visual element that is necessar-ily and politically in tension with the narrative, but he also draws on its ability to add to characterization. He uses the costumes as psychological cues while at the same time undermining their reliability.[6]

An example of his use of an outfit as index of the character's psyche can be found in a scene in which Petra appears stranded in a sea of white shag carpet next to a white telephone. It is her birthday and she desperately desires for Karin to call. She wears a long green off-the-shoulder dress with ruffled top, a blonde curly wig that reminds one slightly of Karin (perhaps a melancholic choice on Petra's part?) and

12.1. Petra takes a drink.

a choker sprouting a bouquet of red flowers, which seems to visualize
Petra's emotional distress very viscerally as a bleeding from the throat.
These same flowers will be held at Petra's genitals during one of the final
scenes, a melancholic tribute to the lost sexual possibilities of her relationship. When Karin is first introduced, her suit of purple and paisley
hints that she is there to do business, but the furry trim (technically
marabou) suggests a sexuality infused with the dynamics of domination
and submission. Notably, the other women in the scene are similarly fur-
trimmed and have just been discussing the power games inherent in any
romantic relationship. In the scene in which Petra and Karin have their
first "date," while Petra's outfit seems true to character, Karin's is not
such a straightforward indication of her interiority. When we see Petra
framed in a doorway she looks like something out of a Klimt painting.
Her skirt makes it almost impossible for her to move, suggesting her
entrapment by the excessiveness of her desire. But the top of her outfit
is a mix between armor and beaded lingerie, between protection and

12.2. Petra and Karin meet for the first time.

exposure ("I had to fight," says Petra to Karin regarding her past). The outfit's oscillation between defense and desire is echoed by Karin's, on whom a sequined metallic bra-top dress hints at self-protection, opening to expose a triangle around her bellybutton, giving her a sense of extreme vulnerability, as well as echoing a vaginal shape, here offered to Petra. Her thick gold choker and armband connote bondage. Although her outfit indicates a servility and vulnerability, this is revealed to be the opposite of stubborn, independent Karin's true character.

In regard to the use of costume in *Petra*, Olga Solovieva argues that "dress replaces the body. Mask-like makeup and ever-changing wardrobes take on a life of their own, representing the dynamics of the characters' personalities."[7] This is not quite so; dress can never "replace" the body for Fassbinder's characters. Fashion provides the means by which his characters attempt to create new personas for themselves, personas that will help them to break from their dysfunctional pasts. Yet the body and its interconnected psyche remain, threatening to undermine the

fantasies expressed by their fashion choices. As indicated in the opening scene, in which Petra's forced enthusiasm toward her mother and
her dishonesty over the phone are accomplished without outfit, wig,
or makeup, the relationship between who you are and what you wear
is not straightforward. Fashion is not to blame for the artificiality and
oppressiveness of sexual and interpersonal relations in the film. Karin's
peek-a-boo gown belies her invulnerability and stubborn independence.
Like many of her words on this first night of passion, Karin's dress, with
its slave band accessories and exposed core, does not reflect who she is.
If anything, her garb is a representation, along with her speech, of the
person she wants Petra to see her as. Although Karin maintains that she
has always been honest with Petra, she seems all too aware of how to get
what she wants from the lonely designer. There are bodies beneath clothing that contradict their outward presentation. The characters are not
what they wear, but often what they wear expresses who they wish they
could be. It is this side of fashion, as a space of self-creation, that must be
read alongside the stigma that fashion carries as inherently superficial.
Fashion is, for Fassbinder, an ambiguous site of multiple meanings that
harbors within it radical potential. The problem, in *Petra,* is not fashion
but the people on whose bodies it is displayed. For Petra, like Germany,
despite the promises of fashion—the potential to re-create the self, individuality, and the possibility of other ways of being—she remains
trapped in her past, repeating dangerous older patterns.

   Nor is artifice an inherently bad thing. As Fassbinder said when
asked about the inspiration for his television productions, "The true *is*
the artificial."[8] Fassbinder's celebration of artifice is evident in the parallel he draws between the world of fashion and the medium of film itself.
In her attempt to connect with Karin on their first night together, Petra
asks Karin whether she likes art, concerts, or films, to which Karin replies, "I love movies. Films about love and suffering." Here the dialogue
explicitly draws attention to the film *as* a film. Just as they love fashion,
the women love film. Just as fashion is a fetishized illusion, so film provides a space for individual and collective fantasies to be given a visual
language. Thomas Kellner also notes this connection when he writes,
"The *mise-en-scène* is marked by cinematic excess that itself calls attention to the artificiality of the cinematic apparatus and in several scenes

12.3. Maria and her sister take a walk.

individuality are being extended to broader and broader spheres of collective life.[15] Fashion's rule extends even into our experience of temporality. Lipovetsky writes, "What is fashion, indeed, if not a modern social
logic instituting a new legitimate temporality—the social present—that
breaks with the traditional order venerating continuity and fidelity to the
past?"[16] *Maria Braun* begins with an explosion: a picture of Hitler comes
flying off the wall as a bomb hits the building where Maria is performing her nuptials. This explosion and the fascist image that it relegates
to the ashes tell us that we are entering a new time. Maria realizes early
in the film that she must use her mastery of appearances to get ahead.
She trades in her mother's brooch for a bottle of bourbon and a dress
ordered exactly to her specifications. The dealer (significantly played by
Fassbinder) handing her the dress states, "Black, size 38, short sleeves,
low cut. Wasn't easy to get." He offers her a valuable edition of the works
of Kleist, but Maria passes saying, "Books burn too fast and don't give

enough heat." Maria rejects the past, represented here by the work of celebrated author Heinrich von Kleist, in one of many moments in the film where she aligns herself with the future-present of fashion, rather than the past.[17] In the scene immediately following, Maria will have her mother shorten the dress to expose her calves. This dress will be Maria's ticket into a relationship with a financially supportive American soldier, and later with Karl Oswald, whose textile manufacturing company will securely establish Maria financially. Initially working as a translator for Oswald (she has learned English "in bed" with her American soldier) she asks for a moment alone with the head of the American firm, reasoning, "I don't know a thing about business. But I do know something about the German woman and the difference between nylon and cotton. I understand quite a lot about the future. You might say I'm a specialist in it." Maria's knowledge of women and clothing are here implied to be to her advantage in the new German order, an advantage she has over the older men for whom she works. Her ability to anticipate what will serve her well in her quest for upward mobility constitutes her key to getting ahead in the world. Maria explains her involvement with Oswald to her husband, who is in jail for a murder that she committed, explaining that she asked Oswald to sleep with her *before* he could have the chance to make a proposition, so that she would have the upper hand. In another scene Maria tells her brother-in-law that "Reality lags behind my consciousness."

Maria's investment in the future seems to feed into the social present of fashion, in that it enables her to prepare for the change and novelty inevitable in the new era of democratic capitalism. Fassbinder and Maria (as Germany) want to break with the past, but in the process they reveal that the past is not so easy to leave behind. Just as an explosion begins the film, the explosion that ends it is followed by a series of negative shots of the post-WWII Chancellors up to the film's production year (1979), with Willy Brandt, with whom Fassbinder had political sympathies, noticeably absent. The visual logic implies that the fascist past (represented by the image of Hitler at the film's beginning) is somehow continuous with the present. This impression is compounded by Fassbinder's use of actual historical radio broadcasts layered in the soundtrack of the narrative. An earlier broadcast of Chancellor Adenauer stating that

Germany is against rearmament is later contradicted when Adenauer announces that Germany must begin the process of rearmament. The radio broadcast of Germany beating Hungary in the 1954 World Cup is the last thing heard in the film. The radio announcer shouts, "Germany is World Champion [*Weltmeister*]," eerily hinting at the forgetting of history that Fassbinder both critiques and participates in through his own filmic reconstructions.

HISTORY LESSONS

As is evident from the visual and auditory links made in *Maria,* Fassbinder was critical of what he saw as the continuities between West Germany in the 1970s and the Nazi era. He argued that because West Germany had been handed democracy and freedom, rather than having fought for it, traces of fascism were still evident in everyday German life. Of his FRG trilogy he said,

> We didn't learn much about German history in Germany, so we have to catch up with some basic information, and as a filmmaker I simply used this information to tell a story. That means nothing more than making reality tangible. I see many things today that arouse fear in me. The call for law and order. I want to use this film to give today's society something like a supplement to their history.[18]

While Fassbinder himself identified the trilogy as a history lesson, Lynne Kirby sees in *The Bitter Tears of Petra von Kant* a critical awareness of the continuities of the present with the fascist past. She argues that many of the costumes worn in the film hearken back to the interwar period when fascism was on the rise; thus the costumes "put fashion on a continuum with fascism."[19] Thomas Elsaesser argues that in Fassbinder's films *"esse est percipi,"* "to be is to be perceived."[20] In Fassbinder's films, the exhibitionism of the characters is a more dominant motif than any spectatorial voyeurism. According to Kirby's reading, this exhibitionism in *Petra* reeks of fascism. She argues that the conformity of fascism is the conformity of the fashion world: "The fashion industry *is* the industry of conformity, of social-sexual uniforms."[21] Kirby tempers her interpretation somewhat, arguing that other costumes in *Petra* would challenge a straightforward reading of the film as strictly about fascism. Rather, the film must be considered as touching on, "the ambiguous survival of outmoded social relations, their coexistence with and survival as incorporation at the heart of contemporary socio-economic structures."[22]

While Kirby's ultimate conclusion falls in line with my analysis, I would challenge her alignment of fashion with fascism and conformity. Undeniably, fascism had an aesthetic and exhibitionist dimension.[23] Walter Benjamin famously wrote that fascism was the aestheticization of politics,[24] and Susan Sontag argued that under National Socialism "politics appropriated the rhetoric of art."[25] I argue, however, that fashion needs to be separated from an easy conflation with beauty or aesthetics. Fashion's meanings are much more complex and contradictory. While fashion can create regimes of conformity, it *also* promises constant novelty and change, the ability to be an individual and to self-fashion.[26] This ambiguity is evident in Elizabeth Wilson's claim that "To dress fashionably is both to stand out and to merge with the crowd, to lay claim to the exclusive and to follow the herd."[27] Wilson points to the paradox that although most people's fashion choices in a given time and place have more similarities than differences, people tend to see their appearance as an expression of their individuality, at least in the capitalist West. Individuality and novelty are somewhat outside of fascism's logic of conformity and the static immortality of the leader, even if the latter ideals are highly beautified and even eroticized. Citing a long lineage of scholars who saw fashion as intrinsic to the logic of capitalist democracy, equality, and social mobility, Yuniya Kawamura argues that "fashion both requires a certain degree of mobility and fluidity within a society and promotes a more egalitarian society and erases class boundaries."[28] Lipovetsky echoes this when he argues, "Fashion must be conceptualized as an instrument for the equality of conditions,"[29] which "marks a . . . limit to the process of social and political domination in modern societies."[30] Also opposing Kirby's emphasis on the conformism of fashion, Eugenia Paulicelli in her study on fashion under Italian fascism argues that something in the way fashion itself works served to undermine the fascist system: "a culture shuttered in by its nationalistic, totalitarian and autarchic modes was anathema to the creativity and change inherent in fashion."[31]

The paradoxical nature of fashion needs to be reined in and channeled if we are to maintain notions of collective social responsibility and ethical principles in modern capitalist democracies. This ambivalence, rather than any straightforward alignment of fashion with fascism or a less authentic way of being, is what is key to understanding the role of fashion in Fassbinder's films. If anything, Fassbinder was concerned to show that while the promises of capitalist democracy's fashion logic were available and operable for Germany, the social and sexual relations of a previous order still lingered in a nation that had had its democracy handed to it in 1945, rather than having struggled for that freedom. Maria, trying to sell her wedding dress for goods early on in the film, tells her mother, "Nobody wants wedding dresses now," of course alluding to the paucity of German men "on the market," but also hinting at a break with tradition. Wedding dresses, while subject on a minor scale to the whims of fashion, are somewhat outside of the fashion logic, and in discarding hers, Maria, like her nation, is eager to show her fashionability, her ability to adapt to the demands of capitalism and democracy.

PERFORMING THE NATION

Thomas Elsaesser suggests that we read the FRG trilogy's focus on women in terms of their ability to embody the spectacle of show business and capitalism.[32] The protagonists are strong women, consciously using their appearance to control the gaze of men in order to get what they want. Maria, Veronika, and Lola are all talented performers. Elsaesser writes of the historical films that, "they are centered on a female heroine, each of whom, perhaps even more crucially, lives her life through the realities and values of show business, which constitutes them, makes them into what they are, and gives them a field of action, *a terrain for being that exceeds the scope their lives might otherwise have had.*"[33] Lola, a sex worker and singer in the local brothel, deftly negotiates the political and economic situation in her town to ensure the financial security of herself and her child. Veronika Voss, whose character is based loosely on the life of interwar film star Sybille Schmitz, who died of a drug overdose in 1955, demonstrates a keen awareness throughout the film of how to best showcase her aging assets. When she first has a drink with the reporter who later becomes obsessed with her, she orders the waiter to dim the lights and uses candlelight to create a more flattering image of herself for her companion. Later, in a flashback, Veronika argues with her husband as she tries to create a mood in their villa with lighting and music. He complains, "It's always the same crap. You always have to be doing something, always setting something up. Can't we just be the way we are?" To which Voss replies, "Why can't you understand me? When an actress plays a woman who wants to please a man, she tries to be all the women in the world rolled into one." The three protagonists all understand the power of appearances in the logic of postwar German capitalism and survive or perish acceptingly within this system.

When Veronika explains that sometimes, "an actress plays a woman who wants to please a man," she reveals a certain meta-awareness of femininity as performance. This level of performativity on the part of Fassbinder's characters is what Johannes von Moltke argues is their availability for certain campy spectatorial pleasures. Where Elsaesser reads the FRG heroines as *performers,* Moltke argues for a reading of their *performativity.*[34] Here we have "the nation and its history as a drag performance, put on by a particular body."[35] Moltke will go on to argue that, "Where the female female-impersonator erases the substantiality of the feminine, the impersonator of national history radically shifts the status of the historical subject, suggesting that *it is only by 'doing' the historical moment that we can access its meanings.*"[36] Perhaps this point provides a better window into the highly self-reflexive *Petra* as well as the more explicitly historical *Maria Braun.* Both Petra and Karin are very much characters who are playing characters, a fact evinced by their usage of fashion to project the selves they want to be or be seen as. If history is in Moltke's analysis rewritten through the body (of the woman/ Schygulla) then we must ask (to rephrase Jane Gaines) if dress tells the nation's story.[37] Caryl Flinn echoes Moltke's claims, arguing that the silence around recent German history for the postwar generation necessitated a performative relationship to history.[38] Flinn suggests that music and other elements of style in the films of the New German Cinema be read as artifacts that produce alternative possibilities for understanding identity and history. Although these artifacts may not correspond with objective historical referents, the often emotionally charged associations they evoke in the viewer enable various forms of identification and the exploration of lost possibilities. Although she does not explicitly discuss

12.4. Maria visits her old schoolhouse.

fashion, as a major element of film style costume must necessarily be considered as just such an "artifact" that signals other ways of seeing Germany. Maria walks through the ruins of her childhood school in a long black dress and a pillbox hat, a strand of pearls around her neck. Of the jacket with animal-print fur trim worn in this scene, Schygulla says, "The trim on the coat was almost like saying the tiger is rising again."[39] In her reference to the lush costumes signifying a glamorous Germany rising from the ashes, Schygulla seems to imply that in the case of *The Marriage of Maria Braun,* dress *was* meant to tell a story, though that story is perhaps a fairy tale, about the nation.

Thinking of fashion in terms of performative reiterations of history and identity points to the ambivalence of Fassbinder's relationship to Germany *and* fashion. Iterability both cites from a catalogue of already available meanings and at the same time reworks them to enable other ways of seeing and doing history and identity to emerge. As was evident in *Petra,* the body will always place limits on the ability to enact

a meaningful (and lasting) reiteration. It would be a mistake to embrace wholeheartedly a reading of fashion as a realm of purely utopian
democratic potential and unlimited individuality. Fashion, too, has its
dangers. However, one of the meanings it makes available is precisely
this realm of fantasy, of imagining other ways of being and of breaking
one's ties to the past. Though Fassbinder, always cynical, may have been
critical of aspects of the fashion world, he was keenly aware of its fantasy-
producing nature and the way it fabricated new selves and possibilities
for action.

Even a cursory viewing of Fassbinder's films reveals their richness as
sources of high fashion inspiration. The world of fashion, like camp spectatorship, works on the basis of deterritorialized readings of its sources.
While a Marc Jacobs collection or certain camp appropriations may
take away from some of Fassbinder's political critique, they pick up on a
celebration of the superficial that is already present in Fassbinder's relationship to fashion and style. While the argument for camp enables the
reading of history as a drag performance to emerge, I would argue for a
reading that reterritorializes these performances, placing them squarely
in the context of Fassbinder's relationship to Germany past and present. Fassbinder was critical of contemporary Germany, of the constant
danger of the nation slipping into past ways of being. Yet as he argued,
"God knows the FRG is not comparable to Hitler's Reich. And although
I can imagine a different government, this is where I do my business."[40]
Although critical of capitalism, Fassbinder was aware that, "some aspect
of venality forms part of every opportunity to be happy."[41] This ambivalence must be read into the role of fashion in his films: fashion, like the
cinema itself, tells *a* truth despite, or perhaps because of, its artifice. The
fantasy realms that fashion gives us access to, the promise of change and
individuality inherent in the way fashion operates enables the creation
of new identities and of a different nation. Dress tells the nation's story:
Germany is writ large in the figure of Maria Braun; it is also written in
the stories of the individuals whose smaller histories, in a film like *Petra*,
combine to offer other possible ways of understanding German identity.
The glamour of Fassbinder's vision must be read as both a celebration
of the possibilities of postwar democracy and as a weary eye turned on
the tendencies of the present to eschew fashion's penchant for change in

its reproduction of the fascist past. Like the faces obscured by the many veils that adorn the hats of Fassbinder's leading ladies, an older Germany lurks behind the promise of the glamorous and the new.

NOTES

1. I put trilogy in quotation marks, because Fassbinder intended to continue making this series of "historical" films before he died of a drug overdose in 1982, having completed only three.

2. Thomas Elsaesser, *Fassbinder's Germany*, 20–21.

3. Lynne Kirby, "Fassbinder's Debt to Poussin," 16.

4. The costumes for *The Bitter Tears of Petra von Kant* are by Maja Lemcke. This is the only film that Lemcke worked on with Fassbinder.

5. Jane Gaines, "Costume and Narrative," 205–206.

6. See Jaspers and Reichmann, "Kostüm als Charakterdarstellung." According to Barbara Baum, who was Fassbinder's costume designer from 1972–1982 and worked on films such as *The Marriage of Maria Braun,* once their relationship was established, Fassbinder gave her a great deal of freedom, generally offering her a few guiding concepts or figures and then often not viewing her creations until the actors were dressed and the shooting had begun. For *Petra,* however, Fassbinder may have had more direct input into the costuming, because it seems to have been his first time working with Lemcke, and especially because costume plays such an important visual role in the film.

7. Olga Solovieva, "You Are What You Wear," 53.

8. Rainer Werner Fassbinder, *The Anarchy of the Imagination,* 198; italics mine. A character in Fassbinder's 1979 film *The Third Generation* also sums up his attitude well when he says, "Film is a lie, twenty-five times a second. Truth is a lie, every film tells us that. In films lies are dressed up as ideas and shown as truths. That's my idea of utopia—the only one there is."

9. Thomas Kellner, "Fassbinder, Women, and Melodrama," 34.

10. Anton Kaes, *From Hitler to* Heimat, 87–88.

11. Juliane Lorenz, ed., *Chaos as Usual,* 156.

12. Lynn Yaeger, "Screen Idol," 512.

13. Ibid., 514.

14. Kaes, 98.

15. Gilles Lipovetsky, *Empire of Fashion*, 131.

16. Ibid., 243.

17. Although it must be noted that the Kleist reference has multiple valences, as the author was an important reference point for many of the directors associated with the New German Cinema.

18. Kaes, 88. The present-day situation in Germany was of course the rise of "terrorism" in West Germany and what was viewed as the crackdown on free speech and freedom of the press. These issues were the subject of a collaborative film in which Fassbinder participated, *Germany in Autumn* (1978).

19. Kirby, 17.

20. Elsaesser, 68.

21. Kirby, 18.

22. Ibid.

23. Apropos the aestheticization of politics under fascism, Visconti's *The Damned,* a highly stylized film about a

wealthy German family's corruption under the Third Reich, ranked first on Fassbinder's list of top ten movies. See Fassbinder, "The List of my Favorites" in *Anarchy*, 106.

24. See Walter Benjamin, "The Work of Art in the Age of Mechanical Reproduction."

25. See Susan Sontag, "Fascinating Fascism."

26. This argument is made by Elizabeth Wilson, *Adorned in Dreams*, 6; Lipovetsky; and Eugenia Paulicelli, *Fashion under Fascism*, 149.

27. Wilson, 6.

28. Yuniya Kawamura, *Fashion-ology*, 24. This is also central to Wilson and Lipovetsky's definition of fashion as a social phenomenon.

29. Lipovetsky, 31.

30. Ibid., 37.

31. Paulicelli, 143.

32. Elsaesser, *Fassbinder's Germany*.

33. Elsaesser, 116; italics mine.

34. He is particularly interested in adding Schygulla as a campy performer of femininity to the already established canon that includes figures such as Judy Garland.

35. Johannes von Moltke, "Camping in the Art Closet," 98.

36. Ibid., 99; italics mine.

37. See Gaines.

38. Caryl Flinn, *New German Cinema*.

39. Yaeger, 514.

40. Kaes, 97.

41. Fassbinder, *Anarchy*, 68 ("'I'm a Romantic Anarchist'").

WORKS CITED

Benjamin, Walter. "The Work of Art in the Age of Mechanical Reproduction." In *Illuminations*, 217–52. New York: Schocken Book, 1968.

Elsaesser, Thomas. *Fassbinder's Germany: History Identity Subject.* Amsterdam: Amsterdam University Press, 1996.

Fassbinder, Rainer Werner. *The Anarchy of the Imagination.* Baltimore, Md.: John Hopkins Press, 1992.

Flinn, Caryl. *New German Cinema: Music, History, and the Question of Style.* Berkeley: University of California Press, 2004.

Gaines, Jane. "Costume and Narrative: How Dress Tells the Woman's Story." In *Fabrications: Costume and the Female Body*, ed. Jane Gaines and Charlotte Herzog, 180–211. New York: Routledge, 1990.

Jaspers, Kristina, and Hans-Peter Reichmann. "Kostüm als Charakterdarstellung: Interview mit der Köstumbildnerin Barbara Baum." *Film-Dienst* 59 (2006): 53–55.

Kaes, Anton. *From Hitler to Heimat: The Return of History as Film.* Cambridge, Mass.: Harvard University Press, 1989.

Kawamura, Yuniya. *Fashion-ology: An Introduction to Fashion Studies.* Oxford: Berg, 2005.

Kellner, Thomas. "Fassbinder, Women, and Melodrama: Critical Interrogations." In *Triangulated Visions: Women in Recent German Cinema*, ed. Ingeborg Majer O'Sickey and Ingeborg von Zadow, 29–42. Albany: State University of New York Press, 1998.

Kirby, Lynne. "Fassbinder's Debt to Poussin." *Camera Obscura* 3 (1985): 4–27.

Lipovetsky, Gilles. *The Empire of Fashion: Dressing Modern Democracy.* Princeton, N.J.: Princeton University Press, 1994.

Lorenz, Juliane, ed. *Chaos as Usual: Conversations about Rainer Werner Fassbinder.* Berlin: Henschel Verlag GmbH, 1995.

Moltke, Johannes von. "Camping in the Art Closet: The Politics of Camp and Nation in German Film." *New German Critique* 63 (Autumn 1994): 76–106.

Paulicelli, Eugenia. *Fashion Under Fascism*. Oxford: Berg, 2004.

Solovieva, Olga. "You are What you Wear in Rainer Werner Fassbinder's *The Bitter Tears of Petra von Kant.*" *Film Comment* (November/December 2002): 53–56.

Sontag, Susan. "Fascinating Fascism." *New York Review of Books,* February 6, 1975.

Wilson, Elizabeth. *Adorned in Dreams: Fashion and Modernity*. Berkeley: University of California Press, 1985.

Yaeger, Lynn. "Screen Idol." *Vogue,* September 2007.

FILMOGRAPHY

The Bitter Tears of Petra von Kant. Dir. Rainer Werner Fassbinder. Costumes, Maja Lemcke. Filmverlag der Autoren, 1972.

Chinese Roulette. Dir. Rainer Werner Fassbinder. Albatros/Les Films du Losanges, 1976.

Lola. Dir. Rainer Werner Fassbinder. Costumes, Barbara Baum. Trio Film, 1981.

The Marriage of Maria Braun. Dir. Rainer Werner Fassbinder. Costumes, Barbara Baum. Trio Film, 1979.

Veronika Voss. Dir. Rainer Werner Fassbinder. Costumes, Barbara Baum. Trio Film, 1982.

THIRTEEN

Subversive Habits: Minority Women in Mani Ratnam's *Roja* and *Dil Se*

SARAH BERRY

This essay will look at how two Indian films from the 1990s use costume to articulate social tensions around gender, nation, and minority Indian cultures. Made by Tamil director Mani Ratnam, the films use dress to depict women as representatives of marginalized social groups with a conflicted relationship to modern Indian nationalism. While the male protagonists in these films seek to transcend cultural difference, the heroines symbolize marginalized groups and embody resistance to the "homogenizing majoritarian discourses" of Indian nationalism.[1] In the films *Roja* (*Rose* 1992, costumes uncredited), and *Dil Se* (*From the Heart*, 1998, costumes by Manish Malhotra), Ratnam focuses on gender, ethnic, and center–periphery divides, using feminine identity as a space of instability from which to explore the conflicted nature of India's contentiously multicultural national identity.

Numerous analyses of Indian film have explored the way that women's roles symbolize issues of national identity. Sumita Chakravarti has described the geisha-like courtesan as a character whose fusion of Hindu and Muslim arts and social graces makes her a "national projection of a literal embodiment of Hindu-Muslim unity."[2] Jyotika Virdi has looked at how the resurgence of romance-centered films in the late 1980s coincided with market liberalization and the rise of Indian consumer culture. Instead of exploring social hierarchies, she notes, heterosexual romance now deals with "redefinitions of the self and subjectivity in relation to the family and community."[3] Ranjani Mazumdar notes that

this trend has revised the feminine dichotomy, long a staple of Indian
popular film, between a chaste heroine and a vamp (often designated
by Western-style or revealing dress). That duality has been replaced by
a new image of the Indian woman as one whose youthful sexual independence and access to consumer culture and fashion have modernized
Indian femininity.[4]

In *Roja* and *Dil Se,* however, Ratnam depicts women with a conflicted relationship to modernity; their costume signifies allegiance to
tradition and a marginalized cultural identity. In contrast to Chakravarti's reading of the courtesan's Hindu/Islamic fusion as a projection
of Indian national unity, Ratnam's women represent current conflicts
between a secular, federal nation and the "ethno-cultural movements"
that challenge that framework.[5] Ratnam's male characters invariably
call for a transcendent, multicultural nationalism but are confronted
with the problematic aspects of that project and the intensity of resistance to it. Ratnam's "terrorism cycle," which also includes *Bombay*
(1995) and *Kannathil Muthamittal* (2002) has been the object of much
political analysis, with many critics seeing the early films as superficially
questioning nationalism and state power only to reaffirm them in terms
of neoliberal, consumerist individualism.[6] I agree, however, with Priya
Jaikumar's suggestion that the films' frequent references to Ratnam's
own Tamil culture and its political subordination to the North and the
Hindi language gives these films a deeply ambivalent perspective on
Indian assimilationism.[7] If the early films show a clear Hindu-centrist
bias, the last two films in the cycle are significantly more critical of Indian majoritarian culture.

While these films never repudiate the basic goals of Indian nationalism, their female characters embody cultural difference and stand as
powerful counterpoints to claims that the Indian state fosters multiculturalism. But their costumes also mark a range of issues central to
these narratives: resistance, exoticism, the controversial gender status of
female warriors, and the use of clothing to defy, disguise, and subvert social identity. In *Dil Se,* the heroine adopts the gender-neutral uniform of
a rebel warrior, becoming a tragic figure. In joining the battle to protect
her community's cultural and political autonomy the female terrorist
comes to represent the potential loss of tradition. These films ultimately

suggest that Indian secular nationalism has alienated cultural subgroups
and created a kind of internal neocolonialism. Women are central to that
critique, and Ratnam's work implicitly asks how the state can recognize
cultural difference within a framework that also grants women full civil
rights—an issue under intense debate with regard to Muslim women in
the period in which the films were made.[8]

ROJA: THE VILLAGERS STRIKE BACK

Anthropologists often point out how Indian women play a central role in
cultural maintenance, acting as "cultural and symbolic bearers of community identity."[9] This has long been particularly noticeable with regard
to dress codes and norms of "decency" or modesty. Similarly, in Indian
cinema a woman's character is often immediately indicated by the way
she dresses. The 1980s and '90s, however, saw an increased eclecticism in
Indian dress. Women's fashion began to reflect greater access to Western consumer goods, which also changed the representation of women
in film. Jyotika Virdi notes that in earlier Hindi films women were "set
up as repositories of an 'Indian' tradition to establish difference, even
superiority, over the west's material affluence"[10] but in the 1990s the film
heroine became a cosmopolitan consumer whose frequent costume and
location changes signified a new degree of autonomy.[11]

In *Roja*, costumes express the dual function described by Ann Rosalind Jones and Peter Stallybrass when they write that, while fashion
marks the rise of individualism, it also continues to refer to prior customs, costumes, and tradition. They distinguish between these two aspects of clothing by describing "fashion" as clothing that is detachable
from social identity, while clothing as "habit" continues to mark "identity, ritual, and social memory . . . a cultural way of life."[12] *Roja* take its
title from the heroine's name; she is a country girl (played by Madhoo)
who is first seen dressed girlishly in long skirts and *choli* blouses or in a
plain, saffron-colored sari (the symbolic color of Hinduism). She mar-
ries Rishi (Arvind Swami), an urbanite who works for the government
but has come to the village in search of a traditional wife. The contrast
between his modernity and her traditionalism is emphasized by their
first encounter: she is herding goats and sends them into the road to

block his car so she can look at him unseen from behind a rock. The scene privileges her appraisal and also sets up the contrast between Rishi's urbanism (she gasps when he lights a cigarette) and Roja's village life (the goats blocking the car).

The film continues to contrast the modern, secularized hero with Roja's simplicity and childlike religious devotion. Rishi works as a government cryptologist who is suddenly required to travel to Kashmir to help with the Indian military counterinsurgency, and Roja insists on coming with him. Kashmir was a common location for Indian honeymoons before the military conflict (tourism is now restricted), so the location of the couple's trip provides a highly nostalgic evocation of an earlier, undivided India. In a musical sequence set in the scenic Himalayas, Roja is first dressed in her traditional saffron sari, but Rishi wears a deep red sweater. Roja is then seen in a red, black, and gold sari or wrapped in a tribal blanket woven with the same colors of the mountain tribes. This is followed by a long shot of a group of women in tribal dress doing a folk dance around a bonfire at dusk framed by the mountains. In the final shots of the song, Roja wears either red or yellow and Rishi wears black or white, uniting the couple with the colors of the region.

By the end of the Kashmir honeymoon sequence, the film has established a framework of values embracing Rishi's modernity (education and professionalism) but also Roja's assertiveness and possession of cultural heritage (Rishi's boss has implored her to make his favorite traditional foods, while Rishi affectionately calls her "villager"). The synthesis formed by their marriage is placed in the context of a divided nation, however, and specifically in a landscape imbued with nostalgic associations with a part of India now off-limits due to the conflict. Kashmiri separatism is presented not just as a threat to national security, but as a symbol of cultural loss. In the film's next, pivotal scene, Roja sneaks out of the guarded hotel early in the morning to find a temple. She kneels and prays to the "Northern God," asking if he will convey her prayer to her God because "all Gods are the same."

But when she stands up to smash a coconut on the temple threshold (a traditional offering), guards quickly pull their guns, thinking a shot has been fired. Roja's line, "You can't even break a coconut here?" became well known as a comment on the extent to which militarization had displaced ritual norms in the region. As Rishi searches for her, ominous music builds and we see that his car is followed by a van full of militants. When he sees Roja and steps out of the car he's surrounded and taken captive while she runs helplessly after the van. The second half of the film details Roja's fight to get her husband released, but the militants insist that they will only release Rishi in exchange for a captive Muslim terrorist, Wasim Khan. The central figures in this half of the film are the commanding Muslim militant Liaqat Khan and his younger sister, who is unnamed (and uncredited) but central to the film's representation of the tribal community's ethnic specificity and visual exoticism.

The film introduces the space of the militant hideout in a long, labyrinthine tracking shot at dusk, accompanied by the oddly displaced music of the Bulgarian Women's choir. The music, like the ominous tones heard as the militants followed Rishi, clearly codes this community as alien and exotic. The camera winds its way up a narrow path bordered by stone walls, and armed soldiers occasionally step out to block its way and then step aside (it's not yet clear whose point of view the camera is conveying). Tense percussion plays under the Bulgarian choir and the camera finally enters a dark building lit only by oil lamps and shafts of light from Arabesque windows guarded by men wrapped in Pakistani headscarfs. This introduction to the hideout codes the militants' Islamic trappings as frightening and foreign. When the camera finally cuts away from the point-of-view shot, the reverse angle shows a trapdoor in the floor opening slowly, accompanied by a crescendo of suspenseful music—only to reveal a young woman in tribal dress carrying a plate of food. The next shot is from Rishi's point of view as he watches her slowly approach and place the food at his feet.

The sudden shift in tone when we discover that the long tracking point-of-view shot into this ominous space actually belonged to a young woman is underscored by the way she is dressed and lit. She wears a long, deep green *churidar* tunic but her headscarf is woven with red and gold thread, bordered with metal ornaments, and she wears two long braids and elaborate gold earrings that catch the light and make a tinkling sound when she moves. As she kneels to untie Rishi's feet and hands, their faces are framed together and he looks at her intently. Her shy gestures of subordination (kneeling, offering food) directly align her with Roja as the innocent female bearer of cultural tradition. After a short silence the sound of a single flute plays quietly, linking the woman to an exotic but pastoral tribalism. Scary music returns, however, when her brother Liaqat enters with an armed guard. When he sees that his sister has untied Rishi he slaps her face and Rishi yells (in Tamil and English) not to hit a woman. Throughout the rest of the film, Rishi's suffering during repeated beatings is always followed by reaction shots from Liaqat's sister, who never speaks but is clearly sympathetic. After Liaqat's younger brother's death in a politically motivated betrayal by the Pakistani army (to whom he was sent for training), Liaqat himself voices anguish over his inability to escape from the pointless proxy conflict that has now subsumed his community's struggle for political representation.

Roja, meanwhile, has been successful in her relentless fight to get her husband released by appealing to the fatherly impulses of a military minister, who orders a prisoner exchange between Rishi and Wassim Khan. Roja is presented as heroically determined and steadfast, but also naively self-interested; a military official gives her the news by describing the number of Indian soldiers who have died trying to capture Khan, who is also held responsible for countless other deaths. Roja's refusal to set aside her personal desires for the "good of the nation" is presented as childlike and selfish, but also emotionally justifiable. She, like the Kashmiri natives, lives in relation to her family and community and rejects the "imaginary community" of the Indian nation, which stands in direct conflict with her own loyalties. Roja and Liaqat's sister represent a village-based subjectivity that rejects both India's militarized national-security state and the local insurgency, in which the fighters have become pawns in the larger battles of Islamic fundamentalism and the India-Pakistan border. Liaqat's sister ultimately resolves the film's moral impasse by helping Rishi escape before Wassim Khan is released.

Most critiques of *Roja* have emphasized the way Roja is presented as morally flawed by her refusal to look beyond her own desires and consider the larger consequences of Khan's release. Nicholas Dirks argues, however, that Roja's position reveals deep rifts in the jingoist ideology of unquestioning nationalism: her "refusal to negotiate her emotional

13.1. Roja (*left*) and Liaqat Khan's sister (*top and right*) wear the same colors as they challenge state/tribal authority from subaltern positions.

demands with the state is presented as more than simple female intransigence and familial isolationism."[13] Moreover, though the motives of Liaqat's sister remain a mystery, "once again, the role of the woman has been to challenge the terms of the state (or counter-state)."[14]

At the end of the film Roja wears a deep green blouse under her red sari, and there is a cut from her to a close-up of Liaqat's sister, who continues to wear green but whose headscarf is woven with red and gold so that she and Roja are chromatically linked to one another and to the colors of the Indian nation (the white/green/orange of the flag and the green and red of military regalia). Liaqat's sister's lip is bleeding and the camera stays on her face as Liaqat, having just discovered that Rishi has escaped, continues to hit her several times. On one level the parallels between Roja and Liaqat's sister can be described as a cliché of feminine alliance (Roja plans, at one point, to search the local houses for Rishi, noting that there must be "a woman like me there" to help her), but I would argue that the film's (albeit ambivalent) critique of the militarized nation presents both Roja and Liaqat's sister as more than objects of pastoral nostalgia. Both women fight for their own principles, which are aligned with prenationalist cultural traditions and values. If the nation cannot exist without destroying those values, the film suggests, perhaps it ought to start losing a few border conflicts.

DIL SE: RETHINKING INDIAN NATIONALISM

Dil Se was Ratnam's first Hindi-language, big-budget film with a major international star. The film follows Amarkanth Varma (Shahrukh Khan), a journalist for All India Radio, as he arrives in Assam to ask local villagers how they feel about the upcoming fiftieth anniversary of Indian nationhood. The film stages his encounter and infatuation with a local woman named Meghna (Manisha Koirala), who, the viewer learns, is a member of the local separatist terrorist group. Assam has been the site of an armed separatist movement since the 1970s (there are seven states in northeast India that are ethnically and linguistically distinct; they are in various states of conflict with the national government, primarily over demands for greater self-governance). The film thus stages an encounter between Amar as a representative of the Indian national media (he is constantly identified with his network, All India Radio) and an indigenous woman who we finally learn has been so traumatized by the Indian military's counterinsurgency that she has sworn to become a suicide bomber. Visually, her clothing associates her with four different identities: her local identity as a young tribal woman; her exoticized image in the fantasy musical sequences; her gender-neutral appearance as a guerilla soldier; and her brief, transgressive appearance in the costume of a Hindu bride.

The film creates a split in our perception of Meghna between Amar's romantic fantasies and her own identity as a suicide bomber. It's never clear how much of Meghna's own desires are depicted in the romantic musical sequences, and her story is never fully narrated. As one reviewer noted,

> The dreamlike song "pictureizations," brilliantly choreographed by Farah Khan ... seem dissociated, even by Hindi-film standards, from the screenplay, further heightening the overall sense of dis-location, and suggesting the impossibility of realizing romantic fantasy in the midst of oppressive contemporary realities.[15]

This bifurcation of the film's perspective essentially splits Meghna into two different characters. One is Amar's fantasy of the exotic, non-Hindu peasant girl who must be rescued from "villains," seen primarily in the musical sequences where she enacts romantic longing and acquiesces to Amar's demands for her affection. The other is the Meghna of the non-musical narrative, who repeatedly rebuffs his advances but is relentlessly pursued by Amar. This bifurcation intensifies midway through the film when the audience sees her revealed as a member of the separatist militant army. The audience now knows, far more than Amar does, how vast is the gulf between his fantasy Meghna and the "real" one.

Amar first encounters Meghna in a scene of unveiling, a familiar Orientalist trope from the "Muslim social" genre, where a glimpse of the forbidden, veiled woman motivates the narrative. On a cold train platform at night, Amar is underdressed for the cold northern climate, and wears only a bright red woolen bomber jacket over a black shirt (Khan became known in his early career for wearing the latest western fashions in his films). Amar pulls out a cigarette, realizes that he has no match, and then sees a dark figure huddled under a blanket at the end of the platform. He calls out, under the assumption that the lone figure must be a man. Getting no response to his request for a match, Amar begins to pace the platform talking loudly to his unresponsive platform-mate.

He's interrupted by a particularly big blast of wind, and as he turns his back to it he sees (in the background, out of focus) that the blanket has blown away from the person ignoring him and that it's actually a woman. She is dressed in a deep red that matches Amar's jacket, and, in a medium shot we see that she is also beautiful. She clutches at the black blanket until she manages to wrap herself in it again; the red and black colors she wears are, as in *Roja,* associated with Northeastern tribal textiles. Amar's reaction is one not only of surprise but of utter captivation.

He walks slowly toward her and, as she pulls the blanket over the side of her face and turns away, he apologizes for thinking she was a man. He tries to flirt with her by talking incessantly in a silly, self-deprecating way that is part of the star's trademark boyishness. Meghna, however, is unresponsive and unsmiling. Finally she allows him to fetch her a cup of tea but then boards the next train and Amar watches, standing despondent in the rain, as she disappears.

This scene sets up the film's basic framework, which consists of Amar's intense and irrational infatuation, his utter miscomprehension of the people he has been sent to interview about the anniversary of nationhood, and the romantic tension between Amar and Meghna. Athough they wear identical colors, it becomes increasingly clear that he sees her as part of his "imagined community" of Indian national unity, and that this relationship with her is based on misrecognition.[16] In her daily life, Meghna wears a plain muslin *churidar* tunic and *dupatta* scarf woven in a local style, or a long black belted *churidar*. But in the musical scenes associated with Amar's fantasies of her, she wears highly fashionable saris, often with her scarf over her head, creating a montage of "Islamicate" femininity.[17] Interestingly, however, it's never clear if Meghna is Muslim or Buddhist (she prays at a Buddhist temple in one scene). Her "otherness" is simply associated with Islamic traditions, since, as Ananya Jahanara Kabir argues, Muslim-Hindu difference "remains the primary index whereby the mutual fascination of 'self' and 'other' is measured" in Indian culture.[18]

Following Amar and Meghna's encounter on the train platform, the film presents one of the most well-known Indian musical numbers of the 1990s, the song *Chaiyya Chaiyya*. The sequence features an odalisque-like dancer (Malaika Arora) in an elaborate dance costume of the same red and black worn by Amar. Her midriff is bare but her head is wrapped in an ornamented scarf, coding her as a non-Hindu. There is a cut to the front of the train, where Amar stands, backlit by the light at the end of the ravine as the train winds through the mountains into the liminal space of India's border. The sequence features elaborately colorful costumes that, as in *Roja*, emphasize the colors of that region, but combines them with the white tunics and male headscarves associated with Punjabi Sufism. Although Amar stands out in his casual western chic, his colors blend

13.2. Amar's utopian, color-coordinated dance in *Chaiyya Chaiyya* (*top*) and Meghna's rejection of his Orientalist gaze (*bottom*).

in with the carefully coordinated patchwork of color and texture worn by the local dancers as they sway and jump in rhythmic unison on the train. The song's joyfulness is further heightened by the constant movement of the train through dramatic mountain landscapes, shot from a variety of high and low angles. The use of a camera dolly to create swift movements among the dancers on top of the moving train creates a kinetic, Busby Berkely–like sense of liberation and coordination. Like the "honeymoon" in *Roja*, which reclaims the landscape of Kashmir for the audience's visual pleasure and nostalgia, *Chaiyya Chaiyya* presents the long-contested territory of northeast India as a happy land of indigenous beauty and folk culture.

According to Ananya Jahanara Kabir, *Chaiyya Chaiyya* is a popularized version of a traditional *quawwali* by Bulleh Shah, a Punjabi Sufi saint.[19] The song also includes an incantatory sequence during which Amar mimes the Muslim ritual prayer of *namaaz*. Kabir mentions the Muslim background of Shahrukh Khan, the choreographer Farah Khan, and the music director A.R. Rahman, wondering if this had some influence on the song's upbeat representation of Muslim practices. But the song's celebratory invocation of *namaaz* seems, as the film continues, more clearly to be simply part of "Amar's fantasy of the northeast."[20] While the secular Hindu hero of *Roja* is treated as a figure of enlightened modernity, Amar is quickly shown to be both naive and arrogant in his assumptions about center–periphery relations in India. Hinting at this, the happy vision of *Chaiyya Chaiyya* cuts to a shot of armed soldiers and barbed wire along the road Amar travels to reach his assignment.

Once Amar begins interviewing local residents it's clear how ignorant he is of the story he's been sent to cover. Standing in a field with an interpreter, he asks a boy who's harvesting crops, "What do you think of the last fifty years of India's independence?" The boy says "We don't have our freedom," and then becomes increasingly irate as Amar stands, looking baffled. In his next interview a middle-aged man explains how his village leaders have become increasingly powerful and simply extort funds from the villagers. Next Amar asks a young man if a free India has made any progress. He replies, "No. The central government threatens us and keeps us cowed down. Atrocities are inflicted on the poor and innocent. And you say we are free! Is this what freedom means?" The only positive response toward India Amar can find is from a few young children, who smile and say "India is the best!" in English. While Amar is later shown to be courageous in his questioning of the terrorist leader, he is also repeatedly shown to be arrogant and ignorant of the reality outside his narrow, Delhi-based existence (at one point his translator makes fun of him for being so excited about all the trees, effectively "provincializing" Amar's urbanity).[21]

Amar is next shown in the local radio studio, where he's offered the chance to tell stories on the air while the men normally on duty take the night off. What he narrates (accompanied by sound effects, music, and dramatic phrasing) is his first encounter with Meghna on the train platform. There is a cut to a shot of a radio in a local shop broadcasting the story and then one of a radio in Meghna's home, where she suddenly recognizes his voice. This sequence is highly reflexive in both form and content. Amar essentially re-enacts the opening of the film, complete with a musical interlude, and thereby positions himself as both author and subject of the film-as-romance. But his role as the personification of the Indian media (evident by his constant self-identification with All India Radio) is also highlighted, and the viewer is encouraged to see the disconnect between the previous scene in a separatist camp and Amar's own preoccupation with the romantic narrative. The film thus sets up a clear bifurcation between its political content, which Amar just doesn't get, and its romantic narrative, in which Amar is the heroically suffering figure of unrequited love (a role in which Shahrukh Khan has specialized). The film continues along this dual pathway, telling both Amar's story of obsessional love and Meghna's story of political strife. As Kabir notes, the film splits into "two superimposed narratives, corresponding to seeing-with-Amar and seeing-against-Amar."[22]

Both Amar's fetishizing gaze and the way that gaze stands in for the Indian national media is illustrated in the following sequence at a folk culture festival in Ladakh, where Amar arrives to record the performance. The dancers are elaborately costumed to display local customs and folkways of the remote Himalayan region, and they wear uniform smiles that make them look almost robotic in their slow, circling movements. Amar's presence, in Western clothing with his microphone and crew, makes the performers seem even more dehumanized, as if they function merely as the display of "acceptable" cultural difference presented for mainstream consumption, like an entertaining travelogue of the Orient. Similarly, throughout the film Amar interacts with a Meghna who is almost purely his own projection, and the viewer must continually negotiate between the two characters' realities. Amar's vision is dominant, while Meghna's is consistently disruptive.

For example, in one scene Amar walks past the door to a room where Meghna is bathing. The shot, reminiscent of countless Orientalist "bathing harem girl" paintings, begins in black as the door slowly opens as if by magic, and Amar, walking past, stops and looks down a dark passageway to the room's dimly lit interior. Meghna, sitting in the tiled pool in a room decorated with rich patterns and Buddhist icons, pours water over herself from a gold vessel. She sees Amar watching and stops. Her expression registers ambivalence, but as he takes a step closer and seems to threaten her privacy even more her face turns defiant, and she picks up the urn to pour more water over her head, staring back at him angrily. The split sensibility of the film thus not only draws attention to Amar's (and hence the media's) fetishizing gaze, it directly criticizes that vision by virtue of Meghna's reaction shot and her continual rejection of Amar. When he drags her into a Buddhist temple and demands that the monk marry them on the spot, she refuses him. He asks why and she says simply, "You never asked *me*." When he responds by proposing to her, she again refuses and states simply, "I don't have the time."

What neither the viewer nor Amar knows at that point is that she doesn't have time because she has pledged to execute a suicide bombing. Although the film only tells Meghna's story as a brief flashback to her childhood, those images (of her own and her sister's rape by Indian soldiers) are clearly intended to justify her rage against the Indian state and its army. As the film's narrative shifts to Delhi and Meghna is commanded to take advantage of Amar's attachment to her, it slowly dawns on him that there is more going on in her life than a battle of mixed feelings about him. Yet this interlude, in which Meghna and her comrade-"sister" live with Amar's family, is the only time Meghna's own commitment to her communal identity seems to waver. Amar's family has chosen a Delhi girl to be his wife (played by Preity Zinta), and in one scene the women gathered for the wedding put Meghna in front of a mirror and hold up the new bride's trousseau of jewels to see them on her. Amar and Meghna have just had a moment in hiding in which he once again declares his love and she weeps. He then walks past and sees her in the mirror "wearing" his new bride's ceremonial jewelry. In a subsequent song, one of the women places a *bindi* on Meghna's

13.3. Meghna as a Hindu bride (*top*) and Amar as he discovers her identity (*bottom*).

forehead, signifying Hindu marriage, and there is another exchange of tragic looks between Meghna and Amar as she is once again figured as the Hindu bride.

Similarly, Amar's moment of realization about Meghna's identity comes when he enters her room and discovers a headband of the type worn by the insurgent fighters. He finds it on a table in front of a mirror, and as he holds it up, stretched between his hands, he lifts it to the height of his own forehead so that we see him in the mirror "wearing" the headband. It's the moment at which the separate realities of Amar

13.4. Meghna's flashback to her militant training (*top*) and preparation for the suicide bombing (*bottom*).

and Meghna finally meet, and in these mirror images they momentarily exchange cultural identities: Meghna is seen as Hindu, Amar as a separatist. Yet when he confronts her and she tries to describe the atrocities suffered by her people (with her flashback superimposed over their conversation), Amar is still baffled, and she simply repeats, "You know nothing."

At that point, in Meghna's flashback there is a cut to a long shot of ranks of young women in camouflage uniforms, green bands tied around

their foreheads. They recite an oath of allegiance, which Meghna has earlier repeated with her comrades, which states that their people's independence is placed above all else: "We sacrifice our bodies for it, our dreams,
our souls." Meghna's sacrifice makes her unknowable because she has
given up her sense of self. Amar is deeply attracted to this absence; in one
early exchange Meghna asks him what he dislikes most about her and he
answers ". . . your eyes. Because I just can't read what's hidden in them,
however hard I try. Now let me tell you what I like most of all. Your eyes.
Because I can't read what's hidden in them. I really like that." But what
for Amar is mysterious allure is for Meghna a life sentence, the culmination of which is her real "bridal" moment when her female comrade
dresses her in front of a mirror with deliberate, ritualistic movements.
But instead of a wedding gown she wears the muslin body suit holding
the explosives that will kill her.

In contrast to Ratnam's earlier film *Roja, Dil Se* presents a clear critique of center–periphery relations in India (particularly with regard to
political and military corruption). But it also comments indirectly on the
problematic aspects of seeing "syncretic" folk culture as a substitute for a
truly democratic federalism.[23] The film's musical sequences continually
offer a form of exotic escapism that, while providing a range of pleasures
for the viewer, are also shown to be entirely out of step with the reality
presented in the narrative drama. Whereas *Roja* is centrist in its nationalism but sees cultural tradition as an alternative framework for identity,
Dil Se is far more critical of a nationalism that is shown to threaten indigenous cultures or reduce them to fantasies like those enacted in the
film's musical sequences.

Dil Se, while dealing explicitly with separatism in Assam and the
Northeastern border states, can also be read as implicitly addressing
India's ongoing battle with Pakistan over Kashmir. In the comments
following a review of *Dil Se* on a film blog, the viewer praises the film
and suggests that

> Amar's relationship with Meghna is also meant to parallel India's relationship
> with Kashmir: ie, he insists they're meant to be and refuses to let her have her
> independence. She wants to be free of him while being attracted to him, and is
> willing to use violence to get that freedom. In the end, since he refuses to let her
> go and she refuses to submit, they both destroy each other.[24]

While *Dil Se* doesn't describe what an inclusive but non-assimilationist Indian state would look like, it does represent the failure of India's militarized center–periphery politics.

Both *Dil Se* and *Roja* reject the repression of border cultures in the name of an ostensibly liberatory nationalist politics. But in addition, their emphasis on marginalized women who embody cultural traditions raises a question central to debates around multiculturalism in India at the time the films were made: how can minority women be liberated from traditions that may deny their human rights without suppressing the cultures they identify with? Ratnam's women stand between two kinds of subjectivity—the traditional and the modern—and these films question the way each position constrains their cultural "habits" and citizenship.

NOTES

1. Ananya Jahanara Kabir, "Allegories of Alienation and Politics of Bargaining," 141.

2. Sumita Chakravarti, *National Identity in Indian Popular Cinema, 1947–1987,* 288.

3. Jyotika Virdi, *The Cinematic ImaginNation,* 179.

4. Ranjani Mazumdar, *Bombay Cinema,* 221.

5. Kabir, 141.

6. These debates are summarized in Nicholas Dirks, "The Home and the Nation," 173–78.

7. Priya Jaikumar, "A New Universalism," 48. She notes that "Ratnam grew up during the height of the anti-Hindi movement in the South, so he did not have the opportunity to learn Hindi" (note 3).

8. In 1986 the controversial Muslim Women Act was passed, which legalized a double standard for Indian women's rights, with Muslim "personal law" granted authority above the constitutional rights that protected

Hindu women. Rajiv Gandhi's Congress Party, which was lobbied heavily by orthodox Muslim leaders, justified the Act in the name of the secular Indian state's recognition of multicultural practices. The Act was, in part, the result of a court case brought by a Muslim woman by the name of Shah Bano, and Ratnam's 1995 film *Bombay* features a Muslim heroine named Shaila Bano who defies her family to marry a Hindu man.

9. Caroline Osella and Filippo Osella, "Muslim Style in South India," 235.

10. Virdi, 207.

11. Emma Tarlo, *Clothing Matters,* 326.

12. Ann Rosalind Jones and Peter Stallybrass, *Renaissance Clothing and the Materials of Memory,* 5–6.

13. Nicolas Dirks, "The Home and the Nation," 174.

14. Ibid., 172.

15. Philip Lutgendorf, "Dil Se."

16. Benedict Anderson, *Imagined Communities: Reflections on the Origin and Spread of Nationalism.*

17. Kabir, 8.

18. Ibid.
19. Kabir, 7.
20. Ibid., 149.
21. Dipesh Chakrabarty, *Provincializing Europe*, 3–6.

22. Kabir, 152.
23. Peter van der Veer, *Religious Nationalism,* 199–201.
24. Posted anonymously on "Filmi Geek."

WORKS CITED

Anderson, Benedict. *Imagined Communities: Reflections on the Origin and Spread of Nationalism.* London: Verso, 1983.

Chakrabarty, Dipesh. *Provincializing Europe: Postcolonial Thought and Historical Difference.* Princeton, N.J.: Princeton University Press, 2000.

Chakravarti, Sumita. *National Identity in Indian Popular Cinema, 1947–1987.* Austin: University of Texas Press, 1993.

Dirks, Nicholas. "The Home and the Nation: Consuming Culture and Politics in *Roja.*" In *Pleasure and the Nation: The Politics and Consumption of Popular Culture in India,* ed. Rachel Dwyer and Christopher Pinney, eds., 161–186. Oxford: Oxford University Press, 2001.

"Filmi Geek." September 23, 2008. http://www.filmigeek.net/2006/11/dil_se_1997.html.

Jaikumar, Priya. "A New Universalism: Terrorism and Film Language in Mani Ratnam's *Kannathil Muthamittal.*" *Post Script* 25, no. 3 (2006): 48(17).

Jones, Ann Rosalind, and Peter Stallybrass. *Renaissance Clothing and the Materials of Memory.* Cambridge: Cambridge University Press, 2000.

Kabir, Ananya Jahanara. "Allegories of Alienation and Politics of Bargaining: Minority Subjectivities in Mani Ratnam's *Dil Se.*" *South Asian Popular Culture* 1, no. 2: 141–159.

Lutgendorf, Philip. "Dil Se." In *Philip's Filums: Notes on Indian Popular Cinema.* http://www.uiowa.edu/~incinema/index.html.

Mazumdar, Ranjani. *Bombay Cinema: An Archive of the City.* Minneapolis: University of Minnesota Press, 2007.

Osella, Caroline, and Filippo Osella. "Muslim Style in South India." *Fashion Theory* 11, no. 2/3: 233–252.

Tarlo, Emma. *Clothing Matters: Dress and Identity in India.* Chicago: University of Chicago Press, 1996.

van der Veer, Peter. *Religious Nationalism: Hindus and Muslims in India.* Berkeley: University of California Press, 1994.

Virdi, Jyotika. *The Cinematic ImaginNation: Indian Popular Films as Social History.* New Brunswick, N.J.: Rutgers University Press, 2003.

FILMOGRAPHY

Dil Se. Dir. Mani Ratnam. India Talkies and Madras Talkies, 1998.
Roja. Dir. Mani Ratnam. Madras Talkies (original Tamil version), Hansa Pictures (P) Ltd. (Hindi version), Kavithalayaa Productions (Telugu version), 1992.

PART FOUR

Epilogue: After Fashion

Fashion in Film honors E. Ann Kaplan for her contributions to film and media studies. In "Un-Fashionable Age: Clothing and Unclothing the Older Woman's Body on Screen," she offers afterthoughts for *Fashion in Film* about a huge lack in the cultural imagination that is reflected in cinema and in the cinema industry. Not only is there a dearth of good roles for older actresses, but those few roles often exhibit a failure of imagination in how to fashion them. At the end of a fashion cycle there is an almost ritualistic clearing of the closet, a purging of clothes deemed unfashionable to make way for new-fashioned costumes. The older actress (to use the here very appropriately gendered term) can also be subject to visual erasure even when she stars in a film. If she is playing an old lady, she is costumed unfashionably, the very clothes signifying the character's obsolescence. Conversely, she may be depicted as frantically covering up signs of age with wigs, makeup, surgical and latex adjustments—all to disguise the culturally distasteful sight of the old lady. Or perhaps she will take a comical or affectionately condescending role, and, if she wears current fashion, the costumes comment on the disparity between fashionable garb and unfashionable age. Kaplan examines two films that star older women, significantly films that are not American, to see how costume designers shape their characters and cameras shoot their bodies in ways that try not to deny their age but to explore it. Kaplan's epilogue to *Fashion in Film* calls for a recognition of the possibilities of inevitable age and demands for a unification of fashion's pleasures with roles for aging actresses.

FOURTEEN

Un-Fashionable Age:
Clothing and Unclothing the
Older Woman's Body on Screen

E. ANN KAPLAN

I am attached to my clothes and rarely give anything away. They have to be forcibly snatched from me when my closets overflow. I keep believing that I can still wear these clothes: I have several nice linen summer suits that on some days I think might still work, except that the padded shoulders don't look right. In fact, the jacket as a whole looks impossible! In other cases, the shoulders of jackets are no longer padded, but then the skirt is not narrowed in the way suit skirts are today. These suits should go. In other cases, given my age, I no longer wear suits with very short skirts. With dresses it's even worse: somewhere in the 1970s a kind of revived 1950s "New Look" was around and I bought several gorgeous dresses with tight waists and flared mid-calf-length skirts. But these don't look right today either. Yet I simply cannot give these dresses away. I won't even start talking about shoes; suffice it to say that piles of high-heeled shoes, some spiked, cram my closets, never to be worn again.

Several questions arise about what makes it so difficult to say good-bye to clothes that are now unwearable, not necessarily because they don't fit but because they are so far out of fashion. What does it mean to be out of fashion? How can I be fashionable in a situation when the fashion industry is not thinking about clothes appropriate for the older woman? Pamela Church Gibson, a sociologist, writing about fashion in Britain (she is one of the few scholars in Fashion Studies to raise issues of fashion and older women), notes the failure of fashion marketers to cash in on what would seem to be a perfect new clothes market niche for the growing number of older women freed to work because of the feminist movement.[1] And this is also the case in the United States. While stores like Chico's and Eileen Fisher attract older women, neither of their contrasting styles provides a solution. Chico's offers colorful, almost garish, outfits but relies less on *clothing* the older body than on *concealing* it. Baggy pants and roomy jackets distract the viewer from the older body through bright, often glossy materials. Eileen Fisher tries harder in regard to design, but the assumption has been that older women's bodies are matronly and ungainly, and must be swathed in flows of cloth. The fact that Fisher is currently rethinking her designs to accommodate younger customers does not do much for the older women she now leaves behind instead of rethinking new designs *for them*. Unfortunately, Fisher's move underscores the ageism that concerns me in this essay and that is often reflected in traditional costume design for older women on screen, to which I return below.[2]

Why be bothered by wearing something that no longer looks right, if I am not aiming to be fashionable? It seems that my worries have to do with not dressing according to the cultural norms about dress that unconsciously govern our fashion choices. To this extent, Roland Barthes is correct in seeing fashion as a sign system, proven by the fact that suits I keep appear to me no longer to "look right." The signifiers of fashion, Barthes tells us, are part of the physical world (the clothing content) while the signifieds (which become cultural norms) include, Barthes says, "romantic, nonchalant, cocktail party . . . feminine youth"—words found in fashion magazines.[3] These "signifieds" relating to romance and sexuality are perhaps what furnish worries about not being age-appropriate: older women signify as non-sexual within cultural norms, so an older woman wearing youthful clothes would seem to defy being age-appropriate and perhaps result (if not in ridicule) in at least raised eyebrows. While some older feminists may deliberately challenge age-appropriate dress, this takes a good deal of courage, as ethnologist Samantha Holland illustrated. Holland interviewed women between thirty and fifty about their conceptions of themselves through how they thought about femininity and dress from childhood through adolescence to young adulthood and finally aging.

relationship—older women engaged in romance with young men—still shocks the public in general, as well as shocking film audiences in the rare cases when such relationships appear on screen. (Mike Nichols's *The Graduate*, 1967, was a brave early attempt, but Mrs. Robinson [Anne Bancroft] is somewhat demonized.) Fashion and the body are central in these biases: at least in the West, the older woman's body is considered sexless, and without any possibility of being fashionable.[11]

Given these traditionally negative attitudes toward the older female body in Western culture and the close tie-in between Hollywood and the youth fashion market and audience, there have been few film narratives centering on older women except in the abject portrayals Brooks discusses, and therefore little need to discuss dress. The narrative function of women's clothes on film was traditionally linked to women's limited roles. Clothes represented older females as sexless and passively watching life go by rather than as objects of desire.[12] Early cinema, especially in the silent era, relied on clothing to designate normalized social roles. David Wark Griffith's films, such as *Birth of a Nation* (1915) and *Intolerance* (1916), set the stage with female images that became convention from then on. The middle-class mother's hair for decades had to be grey and scraped back in a bun, however young she implicitly was in the story. She had to be clothed in a black dress covering her ankles, often constantly wearing a white apron to designate her main domestic function. Women usually had a marginalized role (Lois Weber, an early female director, famously broke this rule, for example in her 1921 film *The Blot*, by making her women central and sympathetic if still fitting many conventions in regard to dress and subservience). A bit later, in the sound era, the mother—as exemplified by Mrs. Vale (Gladys Young) in *Now Voyager* (1942)—might appear in a grey dress with lace around the neck, but it still covered her entire form from ankle to neck. While by the '40s the mother role might be more central to the film, it was not usually a sympathetic one. Mrs. Vale is repressive, arrogant, and puritanical—pretty much the standard for the era. In addition, she was a foil for the daughter protagonist played so elegantly by Bette Davis, fulfilling another typical function of middle-class mothers in film.[13] Working-class mothers, meanwhile, looked untidy in shapeless dresses and took a backstage to their upwardly mobile daughters—see, for example, the mother and Stella (Barbara Stanwyck) in *Stella Dallas* (1937).

If older actresses were marginalized in classical cinema because appropriate roles were lacking, things are not much better in today's Hollywood, and only marginally improved in other national cinemas, which tend to follow Hollywood. (Documentary cinema is another matter altogether, and there is much to discuss in regard to films by one-time maverick directors like the Maysles brothers.)[14] Mass audiences are still not interested in positive or alternative narratives about older people: when elderly women are represented in Hollywood, they usually fall into (and are clothed according to) the old traditional stereotypes, like Jessica Tandy in *Driving Miss Daisy* (1989), or are made somewhat ridiculous, as in *Boynton Beach Bereavement Club* (2005).[15] Indeed, in the first decade of the new millennium, following Woodward's prediction, the older body is often eliminated on screen when designers make older actresses enact the "female masquerade" by dressing them either in an awkwardly youthful way, like Shirley MacLaine in *Rumor Has It . . .* (2001), or again insisting that the mother relinquish a central public role to her daughter, as in *Postcards from the Edge* (1990).[16] In considering images of older actresses in two films, I explore the efforts of designers and directors working against such practices and stereotypes.

FASHIONING OLDER WOMEN IN TWO FILMS

Two films about a love affair between an older woman and a younger man, from different national cinemas (Britain and France), enable me to compare and contrast national attitudes to the aging body as represented not only by the way older female protagonists are clothed but also by innovations on the part of designers and directors as regards imaging the older woman's *unclothed body*—an even more radical and rare image. Given the close links between Hollywood and fashion, and the obsession of the fashion industry with the thin young body, the older woman's body (whether in masquerade or not) offers challenges to the designer. What meanings in defining subjectivity can we deduce from the older actresses' clothes? How did costume designers think about dress for the various scenes with their protagonists?[17] Specifically, how far is the attitude the film takes toward the unconventional love affair represented in costume or in images of the naked body? In what ways does each designer work with or against traditional national stereotypes of older women by refusing to "eliminate" this body (either through the female masquerade or through roomy, oversized clothes)?

Neither of these two films could have been made in Hollywood, although, as the boomer generation ages, one would hope that Hollywood will change. In the case of British Roger Michell's *The Mother* (2003), the affair between a middle-aged grandmother and her daughter's much younger lover would have given Hollywood directors pause; in the case of Josée Dayan's French film, *Cet Amour-là* (*This Love—As It Is,* 2001), it is not only the age gap between a much older woman (Marguerite Duras played by Jeanne Moreau) and her very young lover, Yann Andréa (played by Aymeric Demarigny), but also the fact that Moreau was already in her eighties when she took the part: this might have worried Hollywood, but was acceptable to French director Dayan. Moreau has been exemplary in taking on roles for much older women—roles which are far more available in foreign films than in Hollywood. She has not been afraid to age on film, and in one remarkable film, *La Vielle qui Marchait dans la Mer* (1991), even allowed photos of her young self to become part of the plot.

Costume in *The Mother* has an obvious narrative function in signifying the protagonist May's transformation from a woman who sees herself as old (although she is only middle-aged) and who has accepted a passive retired life with Toots (her older, frail husband) to a woman with renewed energy, vitality, and autonomy inspired by the passionate love affair with her daughter's young lover. While the costume semiology is perhaps predictable, it serves its purpose. It is how the designer, Natalie Ward, works with May's naked (or near naked) body that may be as important as what she does with costume in challenging the "fashionability" of the older body on screen. She clearly thought carefully about how to dress May and use costume to signal changes in subjectivity. Ward chose a bland, washed-out grey/white as the first costume color scheme to represent how British society situates May as old, and how May in turn sees herself. May's styles in the first scenes fit her self-perception: she wears shapeless pants, loose top, and bulky raincoat. In short shrift, the

14.1. May in the bland clothes she wears as a desexualized older woman before her affair and after it is discovered.

director and screenwriter capture England's required early retirement policies, with middle-class couples like May and Toots living in a neat, nicely furnished semi-detached house on a quiet street in the suburbs where there is little to do, not much of a community, and where the days stretch endlessly, especially for couples like this one, who are already alienated from one another.

May's first costume—the off-white raincoat and pants—is a kind of uniform for middle-aged middle-class women analogous to the "uniform" Pamela Gibson described upper-class older women using to avoid the whole problem of being "fashionable."[18] May's hair is lank and unstyled. The drab clothing is a sign of May's lifelessness, lack of interest in the world, and resignation to her invisibility as wife of a retired office worker. Once her husband dies, May insists on living in London with her children, and her clothes at first remain much the same. However, she begins to wear skirts instead of pants, and her hair begins to look more styled, less limp. The main clothing transformation occurs after the first sexually charged meetings with Darren, her daughter's lover. For the first time, May shows interest in how she looks. We see her posing in front of a mirror, surveying her face and hair, and now dressed in a bright

14.2. May tying on a bright orange scarf signifying her growing attraction to her daughter's lover.

blue jacket with a dramatic orange scarf swung with panache around her neck. Her hair is styled and attractively arranged. The designer here allows her heroine to revert (as her daughter notes) to a kind of 1960s look (anti-fashion, as it were); she dresses May colorfully while not aspiring or pretending to make her fall in step with any idea of fashionable youthful beauty. In other words, Natalie Ward has the heroine select an earlier youthful fashion that appeals to May rather than having her adopt the sort of current styles that we see May's daughter (and daughter-in-law) wearing in the film. In scenes where May prepares lunches for Darren, her new subjectivity is expressed in the long white flowing skirt she wears, suggesting freedom of movement, an opening up, while the close-fitting white blouse reveals her shape.

May's growing sexual desire for Darren is communicated to viewers as May watches him at his workbench, his pants slipping down and prompting her sexual arousal. Michell here not only reverses the infamous "male gaze" but makes an older woman the subject of this gaze instead of its abject object.[19]

We do not expect a sixty-plus, widowed woman to feel powerful sexual desire, especially for a man nearly half her age, and if an older woman felt such desire, one would certainly not expect her to act on it. Yet Michell and scriptwriter Kureishi manage to make May's desire seem normal, and, as such, the team challenges prevailing concepts of what is appropriate for whom at what chronological age, yet without making May's desire grotesque. This does not mean that viewers accept or like what they see: formal and informal internet reviews reveal that the cultural codes audiences bring to the film often prevent them from valuing what Kureishi and Michell are doing. For example, one reviewer mocks May as a "sexagenarian," while another, Dennis Lim, writing for *The Village Voice*, sees May as "co-opting her kids' me-me-me ethos. . . ." May's "sweet-old-lady disposition is deceptive," Lim says, and her "viperish potential flickers to the surface in a remarkable scene at Paula's writing group."[20] Clearly, audiences have trouble when May violates the standards of behavior they expect from older women on screen. They view what she does as age-*inappropriate*—behavior that is not expected of her at her age.

Viewers watching *The Mother* are pushed to see beyond the familiar images of popular culture, with complex results. A later scene, when the two age-mismatched characters make love, provides another opportunity for the directing team to challenge stereotypes of the aging body, nakedness, and sex. Since older women are not associated with sexuality, the team faced the issue of how to represent a sexual encounter between an older woman and a younger man. While everyone's body changes in predictable ways as they age, for women, nudity is governed by ideals of the smooth, graceful, and taut body. This ideal female body, passed down from Greek culture and manifested in Western sculpture and the nude in classic painting, is still perhaps what film viewers unconsciously expect to see in sex scenes. Older bodies lose their shape; skin is no longer taut; breasts droop; veins stick out. One might find beauty in such older bodies in lived reality, but our culture would have to change its visual norms (and related unconscious fantasies) before such bodies would be acceptable on screen.

In the sex scenes in *The Mother*, we realize that May is a large woman, but Michell at first refrains from shooting her naked body in full light. Rather, the director softens the scene through careful lighting, the grey/white colors in the room, and the soft curtains blowing in the breeze. Showing her internalized stereotypes, May asks if Darren sees

14.3. May and Darren after sex.

what she thinks she is, namely "a shapeless old lump." He shakes his head. We cut to a deliberately blurred image of the lovers in bed. Perhaps Michell wanted to bring viewers gently into this "taboo-bashing" (as reviewers put it) part of the story. May says she thought "no one would ever touch her again except the undertaker" as Darren brings her to orgasm. In the post-coital sequence, Michell dares to show May in bright light, revealing her bosom as she sits happily in bed talking to (and seemingly admiring) Darren's muscular form as he stands in the room. As the narrative develops, the directing team's nerves perhaps fail (losing sympathy, they show May becoming a kind of sex addict, shamelessly pleading with Darren for sex), and the designer uses clothing once again to signal May's changing sense of herself and her new subjectivity by putting her in long white skirts. Once the illicit relationship is exposed, May returns to her earlier passive self, dressed again in the bland and shapeless beige pants and bulky raincoat she wore when she first entered her son's house—only now she is not asexual but, inevitably, shamed.

Surprisingly, however, once back home, May eventually rallies: we first see her sitting in her drab gray clothes, head down on the table, facing her dead husband's slippers. But she does not want to remain in her

14.4. May, in bright blue, sets off to new adventures.

suburban house defined as "old." Once again, she changes, and clothes signify yet a new subjectivity: the last shots show May leaving on a trip to Europe, dressed in bright blue, scarf once again waving in the wind, as she steps in a lively manner down the road.

The contrast with Josée Dayan's film, *Cet Amour-là,* is striking, partly because of national difference and because the latter film (based on the novel of the same name by Yann Andréa) deals with the last sixteen years of the famous and prolific activist/writer Marguerite Duras and her lover, Yann Andréa, a much longer and more complex relationship.[21] Also significant, while May's affair takes place subversively when she is living with her family and engaged in their world, the affair between Duras and Yann takes place in isolation from friends and family, within the confines of Duras's apartment by the seaside outside of Paris and in her country house. Whereas in Mitchell's film May starts out as a typical middle-class older British woman, Moreau plays Duras as she reportedly was in her late years, an eccentric French woman perhaps more comparable to the British Iris Murdoch than to May. The comparison only underscores how very French Duras's eccentricity is, at least if you draw on a sense of French culture from the 1960s to 1990s. Her utter disregard for public opinion, her *savoir faire* in regard to sex, her determination to live her life for herself—for writing—seems, if not quintessentially French, at least stereotypically Parisian. As Susan Sontag noted, French culture has always seemed more open than Anglo society to women's participation in art and culture, at least until the Women's Movement closed the gap.[22] Indeed, one might argue that women in North America and England needed the Women's Movement in regard to visibility in the arts world more than the French because women were less accepted as intellectuals and artists in the public sphere.[23]

Unlike May, the protagonist in *Cet Amour-là* has enjoyed free sex with different men and women over her long life. Sexual repression is not the issue for her. The issue, rather, is loneliness (something she shares with May, although each experiences it differently). She is living alone and nearing seventy years of age when a twenty-eight-year-old man, Yann Andréa, turns up on her doorstep. Yann is a fan who feels himself to be Duras's soul mate, having read everything Duras has written and having sent letters to her every day for over two years.

The challenge for designer Mimi Lempicka was how to dress such an eccentric older woman and how to use the clothes to convey the different stages and rhythms of the complex, fraught relationship, with the added complication that (for good or ill) she could not avoid taking into account what was known and seen about Duras's actual clothes. Photos of Duras in volumes by Gabrielle H. Cody, Laura Adler, and others show a glamorous, sexy young woman, clearly fashion-conscious in silk blouse, draped skirt, or casual linen dress, and high heeled, open-toe shoes, bracelet and rings added for effect. As this clearly fashionable young woman aged she continued to dress elegantly, now often in dark colors but always with a scarf draped under and down from her collar, or tucked in around her neck. Images also reveal that she often wore a comfortable waistcoat over a cardigan. Usually, but not always, she is wearing streamlined pants: one image close to her death in 1995 shows her in a sweater, smock, and skirt with Scottish design, complemented by boots.

While Lempicka could freely draw on clothing information from photographs and interviews with Duras, there was still the problem of how to film Moreau's clothed body on the screen. An interesting strategy—a sort of corollary to Natalie Ward's idea in *The Mother*—is to focus less on Moreau's body as a whole than on her fascinating older face. Much of the time she is shot from the waist up. One might think that a director would want least of all to focus on such a face, but the designer (perhaps working with Dayan) bravely chose to make Moreau's remarkable visage the object for the audience's gaze. For viewers, this is a welcome change from the plastic, smoothed-out faces of Hollywood with not a line in view or a hair out of place. Instead of participating in the feminine masquerade, the director makes Moreau's older face the object for the audience's gaze without making it over to conform to artificially youthful norms. This is precisely what is essential if Western consciousness about what constitutes feminine beauty is to change. Our reward is seeing Moreau's face convey many emotions: impatience, desire, love, pleasure, frustration, fear, anger. As we see her raising her eyebrows, frowning, pouting, lowering her eyes, or smiling, the character's feelings emerge clearly and the viewer is enthralled.

Moreau is unusually fortunate amongst actresses for being able to play roles appropriate to her age—a result of working in France rather than in the United States. French directors are prepared to make films about older women, and Moreau is the perfect actress for them. Dayan's film studies the intense, conflicted, and remarkable love affair between two people separated in age by nearly forty years—a distance in time and experience quite common (as we know) for affairs between older men and younger women but so rarely seen between lovers like these. The resulting claustrophobic atmosphere conveys the symbiotic intense nature of the almost too close relationship.

At the first meeting, Yann is dressed in black, while Duras, shot from the waist up—as she will be most of the time—looks elegant in a navy blue jacket in soft material, collar stylishly turned up, with a black and white striped sweater that sits well with her shortish blonde hair, cut away from her face. She looks appropriate for her age of sixty-six years, the clothes neither fitting too close nor wide and flowing à la Eileen Fisher. The clothes communicate confidence, sharpness, and vitality, helped by Moreau's use of her body and especially her face to signal independence, with gaze hurried as she examines the young man. Once again, the female protagonist renders the male the object of her gaze.

14.5. A carefully dressed Duras meets Yann for the first time.

Ironically, it is Yann's clothes that come under scrutiny from Duras, who objects to his suit made of flannel material. Shortly after this, in one of the few scenes of the couple outside, and even fewer long shots of Duras, we find the two walking on the boardwalk near the beach. Duras is dressed in soft brown jacket and tan pants with a large brown and white checked umbrella matching her tan blouse flecked with brown. Soon the camera closes in for the usual medium shot. The next several scenes show Duras and Yann working together on her books. Duras wears her black leather sleeveless jacket and a white blouse reminiscent of photos of the historical Duras; Yann at first appears in white or dark blue. Later, their clothes become darker. The words Duras speaks are of death and love as death, so their clothes and the darkly lit space are fitting. Often the camera closes in on Moreau's face as she ponders her next thought. In a second scene outdoors which includes another long shot of the couple, Moreau is dressed in dark pants and coat with a stunning long purple scarf hanging around her neck and down the back as she walks at a lively pace to the bar, where they drink and dance to one of her favorite 1930s Edith Piaff songs, "La Vie en Rose" (this song, together with Hervé Vilard's 1965 "Capri, C'est Fini,"[24] dominate the deliberately sentimental soundtrack). This is one of several romantic scenes between the lovers, when Moreau conveys sexuality, allure—very much against the stereo-

14.6. Duras and Yann stroll on the Boardwalk.

type of the older woman who is presumed to be beyond sex—and Yann conveys love and adoration.

Soon after this trip, Duras throws Yann out of her flat—something that happens more than once. She can't stand their intimacy, she says to Yann's astonished gaze. Later on, Yann starts going out and staying away overnight. In one scene, as Duras waits for him, drinking, she wears a bright red drape over her dark shirt, making a striking contrast. Her bright red lips and white face suggest anger, resentment, if not rage at his cavalier behavior. Red clothing will from this point on be used artfully to convey both Duras's vitality and sexuality and her frustration and rage—which are, perhaps, just the dark side of her vitality. Toward the end of the film, when Duras's alcoholism becomes more serious, the designer softens Moreau's clothing to reflect her new vulnerability—a vulnerability which, while it indeed led her to admit Yann into her life in the first place, she has tried to deny for much of the film. Moreau is dressed in a soft navy blue blouse with a large white chiffon scarf around her neck and draping down from her shoulders on each side. Her face now looks thin and sad, her hair disheveled; her body is all but dominated by the scarf. She tries to dance with Yann and they embrace tenderly. The camera stays at waist level so that the scarf is in full view all the time. She talks of death and rejects the possibility of love—her common theme of

14.7. Duras in white scarf signifying death.

course—and almost predicts falling ill. She collapses during the night, dressed now in grey. The next morning, Duras is at work again, and the designer has chosen a large bright red scarf atop the blue blouse to signify Duras's determination to finish her book before going to the clinic for detoxification. Once again the camera stays waist high before closing in for another embrace with Yann. As illness increases, so tenderness between the two flourishes: the relationship becomes understandably less sexual and more familial so that the always underlying mother–son figuration of the pair now takes precedence over romance.

The color scheme for the entire clinic episode is mainly white or grey-white, as also in the house when Duras feels ill. Yann wears a white shirt, sometimes covered with his black jacket, and Duras wears white or off-white. Here white connotes something quite different from the drab off-white used in *The Mother* to convey May's depressive lack of self-confidence. In Dayan's film, white suggests thoughts of death, the afterworld, as it becomes unlikely that Duras will ever fully recover. On their return home, the bright splash of green as the camera caresses the trees around Duras's house suggests life and vitality: soon Duras is at work again wearing her classic white blouse and sleeveless black leather jacket or the blue blouse now with small blue neck scarf. The camera remains closed in on Duras's face or body waist up, as it has been for most of the film. In episodes where Duras hallucinates she wears grey or white; during the day, she often wears bright colors, sporting a red scarf or shawl, a blue sweater. Still, we only see her from the waist up. As her death draws near, perhaps prompting thoughts again of the afterworld, Duras takes to her bed in white, with the white chiffon scarf around her neck. She now faces a place beyond color, beyond fashion. Yann, dressed in dull green, tries to comfort her. In our last shot of her, she is all in white, arms clutched around her body, insisting on dying alone.

While my analysis of both films has studied the way designers use fashion to express the development of the relationship between an older woman and a young male lover (or, in the case of *Cet Amour-là*, the rhythms, style, and conflicts between lovers over time) I have also shown how these European films, if in different ways linked to national context, have shown that "unfashionable age" can be, in fact, "fashionable," both in the sense of conveying a plausible and acceptable love relationship— older women can be sexual on screen—and in the sense of carrying off aesthetically pleasing clothing. Both heroines defy dress codes that would render them colorless, background to the action, essentially invisible. Instead, they are clothed in ways that communicate their changing subjectivities as their life situations change. Each refuses to accept that any dress other than blandness is age-*inappropriate*. In other words, the films resist the entire concept of screen heroines (or people offscreen for that matter) needing to follow the kind of "age-appropriate" code described by sociologists like Holland. The designers dress May and Duras according to prevailing subjectivities at a particular moment in the narrative, illustrating Wilson's notion that fashion (and anti-fashion as well) enables people to find a coherent though changing subjectivity. As May becomes sexual, so her dress reflects that. As Duras, who has all along expressed herself in dress though she lives away from the public eye, changes—as her moods change, as her feelings toward Yann Andréa change, as her health changes—so does her dress. These films show that older women's dress can be "fashionable" in that it can express their emotions and being. In a different sense, their dress is "anti-fashion" in the sense of moving beyond the normative fashion cycle of designers. In other words, while the literal body of each figure remains the same, each costume designer selects clothes to construct an identity fitting for a particular activity or situation, or to communicate a particular set of emotions.

I have shown that the designers and directors broke the unfashionable age syndrome by not covering up the older woman's body. Rather, Michell allows this body to be shown during sexual intercourse in the case of May, and Dayan focuses for much of her film on the older actress's face. Women, indeed, in these films "wear their bodies through their clothes."[25] Clothes shape and reveal their changing subjectivities, attesting to the importance of dress in asserting and communicating selfhood. To call older women "unfashionable" is only to make the very superficial claim that older women do not fit into current concepts of the ever-changing fashion cycle designed for young women. Once they can refuse to be awed by youth-centered fashion cycles, older women can and do fashion themselves.

A glimpse of prevailing attitudes in the fashion world may be seen in Eileen Fisher's statements about her work. She claims a new awareness of how her styles have been viewed by "the fashion conscious," as "designed for graying bobos who dabbled in ceramics and had lifetime subscriptions to the *New Yorker*." A graduate student interviewed by the *New York Times* says Eileen Fisher's shift is intended to change the concept of her styles as "for an older generation—sort of an upscale Gap."[26] This view reflects the ageism I have been discussing; Fisher seems interested in changing her styles to attract younger customers rather than in designing hipper clothes appropriate for women over fifty (the hurdle of designing for women over seventy is yet to come). Nowhere does Fisher declare her interest in thinking through fashionable yet appropriate designs for the older woman.

So it is left up to us—at least for now. How helpful, then, is my holding on to my old clothes? The problem with aging may be too *much* holding on to the past. At the end of *The Mother*, May puts on colorful clothes and sets out to make a new life for herself. And in *Cet Amour-là*, Duras is dressed with flair to the end, but never seeks to look younger than she is. Perhaps for me the best thing is to forget about my younger self, forget about feet that could fit into sleek high heels, and try something original. The problem will be avoiding the female masquerade, the imbalance that happens when an obviously older woman puts on a dress made for a young adult. Taking these concerns into account, older women have to set the pace with their own creativity about dress. We should not worry about our shape or having the prescribed curves. We have to dress smartly (or not), colorfully (or not) and in what pleases us now. Our focus should be on our sense of what identity we want to express through our clothes—an identity we can own, not one prescribed by an ageist culture. In finally letting go of my old clothes, I intend to create outfits for any subjectivity I want for any activity or situation. I aim to enjoy my current creativity and to give away the younger self locked in my closets.

NOTES

1. Pamela Church Gibson, "Invisible Women."

2. See Ruth LaFerla, "Eileen Fisher's Shifting Silhouette." I will return to this article at the end of the essay.

3. Roland Barthes, *The Language of Fashion,* 42. Throughout the book, Barthes simply assumes that all fashion has to do with young women and their youthful activities.

4. Samantha Holland, *Alternative Femininities,* 127. See Holland's bibliography for details of research quoted. Her final chapter, "Defying the Crone?" is especially relevant to the topic of fashion for older women.

5. Ibid., 2

6. Elizabeth Wilson, *Adorned in Dreams,* 11.

7. Margaret Gullette, "The Other End of the Fashion Cycle," 35–36.

8. Joanne B. Eicher and Mary Ellen Roach-Higgins, "Dress, Gender and Age," 102. I do not see here, however, any criticism of why we need to learn such norms, nor why we need to adhere to them.

9. Jodi Brooks, "Performing Aging/ Performance Crisis," 233.

10. See my 1997 essay, E. Ann Kaplan, "Resisting Pathologies of Age and Race."

11. While this paper is limited to considering women in European and American film, it would certainly be interesting to compare the problems of the older woman's body, fashion, and sexuality in Western and non-Western cultures.

12. In their essay "The Role of Clothing," Jane Workman and Kim Johnson support my notion about stereotypes, dress, and ageism. They note,

> Stereotypes can be traced to a variety of highly visible and distinctive personal appearance characteristics, such as gender, clothing, hair color, height, or weight. An elderly person's appearance because it is distinctive may contribute to the formation and perpetuation of stereotypes.... [Stereotypes] allow people to simplify information and speed mental processes. However, stereotypes may also modify interaction and bias the interpretation of behavior. (129)

In the rest of this brief essay, they note studies of elderly persons in cartoons, magazine ads, and TV programs. These media "serve as effective transmitters of false, but pervasive, stereotypes concerning elderly persons" (130).

13. See E. Ann Kaplan, *Motherhood and Representation* for details of these roles.

14. See for example their film about the eccentric relatives of Jacqueline Kennedy, *Grey Gardens.* These fascinating aging women lived in increasing disarray and isolation, very much fitting the "witch" and "crazy" images noted by Holland in her research on *Alternative Femininities* (see below). As Holland shows, it is extremely difficult to view alternative lifestyles without finding oneself employing a stereotype that empties the originality of its originality!

15. I should note that *Boynton Beach Bereavement Club,* made by a female director (Susan Seidelman), at least shows affection and empathy for the older characters seeking love in their so-called "twilight" years, suggesting hope that film portrayals of older people are evolving over time, and might evolve further with an increase in female directors.

16. Shirley MacLaine in *Rumor Has It* (2001) plays the heroine's grandmother refusing to be called "grandma" and looking like the heroine's sister! Michelle Pfeiffer in *I Could Never Be Your Woman* (2007) is another good example of an actress who is made to look far too young for her supposed age. Believability aside, it is once again a woman director, Amy Heckerling, who broaches the theme of an older woman falling for a young man. However, this affair soon ends; Heckerling in the end seems to accept rather than challenge normative conceptions of older woman / younger man romance.

17. I had wanted to interview the two costume designers involved in the two films to be discussed below, but unfortunately I could not get in touch with them.

18. Gibson, 80.

19. See Laura Mulvey, "Visual Pleasure and Narrative Cinema"; and E. Ann Kaplan, "Is the Gaze Male?"

20. See E. Ann Kaplan, "The Unconscious of Age," for more discussion of reviews of *The Mother* that provide evidence for viewers' difficulties in accepting the older woman / younger lover relationship.

21. This novel should not be confused with the novel Duras herself wrote in 1982 after meeting and living for a couple of years with Yann. Duras's novel is called *Yann Andréa Steiner. A Memoir,* Duras adding to Yann's actual name a surname she had used before with fictional characters.

22. Susan Sontag, "Rélexions Sur La Libération des Femmes."

23. The question of what kind of writing women were trained to undertake, and what sorts of literature by women were acceptable in the public sphere is another issue. Elaine Marks's influential edited volume, *New French Feminisms,* brings together many complaints by French intellectual women about the way patriarchal concepts long dominated the arts in France—a domination the writers hoped to change. On the other hand, while de Beauvoir's *The Second Sex* predated feminist writings in the U.K. and United States, it was taken up with far more alacrity in the latter nations, apparently striking a deeper chord than in France. Paradoxically, as a result, on political, economic, and professional levels women in the United States moved ahead faster than in France. See Sontag's interviews in Leland Poague, ed., *Conversations with Susan Sontag.*

24. While Piaff is well known, Hervé Vilard is less often cited. This song, "Capri, C'est Fini," hit the French charts in 1965, and is mainly what Vilard is known for.

25. J. Craik, *The Face of Fashion,* 2.

26. Both quoted in Ruth La Ferla, "Eileen Fisher's Shifting Silhouette."

WORKS CITED

Barthes, Roland. *The Language of Fashion.* Trans. Andy Stafford, ed. Andy Stafford and Michael Carter. New York: Berg, 2006.

Brooks, Jodi. "Performing Aging/Performance Crisis." In *Figuring Age: Women, Bodies, Generations,* ed. Kathleen Woodward, 232–47. Bloomington: Indiana University Press, 1999.

Craik, J. *The Face of Fashion: Cultural Studies in Fashion.* New York and London: Routledge, 1994.

de Beauvoir, Simone. *The Second Sex.* New York: Alfred A. Knopf, 1952.

Duras, Margaret. *Yann Andréa Steiner: A Memoir.* Trans. Barbara Bray. New York: Scribner, 1993.

Eicher, Joanne B., and Mary Ellen Roach-Higgins. "Dress, Gender and Age." In *Dress and Identity,* ed. Mary Ellen Roach-Higgins, Joanne B. Eicher, and Kim K. P. Johnson, 101–105. New York: Fairchild Publications, 1995.

Gibson, Pamela Church. "Invisible Women, Ageing and Fashion." In *Fashion Cultures: Theories, Explorations, Analysis,* ed. Pamela Church Gibson and Stella Bruzzi, 79–89. New York and London: Routledge, 2001.

Gullette, Margaret. "The Other End of the Fashion Cycle." In *Figuring Age: Women, Bodies, Generations,* ed. Kathleen Woodward, 34–58. Bloomington: Indiana University Press, 1999.

Holland, Samantha. *Alternative Femininities: Body, Age, Identity.* Oxford and New York: Berg, 2004.

Kaplan, E. Ann. "Is the Gaze Male?" In *Women and Film: Both Sides of the Camera,* 3–15. London and New York: Routledge, 2000 [1983/1978].

———. *Motherhood and Representation: The Mother in Popular Culture and Melodrama.* New York and London: Routledge, 2000 [1992].

———. "Resisting Pathologies of Age and Race: Menopause and Cosmetic Surgery in Films by Rainer and Tom." In *Reinterpreting the Menopause,* ed. Philippa Rothfield and Paul Komorasoff, 100–26. New York: Routledge, 1997.

———. "The Unconscious of Age: Performances in Psychoanalysis, Film and Popular Culture." In *Age on Stage,* ed. E. Ann Kaplan, Valerie K. Lipscomb, and Leni Marshall. New York: Palgrave, forthcoming.

La Ferla, Ruth. "Eileen Fisher's Shifting Silhouette." *New York Times,* October 11, 2009: ST1.

Marks, Elaine, ed. *New French Feminisms: An Anthology.* New York: Schocken Books, 1981.

Mulvey, Laura. "Visual Pleasure and Narrative Cinema." First published in *Screen* 16, no. 1 (Winter 1975): 6–18.

Poague, Leland A. *Conversations with Susan Sontag.* Jackson: University Press of Mississippi, 1995.

Roach-Higgins, Mary Ellen, Joanne B. Eicher, and Kim K. P. Johnson, eds. *Dress and Identity.* New York: Fairchild Publications, 1995.

Sontag, Susan. "Rélexions Sur La Libération des Femmes." *Les Temps Modernes* (1972).

———. "Third World Women." *Partisan Review* 40 (1973): 180–206.

Wilson, Elizabeth. *Adorned in Dreams: Fashion and Modernity.* 2nd Edition. New Brunswick, N.J.: Rutgers University Press, 2003.

Workman, Jane, and Kim Johnson. "The Role of Clothing in Perpetuating Ageism." In *Dress and Identity,* ed. Mary Ellen Roach-Higgins, Joanne B. Eicher, and Kim K. P. Johnson, 129–38. New York: Fairchild Publications, 1995.

FILMOGRAPHY

Birth of a Nation. Dir. David W. Griffith. Costumes, Robert Goldstein, Clare West. David W. Griffith Corp, Epoch Producing Corporation, 1915.

The Blot. Dir. Lois Weber. Lois Weber Productions, 1921.

Boynton Beach Bereavement Club. Dir. Susan Seidelman. Costumes, Sarah Beers. Now Productions USA, 2005.

Cet Amour-là. Dir. Josée Dayan. Costumes:Mimi Lempicka. Canal+ and Les Films Alain Sarde, 2001.

Driving Miss Daisy. Dir. Bruce Beresford. Costumes, Elizabeth McBride. Majestic Film International, 1990.

The Graduate. Dir. Mike Nichols. Costumes, Patricia Zipprodt. Embassy Pictures Corporation, 1967.

Grey Gardens. Dir. Ellen Hovde, Albert Maysles, David Maysles. Portrait Films, 1975.

Grumpy Old Men. Dir. Donald Petrie. Costumes, Lisa Jensen. Warner Bros., 1993.

I Could Never Be Your Woman. Dir. Amy Heckerling. Costumes, Shay Cunliffe.

Bauer Martinez Entertainment, 2007.

Intolerance. Dir. David W. Griffith. D.W. Griffith Corp, 1916.

The Mother. Dir. Roger Michell. Costumes, Natalie Ward. BBC Films, 2003.

Now Voyager. Dir. Irving Rapper. Costumes, Orry-Kelly, Mary Dery. Warner Bros., 1942.

Postcards from the Edge. Dir. Mike Nichols. Costumes, Ann Roth. Columbia Pictures, 1990.

Rumor Has It. Dir. Rob Reiner. Costumes, Kym Barrett. Warner Bros., 2005.

Stella Dallas. Dir. King Vidor. Costumes, Omar Kiam. Samuel Goldwyn Meyer, 1937.

Sunset Boulevard. Dir. Billy Wilder. Costumes, Edith Head. Paramount Pictures, 1950.

Up Close and Personal. Dir. Jon Avnet. Costumes, Albert Wolsky. Touchstone Pictures, 1996.

La Vieille qui Marchait dans la Mer. Dir. Laurent Heynemann. Costumes, Catherine Leterrier. Blue Dahlia Productions, 1991.

CONTRIBUTORS

SARAH BERRY teaches film and media studies at Portland State University and writes on fashion in relation to the media and popular culture. She is author of *Screen Style: Fashion and Femininity in 1930s Hollywood.*

GIULIANA BRUNO is Professor of Visual and Environmental Studies at Harvard University. Her books include *Public Intimacy: Architecture and the Visual Arts; Streetwalking on a Ruined Map;* and *Atlas of Emotion: Journeys in Art, Architecture, and Film,* which won the 2004 Kraszna-Krausz Book Award in Culture and History and was named a Book of the Year in 2003 by the *Guardian.* In 2008 Bruno was featured in *Visual Culture Studies: Interviews with Key Thinkers* as one of the most influential intellectuals working today in visual studies.

STELLA BRUZZI is Professor of Film and Television Studies and Chair of the Faculty at Warwick University. She has published *Undressing Cinema: Clothing and Identity in the Movies; Fashion Cultures: Theories, Explorations and Analysis; New Documentary; Seven Up;* and *Bringing Up Daddy: Fatherhood and Masculinity in Postwar Hollywood.* She serves on the editorial board of *Studies in Documentary* and the British Film Institute's Television Classics series.

MARY ANN CAWS is Distinguished Professor of English, French, and Comparative Literature at the Graduate Center, City University of New

York, and has taught at Barnard College, Princeton University, and the Université de Paris at Jussieu. She has held Guggenheim, NEH, and Getty fellowships, and has served as president of the Modern Language Association and the American Comparative Literature Association. Her books include *Glorious Eccentrics: Modernist Women Painting and Writing; Surprised in Translation; Henry James;* and *Pablo Picasso.*

DIANA DIAMOND is Professor in the Doctoral Program in Clinical Psychology at the City University of New York, and Senior Fellow in the Personality Disorders Institute at the Weill Cornell Medical Center. She has published a number of articles in the areas of attachment theory, borderline personality disorder, trauma studies, gender studies, and film and psychoanalysis. She co-edited *Attachment and Sexuality* and has also co-edited several volumes on European and American cinema and psychoanalysis, the most recent of which is *Psychoanalytic Visions of Cinema/Cinematic Vision of Psychoanalysis.* She is a psychoanalyst in New York City.

CAROLINE EVANS is Professor of Fashion History and Theory at Central Saint Martins College of Art and Design (University of the Arts London) where she teaches and writes on twentieth-century and contemporary fashion. She is author of *Fashion at the Edge: Spectacle, Modernity and Deathliness* and co-author of *The London Look: Fashion from Street to Catwalk; Fashion & Modernity; Hussein Chalayan;* and *The House of Viktor & Rolf.* She is currently working on a history of early fashion shows and modernism.

JANE M. GAINES is Professor of Film Studies at Columbia University. She founded and directed the Program in Film and Video at Duke University, and the Oscar Micheaux Society for Studies in Early African American Cinema. She has published articles on intellectual property, documentary theory, feminism and film, early cinema, and critical race theory. Her books *Fire and Desire: Mixed Blood Movies in the Silent Era* and *Contested Culture: The Image, the Voice, and the Law* both won the Katherine Singer Kovacs prize.

KRISTIN HOLE is a doctoral student in the Department of Literary and Cultural Studies at Stony Brook University. Her research is on German cinema, feminist ethics, and visual culture.

E. ANN KAPLAN is Distinguished Professor of English and Comparative Literary and Cultural Studies at Stony Brook University, where she founded and directs the Humanities Institute. She is past president of the Society for Cinema and Media Studies. Her most recent books include *Feminism and Film; Trauma and Cinema: Cross-Cultural Explorations,* edited with Ban Wang; and *Trauma Culture: The Politics of Terror and Loss in Media and Literature.* She is working on two book projects, *Futurist Dystopian Cinema: Trauma Future-Tense,* and *Screening Older Women: Desire, Shame and the Body.*

ULA LUKSZO is currently pursuing her Ph.D. in English at Stony Brook University. Her current interests are eighteenth- and nineteenth-century fiction, women's studies, and film studies.

ADRIENNE MUNICH is Professor of English at Stony Brook University with affiliated appointments in Art, Cultural Studies, and Women's and Gender Studies. She is author of *Andromeda's Chains* and *Queen Victoria's Secrets,* co-editor of *Selected Poems of Amy Lowell,* and co-editor of the journal *Victorian Literature and Culture.* In addition to work on early radio, she writes on fashion, film, and gender, most recently "Architecture and Abjection in Nicole Garcia's *Place Vendôme.*" She is writing a book on cultural meanings of diamonds.

JACQUELINE REICH is Associate Professor of Comparative Literary and Cultural Studies at Stony Brook University. She is author of *Beyond the Latin Lover: Marcello Mastroianni, Masculinity, and Italian Cinema* (IUP, 2004) and co-editor of *Re-viewing Fascism: Italian Cinema, 1922–1943* (IUP, 2002).

MAURA SPIEGEL teaches literature and film at Columbia University and Barnard College, and narrative medicine at the Columbia College of

Physicians and Surgeons. She is co-author of *The Grim Reader: Writings on Death, Dying and Living On; The Breast Book: An Intimate and Curious History;* and editor of new editions of Upton Sinclair's *The Jungle* and Edgar Rice Burroughs's *Tarzan of the Apes.* She has published articles about emotions, diamonds, and death in film and is currently writing a book about the films of Sidney Lumet.

DRAKE STUTESMAN is writing a biography of the milliner/couturier Mr. John. One article from that project, "Storytelling: Marlene Dietrich's Face and John Frederics' Hats," has been published. She is also author of the cultural history *Snake.* She edits *Framework: The Journal of Cinema and Media* and has organized, participated in, and/or hosted many panels, readings, performances, and screenings in New York and London held at venues including MoMA, Film Society of Lincoln Center, Tribeca Film Festival, and the Gate Theater. She has taught courses in literature, cinema, film costume design, and/or creative writing at New York University, Montclair University, School of Visual Arts, the University of North London (UK), and London's Holloway Prison for over a decade. She is on the board of (and presents for) the New York/London *Fashion in Film Festival* and the costume/hair/makeup design awards ceremony, *Designing Hollywood,* and is co-chair of The Women's Film Preservation Fund.

INDEX

Fuller, Loïe: Serpentine Dance, 84–85, 100
Funny Face, 260, 268–71, 272, 276
furs, 276, 278n5, 281, 284–85, 289; representing class, 264–65, *266*
futurists, 241, 249; paintings (mentioned), 237

Galliano, John: "guillotine chic," 203, *205, 206*
Gandolfini, James, 23
Gang of Four: "Natural's Not in It," 211
Garbo, Greta, 24
Gardner, Ava (mentioned), 162
Gaudreault, André (mentioned), 116
Gaumont, 112, 123–24, 129n12
Gavault, Paul: *Le Mannequin,* 124
gaze, 335, 337; vs. the Look, 3; women as object of, 165, 294, 313, 314, 330
genres, 15–16, 40, 55, 115, 281; in early film, 129n18. *See also specific genres*
Gentlemen Prefer Blondes, 4, 7, 22
Gershwin, Ira, and George Gershwin, 270, 271, 279n13
Gibson, Pamela Church. *See* Church Gibson, Pamela
Gilda, 18, 55, 57, 59, 60, 62, 65, 78n17
Gilman, Charlotte Perkins: *Herland,* 185
girl power, fashion equated with, 213
Givenchy, Hubert de (designer, *Funny Face*), 270, 271
The Glass Key (mentioned), 58
The Golden Bed (mentioned), 36n22
Goodbye to Berlin, 8
Grahame, Gloria: in *The Big Heat,* 62
Greenstreet, Sydney: in *The Maltese Falcon,* 59
Greer, Jane: in *Out of the Past,* 62, 70
Grey Gardens (mentioned), 342n14
Griffith, David Wark, 29, 36n22, 326
Grumpy Old Men, 325
Guazzaroni, Emilio: on political movements in Italy, 240–41
"guillotine chic," 203, *205*
Gunning, Tom, 116, 118, 126, 130n27
Gutman, Robert, 142
Guys and Dolls (mentioned), 265

Haas, Phillip: *Angels and Insects,* 192–200
hairstyles: coiffures in *Marie Antoinette* (1938), 145; the Colleen Moore bob, 7–8, *9;* imitating Veronica Lake's in *L.A. Confidential,* 73; "Leo's haircut" (mentioned), 2; in *Mahogany,* 273; in *Marie Antoinette* (2006), *218, 219, 219,* 221; in vampire films, 46
Hammett, Dashiell (mentioned) 58, 68
The Hand, 82, 87, 92, 95; (mentioned), 83
Harden, Marcia Gay: in *Miller's Crossing* (mentioned), 69
Harlow, Jean: in *Dinner at Eight,* 148–49; (mentioned), 72
Hathaway, Anne: in *The Devil Wears Prada,* 268
Hattie Carnegie, 19, 35n9, 145
haute couture, 19, 21–22, 28, 69, 164, 279n11; inspired by Marie Antoinette, 203, 227
Hayes Code. *See* Motion Picture Production Code
Haynes, Todd: *Far From Heaven,* 176–77
Hayworth, Rita: in *Gilda,* 62, *63, 64;* (mentioned), 17, 65, 72, 162
Head, Edith, 8, 24; designs for *Funny Face,* 271; as Edna Mode in *The Incredibles,* 8, *9;* on the New Look, 163; (mentioned), 4, 17, 33–34, 65
Heckerling, Amy, 342n15
Hepburn, Audrey, 279n14; in *Funny Face,* 268–71, 273, 276, 277, 279n11
Hermant, Abel: *La rue de la Paix,* 124
high fashion, 234, 297; vs. low fashion, 21. *See also haute couture*
history movies, film fashion in, 108
Hitchcock, Alfred: *Rear Window,* 165–67, 168, 169, 171
Holland, Samantha, 323–24, 341n4, 342n14
Hudson, Rock: in *All That Heaven Allows,* 175–76; in *Magnificent Obsession,* 170–76
The Hunger, 48–50
Hurt, William: in *Body Heat,* 69

277; in *Marie Antoinette* (2006), 207, 211–12, 218, 227; in New German Cinema, 295; in Ratnam films, 305, 306, 309, 311–12, 317; in *Roberta,* 262–64, 266–67

Musidora, 43, *44*

"Muslim social" genre, 309

Muslim Women Act, 318n8

Musser, Charles, 124, 126, 127, 130n27

Muybridge, Eadweard (mentioned), 237

Nadoolman Landis, Deborah, 21

narrative cinema, 125–26, 128, 131n58

national identity, 6–8, 233–35; in fashion films, 260–77; in Fassbinder's films, 281–98; in Italian silent cinema, 236–54

Neale, Steve: *Genre and Hollywood,* 55, 56

Neilson, Asta, 114

neo-noir, 56, 66–75; portrayal of women in, 66, 79n40

New Look, 17, 108, 160–78; eroticism and, 164, 166, 173

Nicholas Nickleby, 181

Nicholson, Jack: in *Chinatown,* 67, 68

Nike of Samothrace: in *Funny Face,* 270, 271, 272

Ninotchka, 24

No More Ladies, 150

Notebook on Cities and Clothes (mentioned), 87

older women: fashioning of, 321, 322–41; invisibility of, 325, 329; stereotypes, 325, 327–28, 331, 336–37, 341n12

Oldman, Gary: in *Dracula,* 45–46

"ordinary women," 162; movie stars compared to, 136n4, 137–38, 277

orientalism: in Indian film, 309, *311,* 313–14; in *Mahogany,* 274, 277

Orlando (mentioned), 176

"ornate" woman, *189, 199*; compared to the "plain" woman, 182–200, 200n4

Orry-Kelly: designs for *The Maltese Falcon* (mentioned), 65

Oscars. *See* Academy Awards

Oswald, Karl: in *Maria Braun,* 291

Out of the Past, 59, 60, 62, 70

Pagano, Bartolomeo, 233–34. *See also* Maciste films

Papini, Giovanni, 241–42; *Maschilità,* 241

La Parapluie fantastique, 116, *117*

Paris Fashions (mentioned), 123

Pasolini, Pier Paolo (mentioned), 274

Pastrone, Giovanni, 238; *Cabiria,* 242–45; *Maciste,* 245–51; *Maciste alpino* (Maciste the Alpine Soldier), 251–52

Pathé-Frères, 115, 123, 129nn12,18, 130n45

Patou, Jean, 131n60; (mentioned), 125

Patton, Paula, 4–5, 7

Perkins, Anthony: in *Mahogany,* 272, 274

le Petit Trianon, Marie Antoinette's life at, 221–22, *222, 224*

Pfeiffer, Michelle: in *I Could Never Be Your Woman,* 342n16; in *Up Close and Personal,* 325

Pitt, Brad: in *Interview with the Vampire,* 44–45

"plain" woman, compared to the "ornate" woman, 182–200

Poiret, Paul, 17, 28–29, 35n10, 115; marketing strategy of, 110, 119–23, 124, 130n36; "The Thousand and Second Night Party," 120

Polsca, Juliet (designer, *The Sopranos*), 23, 28, 35n17

Postcards from the Edge (mentioned), 327

Potter, Sally: *Orlando* (mentioned), 176

Powell, Sandy: designs for *Far From Heaven,* 176–77

Preminger, Otto: *Laura* (mentioned), 55

Pre-Raphaelites, 181, 199, 201n19

"primitive cinema," 118

protagonists, 118; in Fassbinder films, 294–95; in film noir, 58–59, 67; in *Maciste* films, 245; in *Madam Satan,* 135; older female, 327, 328, 334, 335; in Ratnam films, 301, 302

Queen Christina, 143, 157n14

quick-change artist, 249

This book was designed by Jamison Cockerham at Indiana University Press, set in type by Cathy Bailey, and printed by Sheridan Books, Inc.

The text face is Arno, designed by Robert Slimbach, and the display face is Avenir, designed by Adrian Frutiger, both issued by Adobe Systems.